The Hidden Perspective

DAVID OWEN (Lord Owen) trained as a medical doctor and practiced as a neurologist before being elected a labour MP in his home city of Plymouth. He served as Foreign Secretary under James Callaghan from 1977 until 1979, and later co-founded and went on to lead the Social Democratic Party (SDP). Between 1992–95 Lord Owen served as EU peace negotiator in the former Yugoslavia, and he now sits as an Independent Social Democrat in the House of Lords. He is the author of many books, including *In Sickness and In Power* and *The Hubris Syndrome*.

The Hidden Perspective

The Military Conversations 1906–1914

David Owen

First published in Great Britain in 2014 by
Haus Publishing Ltd
70 Cadogan Place
London SW1X 9AH
www.hauspublishing.com

This first paperback edition published in 2015

A CIP catalogue record for this book is available from the British Library

Print ISBN 978-1-908323-98-9
Ebook ISBN 978-1-908323-67-5

Typeset in Minion by MacGuru Ltd
info@macguru.org.uk

Printed and bound in Spain by Liberdúplex

Cover: *House of Commons in Debate, Spring 1914* by Leopold Braun. Edward Grey is seated
at the end of the front bench and Asquith is standing at the Despatch Box.

Contents

Preface

The Foreign Secretary's room in Whitehall with its big windows looking out west to St James's Park and north across Horse Guards Parade, particularly in the evening cannot but evoke, from time to time, for anyone who has been Foreign Secretary the memorable words of Sir Edward Grey on 3 August 1914. Speaking to a companion as he was watching the gas lights being lit in the street below he said, 'The lamps are going out all over Europe. We shall not see them lit again in our lifetime.'

On my becoming Foreign Secretary in February 1977, my friend the late John Mackintosh, a fellow Labour MP, mentioned Edward Grey when congratulating me. I was not sure what he meant and he guided me to the warnings in Chapter Eleven of his brilliant book on *The British Cabinet*,[1] with its description of the two Cabinet meetings under Asquith in 1911. This was when the Cabinet was first made aware of the secret Military Conversations begun in 1906. The insight I gained from that chapter has never left me; democratic accountability in Cabinet is the very cornerstone of our democracy, particularly when having to judge whether or not to go to war. Only on some occasions is it feasible to take such a decision to the floor of the House of Commons in open debate. Where possible, that is of course the best democratic form. But it was not deemed possible, I think correctly, in 1914 and in 1939. There was a Parliamentary debate in 2003 before the Iraq War. Whether Parliament was misled

---

1 John P Mackintosh, *The British Cabinet* (2nd edition, Stevens & Sons, London: 1968) pp 316–24.

and disingenuous information given to the House of Commons about intelligence information is currently being examined by the Iraq Inquiry chaired by Sir John Chilcot. When I was on the Carnegie Commission on Preventing Deadly Conflict from 1994 to 1997, I started to analyse the Military Conversations, but a book I was writing on illness in heads of government[2] took precedence. Though I did deal in this book with the effect of alcohol on the decision-making of Asquith and the relevance of what I call acquired hubris syndrome on Lloyd George, particularly from 1919 to 1922.

In *The Hidden Perspective* I try to bring political experience to the scholarship and research of others. It contains quotes and actual documents exchanged amongst politicians, diplomats and the military, underpinning the Military Conversations and the Triple Entente involving France, Russia and Britain. Some of these documents are given in full, but the general reader can if they prefer be selective since I bring key words and sentences into the main text. Cross-referencing between Chapters Two and Three is inevitable because of the overlap between diplomacy and politics over the same time period.

Because I am by training a neuroscientist and because doctors of medicine have over the centuries used the post-mortem as a way of learning from their mistakes, I attach much importance to actual documents. In 1979, after the fall of the Shah, I established a year-long inquiry by the diplomat Nicholas Browne into British policy on Iran 1974–78, to learn the lessons of my mistakes and those of others. Senior diplomats have told me that this report, published in 2010, has been invaluable to them over the years. Two recent books analyse my own decision-making in foreign policy through documents, one on the British nuclear deterrent[3] and the other on Bosnia-Herzegovina.[4]

---

2 David Owen, *In Sickness and In Power: Illness in Heads of Government during the last 100 years* (Methuen, London: 2008, revised 2011).

3 David Owen, *Nuclear Papers* (Liverpool University Press, Liverpool: 2009).

4 David Owen (ed.), *Bosnia-Herzegovina: The Vance/Owen Peace Plan* (Liverpool University Press, Liverpool: 2013).

Drawing on published documents and the evidence of the Iraq Inquiry chaired by Sir John Chilcot, *The Hubris Syndrome*[5] examines George W. Bush and Tony Blair's decision-making.

My paternal grandfather, a captain in the Merchant Navy, was killed in an accident aboard his ship during the First World War. My father served as a doctor in the Royal Army Medical Corps, attached to the 9th Lancers in the British Expeditionary Force in 1940. I have long wanted to understand about the 1914 British Expeditionary Force and whether there is much of a historical connection between what lay behind the disaster and the miracle that took place on the beaches of Dunkirk.

Many people have helped me, but a few need special mentions and my grateful thanks. First and foremost my cousin, Simon Owen, for much help working together in Greece. The Library staff in the House of Lords. The Bodleian Library, Oxford, for access to the Asquith and Harcourt papers and permission to print the Harcourt memo of 14 March 1912 in full. The National Archives. Much assistance from Maggie Smart over this and other books. Also Amanda Frost. To my publisher, Barbara Schwepcke, and all at Haus Publishing I am very grateful for many things but especially for coinciding publication with the Adam von Trott Lecture at the German Embassy on 18 March 2014.

The German historian Joachim Fest wrote about the resistance to Hitler: 'opponents of the regime came from various backgrounds: civil servants, clergymen, trade unionists, lawyers and professors. The officers were only the armed wing of the plot: they were to retreat to second place after overthrowing Hitler, and hand over political leadership to the country.'[6]

Limehouse, London, January 2014

---

5 David Owen, *The Hubris Syndrome: Bush, Blair and the Intoxication of Power* (Methuen, London: revised edition, 2012) pp 196–212.
6 Joachim Fest, 'Adam von Trott', *Prospect Magazine*, No 32 (20 July 1998) p 1.

Introduction

On the idle hill of summer,
Sleepy with the flow of streams,
Far I hear the steady drummer
Drumming like a noise in dreams.
Far and near and low and louder
On the roads of earth go by,
Dear to friends and food for powder,
Soldiers marching, all to die.

A E Housman, from *A Shropshire Lad* (1896)

This is not a book about the 1914–18 war but about the military and political impact on that war of conversations between the Chiefs of Staff of Britain and France that formally started in January 1906.

The total number of military and civilian casualties in the First World War was over 37 million. There were over 17 million deaths and 20 million wounded, ranking it among the deadliest conflicts in human history.

The dead numbered about 10 million military personnel and not quite 7 million civilians. The Entente Powers, Britain, France and Russia (also known as the Allies), lost about 6 million soldiers while the Central Powers, Germany, Austria and Hungary, lost about 4 million. At least 2 million died from disease and 6 million went missing, presumed dead.

Chapter One

From Balance of Power to Entente

Great Britain's geopolitical power base was weakened by the Boer War. When it started on 11 October 1899, some believed, as in 1914, that the Boer War would be over by Christmas. Yet it proved to be the costliest, bloodiest, longest and most humiliating war Britain had fought between 1815 and 1914. There were over 100,000 casualties of all kinds amongst the 365,000 imperial and 82,742 colonial soldiers who fought, and 22,000 of them were buried in South Africa.

The central tactical lesson of the Boer War, according to Thomas Pakenham, its historian, drawing on an article in the *Journal of the Royal United Services Institute* of December 1901 by Jean de Bloch, 'was that the smokeless, long-range, high-velocity, small bore magazine bullet from rifle or machine-gun – plus the trench – had decisively tilted the balance against attack and in favour of defence.'[1] That lesson eluded all but a few back in London, whether military or political decision-makers. A notable exception was Winston Churchill, who had been involved in the Boer War. Speaking in the House of Commons on 13 May 1901, he warned that a European war could only end 'in the ruin of the vanquished and the scarcely less fatal commercial dislocation and exhaustion of the conquerors'.[2]

---

1 Thomas Pakenham, *The Boer War* (Weidenfeld & Nicolson, London: 1979) pp 571, 574.
2 Martin Gilbert, *First World War* (Weidenfeld & Nicolson, London: 1994) p 3.

In her recent illuminating book *The War That Ended Peace*, Margaret MacMillan devotes much-needed attention to warnings of experts 'that offensives would end in stalemates with neither side strong enough to overcome the other, while societies were drained of their resources, from men to munitions.'[3] She explains why Bloch's three lectures at the Royal United Services Institute in the summer of 1900, to an audience of largely military men, were dismissed. Bloch was a Warsaw financier, and as a Jew, a pacifist and a banker he was everything they tended to dislike: 'namby-pamby so-called humanitarianism' was one reaction. But according to Bloch's 'meticulous calculations a hundred men in a trench would be able to kill an attacking force up to four times as numerous, as the latter tried to cross a 300-yard wide "fire-zone"'.[4]

Continental Europe had never experienced anything like the carnage of the Boer War. Its last war of 1870 had ended on 10 May 1871 with France having to transfer almost all of Alsace and part of Lorraine to Germany, but the Franco-Prussian War did not involve mass loss of life and devastation, though it contained within it the seeds of a continuing French fear and hatred of Germany. It was a war in which Great Britain deliberately avoided any involvement. Resentment still simmered in France over its defeat by Germany. The statue for Strasbourg in the Place de la Concorde remained draped in black. Every year those graduating from the French cavalry school went to the border to look down the slope in the Vosges mountains which they would charge down when, as they thought, hostilities would inevitably be resumed between France and Germany. For Great Britain there was no need to harbour traditional animosities from across the Channel. The most recent war Britain had fought in Europe was in the Crimea, and so although the French continued to distrust 'Perfidious Albion' there was not

---

3 Margaret MacMillan, *The War That Ended Peace: How Europe Abandoned Peace for the First World War* (Profile Books, London: 2013) pp 594, 305.
4 Niall Ferguson, *The Pity of War* (Allen Lane, London: 1998) p 9.

the intense fear and hatred engendered by a combat with Germany within living memory.

In 1888 the German Emperor Wilhelm I died; he was succeeded by his son Frederik who died 98 days later of cancer of the throat. His son became Wilhelm II. It soon became apparent that Wilhelm, who on succession became known as the Kaiser, had an odd personality – which some analysts put down to an arm withered from birth – for which he compensated by attempting to be even more militaristic than his predecessors. He removed Bismarck, as if to demonstrate that henceforth he would be in charge of foreign policy. Bismarck, the 'Iron Chancellor', had made Wilhelm I Emperor and proclaimed the German (united) Empire in the Hall of Mirrors in Versailles – something the French never forgot and therefore insisted that the peace treaty of 1919 which followed the First World War be signed there too.

In December 1895 the Kaiser unleashed 'a torrent of outrage in the British press and a corresponding wave of jubilation in Germany'[5] with the release of the Kruger Telegram. Addressed to Paul Kruger, President of the Transvaal, it offered congratulations on the defeat of Jameson's raid on the Republic. Although mildly worded, and considered to be gesture politics, the telegram was nevertheless withdrawn under protest. After nugatory British concessions to the Transvaal, Germany was excluded from any further involvement in the future of South Africa. The real casualty of the Jameson Raid, however, was the then Colonial Secretary, 'Joe' Chamberlain, who only survived his complicity because of the steadfast support of Salisbury and Balfour. Another aspect of the Transvaal Crisis was that between November 1885 and June 1886 the Channel Fleet did not leave Portland, a fact observed by the German navy. This should have been a warning to Admiral Tirpitz that his assumption that the British would never assemble

---

5 Christopher Clark, *The Sleepwalkers: How Europe Went to War in 1914* (Penguin, London: 2013) p 146.

the greater part of the Royal Navy in the North Sea was plain wrong, as would be demonstrated from 1912 onwards.[6]

In the spring of 1898 Admiral Tirpitz, who was appointed as a government minister, pushed his Navy Bill through the Reichstag. The size of the German navy then was 78,000; by 1914 it was 1.1 million. Norman Stone, in a stimulating book on the First World War, pithily describes this naval expansion. 'The last thing that Germany needed was a problem with Great Britain, and the greatest mistake of the twentieth century was made when Germany built a navy designed to attack her.'[7]

A brash, immature, strutting bully, the Kaiser, according to the historian Christopher Clark, wrote in a letter to his uncle the Prince of Wales (later Edward VII), 'I am the sole master of German policy.' But he was boasting, for in 1890, without Bismarck at the Kaiser's side, the decision was taken to reject the Tsar's offer to negotiate the three-year Reinsurance Treaty without any reference to him and without his prior knowledge. In January 1904 he told King Leopold that he expected Belgium to side with Germany in the event of an attack and that the Belgians would gain new territories in northern France; otherwise he would proceed 'on purely strategic principles'. In other words invade Belgium. But the boast disguised the fact that this premise was based on the French attacking first. A sober, revelatory assessment from Clark about the Kaiser's actual influence 'suggests a fluctuating and ultimately relatively modest impact on actual policy outcomes.'[8]

British foreign policy was still in 1890 one of 'splendid isolation', a much-used phrase but with less and less meaning as other countries began to gain in strength, in particular the USA, Germany and Japan. In 1892–4 Gladstone formed his last government and, rather

6 Paul Kennedy, *Strategy and Diplomacy 1870–1945* (Fontana, London: 1984) pp 134–43.
7 Norman Stone, *World War One: A Short History* (Penguin, London: 2008) p 11.
8 Clark, *The Sleepwalkers*, pp 181, 183.

too adamantly for some of his fellow Liberals, refused any association with Germany and Austria. Meanwhile Russia, responding
to the German refusal to renew their treaty, signed a Franco-Russian Agreement in 1891 that included a clause obliging France to
give Russia diplomatic support in any colonial conflict with Great
Britain. A Military Convention followed in 1894, covering Russia and
France being attacked by Germany. This Franco-Russian agreement
with specific military clauses[9], what George Kennan would later call
the 'fateful alliance', started to fuel a German sense of encirclement.
When, after the 1904 Entente Cordiale, this agreement was extended
to include Britain in the Triple Entente, that feeling of encirclement,
specifically denied by Germany at the time as one would expect, grew
more intense. It is revealing that Grey in his autobiography explains
the theory of the encircling policy as having been encouraged by the
Germans to hold their public to high levels of defence expenditure.[10]
The dilemma within the Triple Entente is well described in a chapter
on Great Britain and Russia 1907–14. For Russia, the policy would
be a success if it promoted a grand design in Europe, for England
it would be a success if it did no more than stabilise Anglo-Russian
rivalries in Central Asia and Persia, while there could also be an additional benefit for British policy if it steadied the wavering Russian
commitment to the Franco-Russian alliance.[11]

The Triple Entente never had the historic significance of its predecessor, the Entente Cordiale. Militarily Russia never lived up to the
hopes vested in it by France in particular and, although it took heavy
casualties in its share of the fighting from the onset of war in 1914, by
1917 the cracks in Russian society had widened into a ravine. On 12
March the Tsar was due to return to the capital when 17,000 men in the
garrison there demonstrated against him in the streets. By 15 March

---

9 Henry Kissinger, *Diplomacy* (Simon & Schuster, New York: 1994) p 181.
10 Edward Grey of Fallodon, *Twenty-Five Years, 1892–1916* (Hodder &
Stoughton, London: 1925), Vol 1, p 203.
11 F H Hinsley, (ed.) *British Foreign Policy under Sir Edward Grey* (Cambridge
University Press, Cambridge: 1977), p 236.

the Tsar had abdicated in favour of his son. The Bolshevik Revolution was under way and Germany felt vindicated for its 1890 refusal to renew the Reinsurance Treaty. Indeed, Berlin had for some time done much to foment unrest in Russia. Britain had made a poor long-term choice over its alignment with Russia, but fortunately from February 1917 the USA, foreseeing the threat from German submarines, was ready to consider committing troops to the war in Europe.

Henry Kissinger wrote in *Diplomacy* of the Triple Entente,

> It was the beginning of the end for the operation of the balance of power. The balance of power works best if at least one of the following conditions pertains: First each nation must feel itself free to align with any other state, depending on the circumstances of the moment. Through much of the eighteenth century, the equilibrium was adjusted by constantly shifting alignments; it was also the case in the Bismarck period until 1890. Second, when there are fixed alliances but a balancer sees to it that none of the existing coalitions become predominant – the situation after the Franco-Russian treaty, when Great Britain continued to act as the balancer and was in fact being wooed by both sides. Third, when there are alliances and no balancer exists, but the cohesion of the alliances is relatively low so that on any given issue, there are either compromises or changes in alignment.
>
> When none of these conditions prevails, diplomacy turns rigid. A zero sum game develops in which any gain of one side is conceived as a loss for the other. Armament races and mounting tensions become inevitable. This was the situation during the Cold War, and in Europe tacitly after Great Britain joined the Franco-Russian alliance, thereby forming the Triple Entente starting in 1908.[12]

Yet the Triple Entente is often seen as starting on 31 August 1907 with the Anglo-Russian Convention, which covered practical

---

12 Kissinger, *Diplomacy*, pp 181–2.

arrangements over Afghanistan – the Russians accepted that it was in the British sphere of influence and that all Russian dealings with its leaders would go through Britain. On Persia it was agreed that there would be a Russian sphere of influence in the north and a British in the south. Even the term Triple Entente, much favoured by the French, was rarely used by Russia and Britain, and it is not to be confused with the Triple Alliance of 1882 between Germany, Austria-Hungary and Italy.

Lord Salisbury became Prime Minister for the third time in 1895. Unusually, he combined the role with that of Foreign Secretary, but his health was bad, and in 1900 Lord Lansdowne took on that role. He had presided over the Viceregal administration in India, but had not modernised the War Office as Secretary of State. To some surprise the Marquess of Lansdowne as Foreign Secretary was interested and willing to push ahead with organisational changes, 'so ideas were worked, in 1904, into a more detailed reform scheme by a committee, established by Sanderson (the Permanent Under Secretary, PUS) and chaired by W Chauncey Cartwright who, as chief clerk, was in charge of the Foreign Office establishment.'[13] A central Registry was created, with a separate cyphering department, and the new scheme started on 1 January 1906 under the newly appointed Foreign Secretary Edward Grey. The Foreign Office in 1884 was small, its establishment numbering 44 officials, and by 1914 it had risen to only 51 (first-class clerks). The Diplomatic Service by 1914 had 135 diplomats. The Royal Commission on the Civil Service concluded that same year that 'the Foreign Office was the same as it was 50 years ago … still appointed mostly Etonians to vacant posts. Of the 21 entrants between 1907–13, sixteen were educated at Eton.'[14] The Foreign Secretary had power

---

13 T G Otte, *The Foreign Office Mind: The Making of British Foreign Policy 1865–1914* (Cambridge University Press, Cambridge: 2011) pp 241, 243.
14 Fifth Report of the Royal Commission on the Civil Service, 1914, Minutes of Evidence (C7749), 9.9.40972, 41018 and app.84

of patronage until 1907, when nominations were transferred to a Board of Selection.

Lansdowne agreed with 'Joe' Chamberlain, the Colonial Secretary, that 'splendid isolation' had to be reviewed. Never a man shy in stating his opinions, at the Imperial Conference of 1902 Chamberlain depicted the British Empire as a 'weary Titan staggering under the too vast orb of its own fate'. Described by Roy Hattersley in *The Edwardians* as having a mind which was 'as capricious as it was fertile', [15] Chamberlain argued in a speech at Leicester reported in *The Times* on 1 December 1899 for an alliance of Great Britain, the United States and Germany; what he called 'a new triple alliance between the Teutonic race and the two great branches of the Anglo-Saxon race'. Hattersley, like Chamberlain MP for Birmingham for many years, writes perceptively about him as a thruster who by the age of 40 had made a fortune. For Chamberlain, the underlying issue was Germany's growing industrial strength. He saw geopolitics through the prism of having been a manufacturer of goods,[16] while other politicians were listening to a public opinion hostile to Germany and a diplomatic class more in favour of accommodating France. On 10 December 1900 Lloyd George attacked in Parliament Arthur Chamberlain, Joe's younger brother. He treated the entire family as profiteers from the Boer War fomented by the head of the clan, though he did not attack Joe or Austen, both themselves members of the government, by name. Joe Chamberlain, no shrinking violet, seeing on the Liberal Opposition benches many members of the privileged classes, landed gentry and legal profession, hit back. 'My relations are all men of business. They are all men who have to make their own fortunes or obtain their own subsistence. I come of a family which boasts nothing of distinguished birth, or of inherited wealth but who

---

15 Roy Hattersley, *The Edwardians* (Little Brown, London: 2004) p 106.
16 Peter T Marsh, *Joseph Chamberlain: Entrepreneur in Politics* (Yale University Press, New Haven: 1994).

have a record – an unbroken record of nearly two centuries – of unstained commercial integrity and honour.' He knew more than most in Parliament that Germany was posing an increasing threat to England's prosperity. In 1862 German manufacturing had held the fifth largest share of world industrial production at 4.99 per cent while Britain held first place with 19.29 per cent. Between 1880 and 1890 Germany rose to third place and in 1913 it was second only to the USA, Britain having slumped to third place.

Count Bernhard von Bülow, then still German Foreign Secretary, who Chamberlain had met in Britain before he made his speech on 11 December 1899, then spoke to the Bundesrat and in effect replied negatively to Chamberlain and those who thought like him by simply advocating increases in German naval expenditure. Salisbury, too – as soon as he returned from the official period of deep mourning following his wife's death on 3 November – replied to Chamberlain and 'politely put paid to any German alliance proposals', according to his recent biographer.[17] To Salisbury, Bülow's response was an all or nothing gambit; to Bülow, Salisbury's attitude was provincialism.

It is worth recording Bülow's thoughts on a country it was not at that time an exaggeration to call Great Britain: 'English politicians know little about the Continent. From a continental point of view they know as much as we do about ideas in Peru or Siam. They are naive in their conscious egotism and in a certain blind confidence. They find it difficult to credit really bad intentions in others. They are very quiet, very phlegmatic and very optimistic ...'[18]

Whereas Salisbury thought, 'Except during his [Napoleon's] reign we have never even been in danger; and therefore, it is impossible for us to judge whether the "isolation" under which we

---

17 Andrew Roberts, *Salisbury: Victorian Titan* (Weidenfeld & Nicolson, London: 1999) p 749.
18 Sir Valentine Chirol, *Fifty Years in a Changing World* (Jonathan Cape, London: 1927) p 284.

are supposed to suffer, does or does not contain in it any elements of peril. It would hardly be wise to incur novel and most onerous obligations, in order to guard against a danger in whose existence we have no historical reason for believing.'[19]

Thereafter Lansdowne tried to keep talking to Germany, with the support of Balfour, who was to become Prime Minister in 1902. Balfour did not lack experience of foreign affairs since in the late 1890s, with Salisbury not always able to carry out his responsibilities as Foreign Secretary to the full, he had deputised for his uncle. As Leader of the House of Commons Balfour patiently negotiated an agreement with Germany with Chamberlain's help where both countries were to help Portugal financially.[20] The Portuguese backed off that agreement, but it was a positive sign that cooperation over Africa with Germany was feasible and sadly not utilised to the full during the Haldane Mission in 1912 (see Chapter Four). The Salisbury Cabinet was ready to consider an entente with Germany but not an alliance, the distinction being that a full-scale alliance with commitments was too inflexible, whereas an entente was no more than an understanding. That distinction was important in order to keep open the possibility of improving relations with Germany and also to allow public opinion to adapt to the reality that the Germans were bound to want more respect and influence while becoming a major European power. Yet an entente would not automatically carry the weight to demand a dramatic reduction in Germany's naval shipbuilding programme. While the emergence of a strong German navy was inevitable therefore, its pre-eminence was neither inevitable nor desirable.

The emerging Germany of this period was very different from the Germany that developed in the 1930s under Hitler and to elide

---

19 Memorandum from the Marquess of Salisbury, 29 May 1901, in G P Gooch and H W V Temperley (eds.), *British Documents on the Origins of the War: 1898–1914, Vol II, The Anglo-Japanese Alliance and the Franco-British Entente* (HMSO, London: 1927) p 68.
20 R J Q Adams, *Balfour. The Last Grandee* (John Murray, London: 2007) p 155.

the two is a grave error of judgement. But it is very easy in the 21st century to do so, subconsciously at least. In truth, what Germany became under Hitler was heavily influenced by the effect of the First World War and its aftermath. Defeat on the battlefield, humiliation in the reparations and the global restructuring of the Paris Treaty of 1919 had a huge impact on the German psyche.

The political and diplomatic priority in both countries at the turn of the century should have been to build upon those many aspects of German and British life and attitudes which the peoples had in common through music and art, medicine and philosophy, and bypassing Prussian military attitudes through friendships. Instead of which British leaders chose to engage in Military Conversations with the French while German leaders followed Tirpitz's advice to challenge Royal Navy supremacy between Heligoland and the Thames.

Much of the history of the First World War, written in the period before the Second World War, was influenced by a refusal to analyse mistakes in British policy lest it call in question the immense sacrifices made for victory. After the Second World War history had to overcome the by then entrenched public view that the German people themselves were different from everyone else in Europe in being intrinsically brutal and anti-Semitic, a nonsense that took until the 1970s to dispel. Anti-Semitism in France before 1914 was far stronger than in Germany; witness the Dreyfus Affair recounted in the recent Robert Harris book *An Officer and a Spy*.[21] Nor was anti-Semitism absent in Britain.

The post-Second World War educative process was not helped by the German historian Fritz Fischer writing *Griff nach der Weltmacht*[22] in 1961, with its 'implication that German war aims in the First World War had been little different from those pursued by

---

21 Robert Harris, *An Officer and a Spy* (Hutchinson, London: 2013).
22 Fritz Fischer, *Germany's Aims in the First World War* (W W Norton & Co, New York: English version, 1967).

Hitler in the Second.'[23] Niall Ferguson has persuasively argued that it is an inescapable fact that no evidence has ever been found by Fischer or his pupils that the September 1914 programme of the German Chancellor with its objectives ever existed before 4 August, when the war started.[24] Wars create new objectives. Few would have thought in December 1941 when the US entered the Second World War that unconditional surrender would become by 1943 the policy of the Allies.

As Tony Barber pointed out in a review article in the *Financial Times* on 4 October 2013 entitled 'The causes of the First World War. How recklessness, unstable alliances and bad luck plunged Europe into crisis', it has become 'more usual to blame the war's outbreak, in descending order of culpability, on Germany, Austria-Hungary, Russia, Serbia, France and Britain.' But culpability for not preventing war, as distinct from its immediate outbreak, puts Great Britain nearer the top, certainly not the bottom of that list. Simply because Great Britain was in a stronger position to prevent that war than any other European country for at least a decade before its outbreak.

Remembering Kissinger's masterly summary of the balance of power it is worth spending time examining whether Great Britain could have done more to keep the balance of power going in Europe as a way of avoiding the First World War. In particular, whether Edward Grey, as British Foreign Secretary from 1905 to 1916, might have conducted a very different foreign policy.

First, it is necessary to examine Grey's earlier views on foreign affairs. He was a Liberal MP who had been sent down from Balliol College at Oxford for idleness, and had returned to obtain a Third in Law. He first served in the Foreign Office under Lord Rosebery

23 Fritz Fischer, 'Kontinuität des Irrtums: Zum Problem der deutschen Kriegszielpolitik im Ersten Weltkrieg' *Historische Zeitschrift*, Bd. 191, H1 (Aug, 1960) pp 83–101.
24 Niall Ferguson, *The Pity of War*, (Allen Lane, London: 1998) p 169–70.

in Gladstone's government and then under Lord Kimberley when Rosebery became Prime Minister in March 1894. He dealt mainly in this period with Uganda and the Upper Nile.

In Opposition he was a strong supporter of the Boer War. His views were, in the words of a recent biographer, Michael Waterhouse, 'diametrically opposed to those of Lloyd George',[25] and he became leader of those Liberals who backed the Conservative government's position. Through a series of speeches in favour of the war both inside and outside Parliament he came to be seen as a Liberal imperialist. When Sir William Harcourt, the Liberal leader, resigned, Grey wanted Asquith to follow him. Later he hoped for the return of Rosebery as leader rather than to continue with Campbell-Bannerman (often hereafter referred to as 'CB').

Lloyd George's opposition to the Boer War has, however, frequently been misrepresented. He was 'never a pacifist, and always an enthusiastic upholder of the British Empire more especially of the maritime supremacy on which it was based ... he regarded that particular war as unnecessary and damaging not least to the interests of the British Empire'.[26] There was a certain political opportunism present, also sentiment about small nations. As Leader of the Opposition, CB only just managed to hold the Liberal Party together, deeply divided as it was over the Boer War. His impatience with Grey took the form of referring to him as 'Master Grey'.

Edward Grey while still an Opposition MP was not in favour of either 'entente' or an alliance with Germany. His most detailed biographer Robbins highlights a private letter Grey sent to Henry Newbolt, a close friend and author of the poem 'Drake's Drum'. The letter, sent on 5 January 1903, before he became Foreign Secretary,

---

25 Michael Waterhouse, *Edwardian Requiem: A Life of Sir Edward Grey* (Biteback Publishing, London: 2013) p 99.
26 John Grigg, *Lloyd George: From Peace to War, 1912–1916* (Methuen, London: 1985) pp 128–9.

is of great significance in analysing Grey's actions as Foreign Secretary:

> I have come to think that Germany is our worst enemy and great-
> est danger. I do not doubt that there are many Germans well dis-
> posed to us, but they are a minority; and the majority dislike us so
> intensely that the friendship of their Emperor or their government
> cannot be really useful to us ... I believe the policy of Germany to
> be that of using us without helping us: keeping us isolated that she
> may have us to fall back on. Close relations with Germany mean for
> us worse relations with the rest of the world especially with the US,
> France and Russia.[27]

In this view Grey found himself at that time up against his mentor Rosebery, who believed that Britain should seek out the strongest nation, Germany. Rosebery was, as Waterhouse makes clear, 'not an anti-French Germanophile'.[28] He was a lover of France and a biographer of Napoleon; a student of continental Europe and frequent visitor; the very things that Grey was not.

The German Chancellor was now Bülow and he felt, along with other influential Germans, that only if the British agreed to join the Triple Alliance of Germany, Austria-Hungary and Italy would German public opinion no longer feel encircled by Russia and France. Then, and only then, would it give support for a slow-down of the German naval building programme. A mere entente was not enough for the Germans, but it was all that Lansdowne could have offered.

In May 1902 the Boer War ended and in July of that year Salisbury delivered up the seals of office as Prime Minister and Balfour succeeded him. Lansdowne, meanwhile, rebuffed by Germany in 1902,

---

27 Keith Robbins, *Sir Edward Grey: A Biography of Lord Grey of Fallodon* (Cassell, London: 1971) p 131.
28 Waterhouse, *Edwardian Requiem*, pp 105, 109.

according to Kissinger 'stunned Europe by forging an alliance with Japan, the first time since Richelieu's dealings with the Ottoman Turks that any European country had gone for help outside the Concert of Europe.'[29] This is a reference to the Congress of Vienna starting in September 1814, where the British Foreign Secretary, Lord Castlereagh, had negotiated with Metternich for Austria, Hardenberg for Prussia, Talleyrand for France and Tsar Alexander I for Russia in a forum which was described as the Concert of Europe. When war erupted between Russia and Japan in February 1904 the significance of that alliance became clearer. Balfour believed, in contrast to many Europeans who anticipated a decisive Russian victory, that 'Japan would give the Tsar no peace in Asia.' But he was also determined that Britain should not be dragged into the conflict, which for a short time, when the Russian fleet fired on unarmed British fishing vessels on the Dogger Bank in the North Sea, looked possible. But after some bluster the Russians backed down. The Russo-Japanese conflict was ended by President Theodore Roosevelt in May 1905 with the Japanese victorious.[30]

In 1903 Lansdowne started to repair relations with France, initially dealing with colonial tensions and leading to the series of agreements that constituted the Entente Cordiale of 8 April 1904. Also that year a new Committee of Imperial Defence (CID) was established by Balfour to co-ordinate defence planning and budgets. Reform of the forces after the Boer War was inevitable and in the next Liberal government Haldane, the new Secretary of State for War, moved that agenda forward for the Army, while for the Navy Lord Selborne and Admiral 'Jacky' Fisher did likewise.

One of the CID's early studies looked at Great Britain's capacity to handle an invasion, and the findings were very reassuring. Sending troops to France was not considered necessary for Britain to resist invasion. This should have given strategic thinkers the opportunity

---

29 Kissinger, *Diplomacy*, p 187.
30 R J Q Adams, *Balfour*, p 187–9.

to examine alternative options for preventing war and establishing a peace in Europe if war broke out. However, there is scant evidence that much was done. It was vital for Britain in the coming era of submarine warfare to build a Navy that could enforce a distant maritime blockade, not a close blockade, to battle or bottle up the German navy in their own ports – action in which Britain's Dreadnought battleships would need to play their part. If Britain decided not to engage militarily on the continent it had to be able to step in and enforce a ceasefire and reach a peace settlement by other means. This meant having an interception capability some distance from the home ports to which the target merchant ships were heading, whether German, Russian or French. Such naval strategies have a long history but were out of fashion at the start of the 20th century.

In part the problems of a naval blockade depended on legal interpretations of what respecting neutrality really meant. In 1831 a conference of the five Great Powers (Austria, France, Great Britain, Prussia and Russia) had laid down 25 articles to determine relations between Belgium and Luxembourg incorporated in treaty language. In 1839 a separate treaty was made between the five Powers and Belgium in which each Power acting individually guaranteed the independence of Belgium; but the Prussian Minister asked for a collective guarantee of the integrity and independence of Luxembourg and this was agreed. The legal situation was further complicated by the Declaration of Paris of 1856 which stated a belligerent power could not seize enemy goods in a neutral ship or neutral goods in an enemy ship, with the exception of contraband, a traditional term which was not defined. Then in 1892 the Chief of the German General Staff Alfred von Schlieffen changed the fundamental concept of his predecessor Helmuth von Moltke. Instead of mounting a two-front war on Russia and France he decided to destroy the French army first before the Russian army had fully mobilised, estimating that this would take six weeks. The whole concept was built on violating the neutrality of Belgium, which Britain and France were long pledged to defend. It was premised

17

on two victories in quick succession. When the younger Helmuth von Moltke took over from Schlieffen he ruled out going through Holland to Belgium, a factor in that it was his wish to go on being able to import goods for Germany through Dutch ports. All of these legal limitations were compounded by Edward Grey and the British Foreign Office, whose initiative it was to call the London Naval Conference in 1908–9; with the aid of some so-called naval experts they were ready to abolish the right of capture of contraband in the run up to the 1914 war, the very power which was to become a key economic weapon in that war. Indeed, some began to refer to the Foreign Office during that war as the 'Ministry of Contraband'.

Naval blockades are still controversial in the 21st century. Many people were amazed when, in 1962, President Kennedy turned to what he called a naval quarantine to help solve the Cuban Missile Crisis. This was using sea power as the least provocative and most flexible method of exercising the military power of the United States over the Soviet Union when Khrushchev, as we now know, had already put missiles with nuclear warheads in Cuba. Kennedy set the point of armed interception of Russian vessels 500 miles off the coast of Cuba.

Another example was the secret deployment, during what were expected to be tense negotiations with Argentina, of a single Royal Navy nuclear-powered submarine off the Falklands in late November 1977. If provoked, the Rules of Engagement allowed the submarine 'to protect British lives and property by deterring or countering Argentine aggression'. This was to be accompanied by a 12-mile extension of the territorial sea plus the innovatory notion of an identification zone to be set some 50 miles out from the Falkland Islands and that might have gone further out to 100 miles.[31] The Ministry of Defence was not keen to send a submarine and wanted surface ships only. In the event two frigates were also sent but were ordered to stay outside the normal Argentine search area. Had that same secret

---

31 Sir Lawrence Freedman, *The Official History of the Falklands Campaign*, Vol 1, *The Origins of the Falklands War* (Routledge, London: 2005) pp 82–8.

deployment been made in early 1982 the Argentinians would never have been able to land from ships on the Falkland Islands.

Balfour wrote to Lansdowne on 12 December 1904, 'There is only one policy which will prevent wild schemes developing into dangerous acts – the policy, I mean, of a big Navy, an efficient Indian Army, and a perfectly clear intimation to Russia that the invasion of Afghanistan means war with England.' Balfour was cautious over the Entente Cordiale and did not exaggerate its usefulness, and importantly did not – according to his biographer – pretend that 'France's enemies necessarily were Britain's.'[32] Lansdowne was well aware that Great Britain's move away from balance of power politics was a new policy. By using the word 'entente' to describe the 'cordiale' relationship with France, he gave the impression to the press that this was a continuation of the balance of power, and this ensured there was little political controversy at home. But within the Entente's terms, in the minds of senior British diplomats, were the ingredients of an alliance, even a military alliance.

In January 1905, the younger Moltke, head of the military, warned the Kaiser that a war with France could not be 'won in one decisive battle, but will turn into a long and tedious struggle with a country that will not give up before the strength of its entire people has been broken.'[33] He was 'an unexpected general, a Christian Scientist who played the cello and was prey to deep melancholy'. A highly intelligent and cultured man, he rose through a close association with the Kaiser, which began when he served as an adjutant to his uncle, 'the Great Moltke', victor over France in 1870–1.[34]

The German decision in March 1905 to turn a cruise by Kaiser Wilhelm into a demonstration that Morocco was not the sole preserve of the French started the process of changing the way Britain

---

32 R J Q Adams, *Balfour*, p 186, 189.
33 Ferguson, *Pity of War*, p 97.
34 Max Hastings, *Catastrophe: Europe Goes to War 1914* (William Collins, London: 2013) pp 26–7.

and France saw their Entente, particularly among the diplomatic class. The *Hamburg* was too large a ship to moor up at Tangier, but upon instructions from Berlin to put the Kaiser ashore, Wilhelm agreed to land in a small boat, whereupon he was met by a white Arab stallion on which he rode through the streets. To the Sultan's adviser, a former British Army officer, he said, 'I do not acknowledge any agreement that has been come to. I come here as one Sovereign [*sic*] paying a visit to another perfectly independent Sovereign. You can tell [the] Sultan this.'[35]

The French reluctantly agreed to an international conference on Morocco starting in July at Algeciras in the south of Spain, but made no secret of their belief that the threat to peace was Germany and that an alliance between France, Great Britain and Russia was the key to keeping German designs in check.[36] In 1905, the French Naval Attaché had been unofficially in conversation with the British Admiralty. This was reinforced when Major-General Grierson had a chance meeting with the French Military Attaché after the Liberal government took office. Many of these records have been collected in *British Documents on the Origins of the War, 1898–1914*.[37]

Balfour, with his government in disarray and amid rows over Tariff Reform, decided not to seek a dissolution as was established constitutional practice. He resigned on 4 December 1905 and Campbell-Bannerman became the Prime Minister of the new Liberal government the next day. He had been first appointed to the Cabinet in February 1886. Queen Victoria told Gladstone at the time that Britain now had 'a good honest Scotchman at the War Office'.[38] Campbell-Bannerman received the invitation

---

35 MacMillan, *The War That Ended Peace*, p 354.
36 Paul Birdsall, *Versailles, Twenty Years After* (Reynal & Hitchcock, New York: 1941) p 128.
37 G P Gooch and H W V Temperley (eds.), *British Documents on the Origins of the War: 1898–1914, Vol III, The Testing of the Entente 1904–6* (HMSO, London: 1928)
38 John Wilson, *CB: Life of Sir Henry Campbell-Bannerman* (Constable, London: 1973).

from Buckingham Palace at 4.45 pm on the afternoon of 4 December to go and see the King the following day. After talking to his wife, the final arbiter, CB rejected the demands of Asquith, Grey and Haldane that he lead as Prime Minister from the Lords, a place which he had little time for. According to Margot Asquith's diary,[39] the next day, having declined to take the King's hint – 'We are not as young as we were, Sir Henry!' – CB deflected the suggestion of going to the Lords by saying that ultimately he would go, but he would prefer to start in the Commons. The King then confirmed him as Prime Minister. Hearing this, Asquith's opposition folded and he became Chancellor of the Exchequer. Sir Robert Reid was already Lord Chancellor.

Grey was not CB's first choice to go to the Foreign Office. Not surprisingly, since Grey had spent six years trying to remove him as party leader. CB offered the position formally to the vastly experienced diplomat Lord Cromer, Consul-General in Cairo. He was a Baring, but neither a banker nor particularly political. He was nicknamed the 'Vice-Viceroy' of India since he had been so close to Northbrook, the Viceroy, and was recognised for brusque self-confidence and certainty of opinion. But at the age of nearly 65 he refused next day on grounds of health.

Cromer had been frequently consulted over the Egyptian aspects of the Anglo-French Entente. In June 1903, for instance, he was strongly supportive of an 'understanding as cordial as possible – yes, but hardly more!'[40] In November 1903 with evident satisfaction Cromer noted 'that we are really asking for a good deal more than we offer in return.'[41] It is improbable that Cromer would have agreed as quickly as Grey did to military links with France. The popular visit of Edward VII to Paris in May 1903, and the return

39 Margot M Asquith, *Autobiography* (Thornton Butterworth, London: 1922), Vol II, p 72.
40 Cromer to Bertie, 26 June 1903. Bertie Mss, Add Mss 63015.
41 Cromer to Lansdowne (private), 6 November 1903, Lansdowne Mss, FO 800/124.

visit of President Loubet two months later, had created a differ-ent atmosphere across the Channel, but Cromer, experienced in India and Egypt, had a global view which he would have carried into the Foreign Office. He had also been closely involved in 1898 when a French attempt to claim Fashoda, a village on the Upper Nile in South Sudan had, in the words of MacMillan, 'nearly caused a war between France and Britain'.[42] Since Italy and Germany saw this as a situation to exploit, there were dangers until the French withdrew. Whether or not it could ever have developed into a war, it was a 'salutary' experience. To Cromer it might well have been that friendship with France was one thing, joint military planning within eight years of such a confrontation another. He had also witnessed Salisbury's decision not to send an ultimatum to France over Fashoda; instead Salisbury had mobilised the Mediterranean fleet and part of the Channel fleet was sent to Gibraltar to put pres-sure on the French navy in Toulon. The French then decided to leave Fashoda. Cromer would have been a very different Foreign Secretary to Grey. So it was that Grey was destined to play the most crucial role in the next stage of the Entente Cordiale.

The Entente Cordiale has flickered over Anglo-French rela-tions for 110 years, sometimes burning brightly for a few years, but never at full glow for even a decade. It remains full of ambivalence, hesitation and doubt. But in its finest moments there has always been a legacy of unfilled potential. Churchill's personally drafted message to the French government from the British Government of 13 June 1940, 'We take this opportunity of proclaiming the indis-soluble union of our two peoples and of our two Empires'[43] and Mitterand's presidential rebuke to the Quai d'Orsay worried about the impact of a battle in the Falkland Islands on 1 May 1982, 'If there isn't a reflex of solidarity between England and France then

---

42 MacMillan, *The War That Ended Peace*, p 131.
43 Martin Gilbert, *The Churchill War Papers, Never Surrender*, Vol II, May 1940–December 1940 (Heinemann, London: 1994) p 323.

between whom could such a reflex exist?'[44] are but two of the most memorable. At the turn of the year of 1905 was its first potential moment for fulfillment or disappointment.

Edward Grey, ever reluctant to appear to want preferment, was eventually appointed Foreign Secretary, but only after Asquith had convinced CB to invite Haldane to be Secretary of State for War. Richard Haldane had attended Edinburgh University and had studied Philosophy in Germany. It was Haldane who then convinced his friend Grey to accept the Foreign Office. The trio who had agreed the 'Relugas Compact' in September 1905 (named after the place in Sutherland, Scotland) not to serve under CB as leader in the House of Commons were now all doing just that. The Foreign Office, according to Margot Asquith's autobiography, 'adored Edward Grey and was in a state of trembling anxiety lest he should stand out'.[45] Haldane became a peer in 1911 and four years later, due to the strength of anti-German feeling in the country, was forced by Asquith to resign because of a whipped-up sense of public outrage at his supposed German sympathies.

CB's problem, as his authoritative biographer Wilson put it, was that he had acquired a Foreign Secretary with whom he had very little in common, and between the two men there was a certain mutual antipathy, intensified by a War Minister who had been even more antagonistic.[46] When the Prime Minister presented his Cabinet list to the King on 10 December 1905 he must have known that he was going to have to tread delicately with Grey and Haldane. CB himself was one of our better Prime Ministers and not in the least vindictive. He had arguably bent over too far to accommodate both men in order to win over votes in the General Election, which in the landslide that followed he could have done

44 Lawrence Freedman, *The Official History of the Falklands Campaign: Vol II, War and Diplomacy* (Routledge, Oxford: 2005) p 491.
45 Margot Asquith, *Autobiography*, Vol II, p 76.
46 John Wilson, *CB*, p 457.

without. Neither represented mainstream Liberal opinion within his Cabinet, but he had saddled himself with them and made the relationship work.

Edward Grey was once famously described by Balfour as a 'curious combination of the old-fashioned Whig and the Socialist'. Though he was, like Rosebery (Foreign Secretary from 1892–94), an 'expansionist' abroad, and not a 'consolidator' concerned that the price of Empire should not slow social reforms, he was not an uncritical one. Grey wrote to a friend, Paul Herbert, in 1895 about the sort of malevolent and bastard enthusiasm which existed in France and Germany for large slices of Africa, for which they would eventually derive no other satisfaction than having kept other people out, and for that, he warned, they would have to pay a heavy price.

Churchill's realism over the shape of any future war after the Boer War was never absorbed by Edward Grey. Despite being Foreign Secretary for over eight years, he was still by 1914 unaware of what would unfold militarily. Although he frequently expressed his hatred of war, Grey never understood that a continental land battle would drag Britain into a protracted war with deaths and casualties beyond imagining. He was dismissive of technical and strategic questions and had no experience of military life. By contrast, the two Foreign Secretaries from December 1940 to March 1951, a period which covered the Second World War and the start of the Korean War, had considerable experience. Anthony Eden had fought in the First World War I, receiving a Military Cross, and was War Minister in 1940. Ernest Bevin had served in the War Cabinet from 1940 to 1945.

It is a particular help that the biography of Grey, *Edwardian Requiem* by Michael Waterhouse, is perceptive and unusual in its lengthy chronicling of Grey the fisherman, ornithologist and countryman. This gives the author's comments on Grey's character and his wife's frigidity an insight and objectivity that sets him apart from other biographers whose focus is mainly on the politician. He mentions Grey's secretiveness as being part of his character, and his complicated private life as a factor in that secretiveness. 'Although there was no physical side to the Greys' marriage, their love and affection was close and immensely strong.'[47] Grey's wife was seriously hurt when her horse shied and she was thrown from her dogcart. She died on 4 February 1906. Grey was devastated but he had a number of other women in his life, with one of whom he had a child. His colourful love life was conducted with great discretion, including with his long-time lover and second wife Pamela Glenconner.

On the big social question of the day, votes for women, Grey was a reformer. In May 1913, a Private Member's Bill, which would have given a modest number of women the right to vote, was supported by Grey but not by Asquith or Churchill. Grey could not see 'On what grounds of justice, logic, reason or even expediency' women's suffrage could be opposed.

In addition, Grey was a politician with a welcome hinterland; he wrote a classic and bestselling book *Fly Fishing*, published in 1899. He spent, all his life, an amazing amount of time fly fishing; whether on the Itchen from his days at Winchester College, and where he later had a cottage, or on the Cassley river, staying at the post office in Rosehall, Sutherland, Scotland. He was also an amateur 'real' tennis champion, winning at Queen's Club in 1889 and 1891, though he gave up playing when Foreign Secretary.

Hard though it is to conceive, before going to the Foreign Office, there is no record that Grey ever visited the continent of Europe. Even in office, though he worked very hard, it appears he only made one visit abroad, and that was to France for a few days in the spring of 1914; an extraordinary and unparallelled record among Britain's Foreign Secretaries. The famous historian Trevelyan's view was, 'He was more complex in character than people knew.'[48] For

---

47 Waterhouse, *Edwardian Requiem*, p 138.
48 George Macaulay Trevelyan, *Grey of Fallodon: Being the Life of Sir Edward Grey, Afterwards Viscount Grey of Fallodon* (Longmans, Green & Co, London: 1937) p 365.

Margot Asquith, 'I am always happy with Sir Edward Grey and have a deep affection for him. His reality, thoughtfulness, and freedom from pettiness give him true distinction. He is unchangeable and there is something lonely, lofty and even pathetic about him which I could not easily explain.'[49] All in all, a very complex man.

---

49 Margot Asquith, *Autobiography*, Vol II, p 114.

Chapter Two

The Military Conversations

As Foreign Secretary, Edward Grey, at the age of 43, within five weeks of taking office in December 1905, made a crucial reinterpretation of the meaning of the 1904 Entente with France. By 15 January 1906 he and Richard Haldane, the Secretary of State for War, had specifically authorised Military Conversations with the French generals. Analysing the significance of the Military Conversations necessitates drawing on the key documents available from that time. They show the hidden perspectives of this group of decision-makers. The documents help to put the reader back in time, to sense the mood, the fears and the prejudices. In the main, within this chapter the documents are numbered from *British Documents on the Origins of the War*, and they help to convey the authentic flavour of the diplomatic exchanges. Chapter Three, 'The Cabinet Asserts Itself in 1911', draws mainly on politicians' exchanges in their political world, and in Chapter Four, 'Last Chance for Peace', there are some diplomatic exchanges, but the main focus is on the Haldane Mission to Berlin in 1912, and Tyrrell's attempted political discussions just prior to the decision to go to war in the Cabinet.

George Macaulay Trevelyan, in his biography of Grey written in 1937, gives the immediate postwar defence and support of Grey's record as Foreign Secretary, arguing that 'Had it not been for the policy of the Military Conversations of 1906 and the Haldane Army Reforms that were built on them, Paris would have fallen within a few weeks of the outbreak of war before a British expeditionary force had crossed the Channel by routes previously arranged.'[1]

The problem with that argument, apart from its contentious assertion about the August and September 1914 impact of the British Expeditionary Force, is that eight years were to elapse before the war started. Expeditionary force planning could have started if it had been discussed by the Cabinet in October 1908 after the Committee for Imperial Defence (CID) advised that an expeditionary force should be sent to reinforce the left flank of the French army. Or in the autumn of 1911 when the Cabinet was first told about the Military Conversations of 1906, and were in a better position to decide whether it was in the British interest to intervene on the continent. By entering a one-sided military dialogue so early, Great Britain alerted Germany to the fact that it definitely intended to support France. This limited both Great Britain's military and diplomatic clout with Germany, and the potential to create a better political climate between Germany and France so that neither would declare war on the other. It also meant the French had neither the incentive to build up the level of their forces to contain the German army in northern Europe, nor the need to prioritise an arrangement with Belgium for forward defence. British diplomacy suddenly acquired a continental rigidity that had been absent for many decades.

Nor is it correct for Trevelyan and others simply to praise the thoroughness of the timetable planning. It has now been established that there was, by 1914, 'a well-nigh fatal central defect in the British planning. Despite the meticulous drawing up of military railway timetables and the placing of guards on stores of naval cordite, it had never been decided, not only what should constitute

---

1 George Macaulay Trevelyan, *Grey of Fallodon: Being the Life of Sir Edward Grey, Afterwards Viscount Grey of Fallodon* (Longmans, Green & Co, London: 1937) p 117.

a *casus belli*, but where to fight the predictable and known enemy and how to direct the strategy of the campaign.'[2] That was only done in late July and early August 1914 in the Cabinet meetings.

On 29 December 1905 the military correspondent of *The Times*, Colonel Repington, wrote to the new Foreign Secretary Edward Grey about a confidential talk with Major Huguet, the French Military Attaché, on the 28th:[3]

> Major Huguet confessed that his Embassy felt anxious upon the question of the attitude of the new Government in England. His people, he said, had nothing to complain of, since the speeches of Sir Henry Campbell-Bannerman, as well as yours had produced an excellent effect. It was not a question of sympathies but rather of acts, and of what the British government were prepared to do in a situation which presented dangerous aspects.

To which Grey replied 'I can only say that I have not receded from anything which Lord Lansdowne said to the French, and I have no hesitation in affirming it.'

It may be that Repington was a semi-official intermediary under Lansdowne, as concluded by a French writer studying this in 1932, but there are no documents to prove it. Repington's own memoirs say the information only began to flow on 27 December. Professor Temperley wrote in 1939: 'That unofficial conversations took place between military and naval experts in Lord Lansdowne's time has long been known.' But the status of any such conversations is questionable. We know all this from the work of J D Hargreaves

---

2 Clive Parry, Chapter 4, 'Foreign Policy and International Law', in F H Hinsley (ed), *British Foreign Policy Under Sir Edward Grey*, (Cambridge University Press, Cambridge: 2008) p 92.
3 Referred to in an editor's note in G P Gooch and H W V Temperley (eds.), *British Documents on the Origins of the War, 1898–1914, Vol III, The Testing of the Entente 1904–6* (HMSO, London: 1938) p 827.

published in *History* in October 1951.[4] Apparently on 18 November 1905 Major Huguet sent to Paris his own estimate of the size, composition and speed of mobilisation of a possible British Expeditionary Force.[5] His figures corresponded with the figures of a then recent British War Office study, but his message contained no information that was not publicly available. Cambon, the French Ambassador in London, also said explicitly that Huguet had relied on personal observations and not on the War Office.[6]

Not until 20 and 21 December were Huguet's estimates authoritatively confirmed, and that meant under Edward Grey. What had gone before was probably just 'loose talk', an expression used by the former Permanent Under Secretary Lord Sanderson, present at the time, who made a statement in 1922 after he retired, approved by Lansdowne, the Foreign Secretary in 1905. Hargreaves's own summary is an important one: 'the evidence for military conversations between British and French war offices under the Balfour government dates from the 1920s and is of doubtful validity.' It appears that an attempt to shift and share responsibility was made after the war by some diplomats and Liberal politicians.

Grey was well aware very soon after taking office that the French Embassy was anxious about the new government's readiness to match actions to words. Ambassador Cambon could not speak English well and the Embassy believed that Grey's French was not as good as Lord Lansdowne's and that he might have difficulty in handling all the nuances of forthcoming conversations on delicate matters. Some say his French was not bad, only his pronunciation was very English. On 9 January 1906, the night before his first meeting with Cambon, Grey wrote to the Prime Minister to brief him in general but not on the specifics. (See Chapter Three, p 84.)

---

4 J D Hargreaves, 'The origins of the Anglo-French Military Conversations', *History*, Vol 36 (October 1951).
5 French Archives, Bibliothèque Nationale, Paris: DDF, Vol VII, p 137.
6 French Archives, Vol VII, p 366.

It is interesting that Trevelyan gives a warning about relying too much on official documents, stressing that it was Grey who made the decisions, not his officials. The tradition is that all despatches, and later telegrams, have gone out from the Foreign Office with the surname of the Foreign Secretary always at the bottom. That does not mean that he or she has agreed every word or even given specific guidance. From abroad they are signed off by the Ambassador or Head of Mission. Memoranda usually carry the name of the writer. Studying these documents shows how considerable were Grey's interactions with his ambassadors and diplomats in the Foreign Office. Yet in December Grey made no attempt to commission any internal governmental review over the Christmas recess as to how he should respond to Cambon in January, and made no request to have an options paper prepared. A man with no experience of either the War Office or the Admiralty was about to make a momentous decision with Haldane, the new Secretary of State for War, which by any standard of good governance both were ill-prepared to make. Grey's meetings with the French Ambassador both on 10 January and, more importantly, on 31 January had crucial long-term consequences. It is not an acceptable explanation to say that they dealt only with technical matters. They went into the core question of Britain's continental commitment, a debate not confined to the pre-1914 era, but which went on into the 1930s when Neville Chamberlain's aversion to a 'continental campaign grew out of his six-year struggle as Chancellor of the Exchequer to tailor the defence programme to what the Treasury believed the capacity of the national economy to be'.[7]

When Grey met Ambassador Cambon on 10 January they discussed Morocco and the Algeciras Conference, but the main French request, endorsed by the Prime Minister Rouvier, was that

---

7 Michael Howard, *The Continental Commitment: The dilemma of British defence policy in the era of the two world wars* (Temple Smith, London: 1972) p 135.

'The French Gov[ernmen]t should know beforehand whether, in the event of aggression against France by Germany, Great Britain w[oul]d be prepared to render to France armed assistance.' Grey could only reply that he must consult his Prime Minister, and Cambon said that he understood and would repeat his question after the British General Election was over.

Grey reported on this important meeting direct to the British Ambassador in Paris, Sir Francis Bertie. It is interesting, in view of what happened over the Haldane Mission (see Chapter Four, p 144), that he should use the term a 'benevolent neutrality if such a thing existed' (fourth to last paragraph):

No. 210 (a)

Sir Edward Grey to Sir F. Bertie

F.O. 371/70
(No. 22) Very Confidential.

Foreign Office, January 10, 1906.

Sir,
After informing me this afternoon of the nature of the instruc-tions wh[ich] M. Rouvier was addressing to the French Plenipotenti-ary at the Conference about to meet at Algeciras on Moorish affairs (as recorded in my immediately preceding dispatch) the French Amb[assado]r went on to say that he had spoken to M. Rouvier on the importance of arriving at an understanding as to the course wh[ich] would be taken by France and Great Britain in the event of the dis-cussions terminating in a rupture between France and Germany. M. Cambon said that he did not believe that the German Emperor desired war, but that H[is]- M[ajesty] was pursuing a very danger-ous policy. He had succeeded in inciting public opinion and mili-tary opinion in Germany, and there was risk that matters might be brought to a point in which a pacific issue would be difficult. During

the previous discussions on the subject of Morocco, Lord Lansdowne had expressed his opinion that the British and French Gov[ernmen]ts should frankly discuss any eventualities that might seem possible, and by his instructions Y[our] Exc[ellenc]y had communicated a memorandum to M Declassé to the same effect. It had not been considered necessary at the time to discuss the eventuality of war. But it now seemed desirable that this eventuality should also be considered.

M. Cambon said that he had spoken to this effect to M. Rouvier who agreed in his view. It was not necessary, nor indeed expedient, that there should be any formal alliance, but it was of great importance that the French Gov[ernmen]t should know beforehand whether, in the event of aggression against France by Germany, Great Britain w[oul]d be prepared to render to France armed assistance.

I replied that at the present moment the Prime Minister was out of town and that the Cabinet were all dispersed seeing after the Elections, that we were not as yet aware of the sentiments of the country as they would be expressed at the polls, and that it was impossible therefore for me in the circumstances to give a reply to H[is] Exc[ellenc]y's question. I could only state as my personal opinion that if France were to be attacked by Germany in consequence of a question arising out of the Agreement wh[ich] our predecessors had recently concluded with the French Gov[ernmen]t public opinion in England would be strongly moved in favour of France.

M. Cambon said that he understood this, and that he would repeat his question after the Elections.

I said that what Great Britain earnestly desired was that the Conference sh[oul]d have a pacific issue favourable to France.

H[is] Exe[ellenc]y replied that nothing w[oul]d have a more pacific influence on the Emperor of Germany than the conviction that, if Germany attacked France, she would find England allied against her.

I said that I thought the German Emperor did believe this, but that it was one thing that this opinion sh[oul]d be held in Germany, and another that we should give a positive assurance to France on the subject. There could be no greater mistake than that a Minister sh[oul]d give such an assurance unless he were perfectly certain that it would be fulfilled. I did not believe that any Minister could, in present circumstances, say more than I had done, and however strong the sympathy of Great Britain might be with France in the case of a rupture with Germany, the expression which might be given to it, and the action which might follow, must depend largely upon the circumstances in which the rupture took place.

M. Cambon said that he spoke of aggression on the part of Germany, possibly in consequence of some necessary action on the part of France for the protection of her Algerian frontier or on some other grounds wh[ich] justified such action.

I said that as far as a definite promise went I was not in a position at present to pledge the country to more than neutrality – a benevolent neutrality if such a thing existed.

M. Cambon said that a promise of neutrality did not of course satisfy him, and repeated that he would bring the question to me again at the conclusion of the Elections.

In the meanwhile he thought it advisable that unofficial communications between our Admiralty and War Office and the French Naval and Military Attachés should take place as to what action might advantageously be taken in case the two countries found themselves in alliance in such a war. Some communications had he believed already passed, and might he thought be continued. They did not pledge either Gov[ernmen]t.

I did not dissent from this view.

I am, &c.
EDWARD GREY. [8]

On 11 January Lord Sanderson, still for a short time longer the Permanent Under Secretary of State and the most senior diplomat in the Foreign Office, had sent a memo to Sir Edward Grey and annexed a letter from Major-General J M Grierson aimed at

---

8 *British Docs*, Vol III, p 170.

finding out exactly what formal or informal Military Conversations had taken place after Grey's talk with the French Ambassador at which Sanderson had been present. Major General Grierson worked for Neville Lyttleton, the Chief of General Staff, the most senior figure in the Army, who was a social friend of Balfour and of Grey. Lyttleton was later written to by Haldane on 17 January with full instructions to delegate a senior officer so that the French Military Attaché would be able to know who to approach. Lyttleton nominated Grierson; this was copied to Grey, and Haldane repeated in his instructions the agreed formula 'I made it clear that we were to be in no way committed by the fact of having entered into communication', which had been agreed when Haldane and Grey talked together earlier about authorising the Military Conversations. Grey referred Sanderson to his note on Gambon's memorandum in French. He mentions speaking to Haldane and writes that he gathers that whatever is being done is known to Sir J Fisher.

No. 210 (b)

Minute by Lord Sanderson

F.O. 371/70

Foreign Office, January 11, 1906.

Sir E. Grey,
*   I noticed that in your conversation yesterday with the French Ambassador the latter stated that unofficial communications had already passed between our Admiralty and the French Naval Attaché as to the methods in which the two countries might assist one another in case of a joint war against another Power, and that he added that some similar communications had taken place between the Military Authorities and the French Military Attaché, not directly but by intermediaries. I thought this latter remark looked very much as*

if the conversations which we know that Col. à Court-Repington has had with the French Military Attaché had been taken by the latter and by the Embassy as being authorised by our General Staff.

I therefore asked General Grierson today whether he had made any inquiries of the kind directly or indirectly.

He told me that he had not done so, but that if there were any probability of his being called upon at short notice to furnish plans for joint operations it would be important that he should obtain information on several points.

I asked him to write a letter to me on the subject which I could send to you for your instructions, and suggested to him that if he should have an opportunity he should inform the French Military Attaché that he [had] not authorised anybody to communicate on these subjects on his behalf.

I annex his letter just received. Are you disposed to authorise him to commence unofficial communications with the French Military Staff?

Do you think that any similar communications should be commenced with Belgium? They would have presumably to be carried on through our Military Attaché at Brussels. The Belgians would, I suppose, let the Germans know.

S[9].

No. 211

Major-General J. M. Grierson to Lord Sanderson

F.O. 371/70

Winchester House, St. James's Square, S.W.,
January 11, 1906.

Dear Lord Sanderson,

As I told you today in our conversation, I have had no

---

9 *British Docs*, Vol III, p 171.

communication with the French Military Attaché on the subject of British military cooperation with France except, to a certain extent, about the 16th or 18th December when I rode with him in the Row (a chance meeting), and he told me of the French fears as to an attack by Germany. He asked me some questions about our war organisation, and I referred him to the Army List, which shows it and actually gives the composition on mobilisation of a division which does not exist in peace. He also asked if we had ever considered operations in Belgium, and I said that, as a strategical exercise, I had worked such out last spring. That, to the best of my recollection, was all that was passed between us, and I have not seen him since that date.

At the same time I think that, if there is even a chance of our having to give armed assistance on land to France or to take the field on her side in Belgium in consequence of a violation of Belgian territory by the Germans, we should have as soon as possible informal communication between the military authorities of France and/or Belgium and the General Staff. There are a great many points which we must settle before we can make our plans for the despatch of a force to join either the French or the Belgian armies, and these we cannot settle without information which the staffs of these armies alone can give us. Then there are arrangements to be made as to the utilisation of railways, harbours, billets, transport, and supplies, which would be quite different in a friendly country from those we should have to make 'on our own' in a hostile country, and these greatly influence our establishments and consequently the numbers we can put in the field. All these take a great deal of time, and it is exactly that factor which will be wanting on the outbreak of war. To make our help effective we must come at once with every available man. First successes are everything, and if the French could gain those they would 'get their tails up' and all would go well.

For all these reasons I urge that, if there is a chance of such operations, informal communication should be opened between the General staffs on both sides, and I see no difficulty in such communication *being made on the express understanding that it commits the Government to nothing.*

I remain, &c.
J. M. GRIERSON.[10]

On 11 January, the same day as the French Military Attaché returned from Paris bearing the detailed replies of the French General Staff to the questions put by Clarke and Esher through Repington, Louis Mallet, Grey's private secretary, used one of the tactics much loved by diplomats to this day – the prompted despatch or telegram – writing with brutal frankness to the Ambassador in Paris and in the process disparaging his political boss, Grey. Using so-called private correspondence he wrote a letter which has been copied here from the original document held in the National Archives.

Very confidential

Louis Mallet Esq.
To
Sir Francis Bertie.

Foreign Office.
Jan. 11. 06

My dear Bertie,
  Sanderson is sending you in a private letter a conversation Grey has had with Cambon in which the latter put the crucial question – whether France can depend on our armed support in the event of 'aggression brutal' on the part of Germany.
  There is of course only one possible answer & that is that if the aggression arises out of the Entente with us & if we are given an equal voice with the French in the negotiations which result in the attack, we will take our share of the fighting. There is however no

---

10 *British Docs*, Vol III, p 172.

certainty that the Gov[ernmen]t will give such an answer. Sir E. Grey is, between you & me, much upset at being asked the question & is writing to the Prime Minister, who alone of the Ministers is at present to know of the conversation, he gives no opinion at all himself.

In speaking to me he seemed very nervous & said it was a great step to take without Parl[iamen]t about a secret engagement, that if Parl[iamen]t refused supplies, the Govt. would resign & be returned at once by an enormous majority. He said that if Parl[iamen]t were sitting, you could find out opinion by consulting M.Ps. in the Lobbies. I was secretly horrified at such a proposal & again said I thought that H.M.G. should certainly answer in the affirmative & be prepared to resign if necessary.

There is no possible risk in taking this engagement. There will certainly be no war & we stand to gain heavily in France & everywhere by pursuing a logical course. It is expected everywhere abroad.

If we refuse on the other hand, we lose at once all that the Entente has given us – be looked upon as traitors by the French and needs be despised by the Germans – I pity the task of a Foreign Minister after a refusal.

I am writing because I want you if you agree to write a very strong personal letter to Grey <u>on the receipt of his dispatch which I think goes in this bag.</u> It will go to the King, Campbell Bannerman & Ld. Ripon will you also prime C. Harding[e]. He must, supposing he agrees, do everything he can to buck up these miserable creatures.

There are other things also about which I am not happy, Persia e.g. we may be right in refusing them any more money but if so, it should have been done as part of a well considered foreign policy. Gorst is responsible.

Then there is the raising of the Turkish Custom by 7%. O'Conor is urging us to give way. He is of course wrong but I don't know whether he won't succeed.

Yrs. ever

L.M.[11]

---

11 National Archives PRO, FO 800/164 f. 78.

This pernicious practice of a private network of telegrams was still operating in 1977 in the Foreign Office. When the then PUS claimed to the Foreign Secretary it was perfectly all right to have a private telegraphic network, he had no answer when asked 'Who pays for it, the taxpayer?' The problem was that a telegram had been sent criticising the conduct of an MP on a Select Committee visit that had found its way to the satirical magazine *Private Eye*. The Foreign Office Press Department had denied the existence of any telegram. So had Ministers, believing the denial was true, in answers to Parliamentary questions. The Chairman of the Select Committee demanded that the Ambassador responsible should be called before the Committee in public session when it would become obvious that the Embassy, the Department and Ministers had misled Parliament. Eventually the Foreign Secretary (the author of this book) had to see the two senior members of the Committee, both of whom he knew, having earlier served on that Committee. The Ambassador was saved the embarrassment of having to explain this situation before the Committee when they were told he would, for a variety of reasons, soon be leaving his post, and they decided not to insist on his attendance. The practice was then banned in 1977 and all telegrams had to go through open mechanisms. Now with the internet as the main, instant communication it is easier to continue such private prompting but there is the risk of disclosure through Wikileaks.

The lesson from Mallet's behaviour in 1906 is that he was being grossly disloyal to Grey within weeks of Grey having been appointed. Mallet should never have served Grey in his Private Office if he could not be loyal and frank, two qualities which allow the Private Office to function as a powerhouse for a Foreign Secretary wishing to assert his authority over the Foreign Office. Not by any means do all Foreign Secretaries wish to challenge the Foreign Office view, but if they do the answer lies not in the importation of a large number of political advisers, but in creating a powerhouse from the intelligent, hard-working young diplomats ready to serve loyally in the Foreign Secretary's private office. Nicholas Henderson, who was in Ernest Bevin's private office, summed the private office up as 'the place where politics and diplomacy come together, Minister and the machine interlock, home and abroad meet, a clearing-house for papers, a crossroads, a meeting point, a bedlam. It is the most exciting room in the whole Foreign Office. There is always something going on there and enough static in the air to produce a shock at any time.'[12] The tempo in the Foreign Office changes with the incumbent. The first to occupy it was Lord Stanley from 1866–8 and his policy was likened by Lord Salisbury, who preferred to work from the Locarno Room, to floating 'down a stream occasionally putting out a diplomatic boat-hook to avoid collisions'. Edward Grey, always a lonely figure, described being Foreign Secretary in his memoirs in rather morose terms: 'The work besets and besieges like a man in deep water who must keep on swimming or be submerged.'[13] The Mallet letter shows that Trevelyan's claim that Grey made all the decisions is not the whole story and that at this early juncture Grey was initially far more indecisive and uncertain about the Military Conversations than has been claimed. Also that over relations with France there was a small group of highly motivated diplomats in the Foreign Office who were intent on manipulating the new Foreign Secretary.

Sure enough, Bertie in Paris obliged Mallet and sent a despatch (No. 213, *British Docs*, Vol III, p 174) on 13 January which was received on 18 January. Grey was told it was marked to go to the King and Prime Minister in a note from his very experienced, soon to be retired Permanent Under Secretary Sanderson. Grey replied to Sanderson's suggestion that it might be copied to the Cabinet along

---

12 Anthony Sheldon, *The Foreign Office: The Illustrated History* (HarperCollins, London: 2000).
13 Edward Grey of Fallodon, *Twenty-Five Years, 1892–1916* (Hodder & Stoughton, London: 1925) Vol 1, p 64.

with Grey's despatch (No. 22) that same day: 'Nothing is to go to the Cabinet but both documents should go to Ripon and the Prime Minister.' His private secretary, Mallet, without Grey knowing, had however achieved his objective and elicited a tough warning of adverse French reaction to any rejection of their request:

> I consider it my duty to warn His Majesty's Government that, in the event of the answer to be given to the enquiries of the French Ambassador not assuring to France more than a continuance of diplomatic support, or of neutrality in the event of a war provoked by Germany, there is serious danger of a complete revulsion of feeling on the part of the French Government and of public opinion in France. The Government would consider that they had been deserted and might, in order to avoid the risks of a war without ally, deem it advisable to make great concessions to Germany outside Morocco in order to obtain liberty of action in that country.
>
> Such concessions might not be very great sacrifices for France, but they might well be very detrimental to the interests of the British Empire, for, in the temper in which France would then be, it could not be expected that she would give them much consideration.

Bertie's telegram read as follows:

No. 213

Sir F. Bertie to Sir Edward Grey

F.O. 371/70
(No. 30) Confidential.

Paris, D. January 13, 1906.
R. January 18, 1906.

Sir,
I have had the honour to receive your despatches Nos. 21 and 22,

*very confidential, of the 10th instant, in which you record a conver-
sation with the French Ambassador on the subject of the coming
conference at Algeciras in the course of which he spoke of the importance of arriving at an understanding as to the course which should
be taken by France and Great Britain in the event of the discussions terminating in a rupture between France and Germany. Monsieur Cambon stated that the Marquess of Lansdowne had, during
the previous discussions on the subject of Morocco, expressed the
opinion that the British and French Governments should frankly
discuss any eventualities that might seem possible, and His Excellency informed you that by His Lordship's instructions I had communicated to Monsieur Delcassé a memorandum to that effect; that
it had not been thought necessary at the time to discuss the eventuality of war, but that it now seemed desirable that this eventuality
should also be considered. Monsieur Cambon went on to say that
Monsieur Rouvier agreed in this view; that it was not necessary nor
indeed expedient that there should be any formal alliance but that it
was of great importance that the French Government should know
whether in the event of aggression against France by Germany, Great
Britain would be prepared to render to France armed assistance.
The Ambassador said that there might be aggression by Germany in
consequence of some necessary action on the part of France, for the
protection of her Algerian frontier or on some other grounds which
justified such action.*

*The instructions to me to which the French Ambassador referred
in his conversation with you, were contained in a telegram from
Lord Lansdowne dated 23 April. My report of the interview, which
I consequently had with the French Minister for Foreign Affairs, is
given in my despatch No. 156 Confidential of the 25th of that month.
The memorandum which I left with him said: 'Le Gouvernement de
Sa Majesté Britannique trouve que les procédés de l'Allemagne dans
la question du Maroc sont des plus déraisonnables vu l'attitude de
Monsieur Delcassé, et il désire accorder à Son Excellence tout l'appui
en son pouvoir.*

'Il ne paraît pas impossible que le Gouvernement Allemand fasse la demande d'un port sur la côte du Maroc.

'Le Gouvernement de Sa Majesté Britannique serait pret â se joindre au Gouvernement de la République pour s'opposer fortement à une telle proposition, et prie Monsieur Delcassé, dans le cas où la question surgirait, de donner au Gouvernement de Sa Majesté Britannique toute occasion de concerter avec le Gouvernement Français les mesures qui pourraient etre prises pour aller à l'encontre de cette demande.'

The telegram of the 13th instant from His Majesty's Ambassador at Berlin which was repeated to me from the Foreign Office, and reached here last night, states that Herr von Holstein fears that if the results of the initial discussions at the conference be unfavourable to France, she may, relying on the support of England, attempt to create a 'fait accompli' by invading Morocco.

If there be an invasion of Morocco by French troops, it will not, I am convinced, be consequent on the initial discussions at the Conference being unfavourable to France; but as an act of self-defence in order to counteract an inroad from Morocco, either spontaneous on the part of some Moorish tribe, or promoted by persons acting in the interests of Germany with a view to bringing about the situation anticipated by Herr von Holstein and giving to Germany a pretext to consider that France had given her a provocation entitling Germany to resort to extreme measures.

France cannot be expected not to take the measures necessary to repel raids into her Algerian territory, and if Germany should treat such measures as a provocation it could only mean that she was seeking a pretext for War. There is no desire in France for war. Far from it. The French people earnestly wish for peace, but the proceedings of Germany in the question of Morocco and her whole attitude towards France, have created such a condition of distrust and irritation in the French people towards Germany, that their patience is well-nigh exhausted. The feeling in the spring and early summer was one of fear lest France, in the state of her military unpreparedness, might suffer immediate disaster if Germany attacked her. Since then every preparation has been made to resist attack and the French Government,

Army and people have become less apprehensive as to what might be the result to France of a war if Germany were the aggressor, for there is a feeling in this country that England, for her own sake, would give armed support to France. It is true that the second article of the Anglo-French Declaration respecting Egypt and Morocco only says that His Majesty's Government will not obstruct the action taken by France for the purposes of the conditions of the Declaration, and that the 9th Article only binds Great Britain to afford to France diplomatic support in order to obtain the execution of the clauses of the Declaration; but if diplomatic support failed to remove the opposition made by another Power without political interests in Morocco to France acting within the conditions of the Declaration, it is felt that the natural sequence would be that France should receive from her partner in the Declaration more than the diplomatic support that had proved insufficient for the purposes of the agreement.

The question has now been put to His Majesty's Government whether, in the event of aggression against France by Germany, Great Britain would be prepared to render to France armed assistance.

It is generally held here that Germany will not go to war if she be convinced that England will side with France, but that if she come to the conclusion that England will abstain from giving armed support to France, she will consider the present moment propitious for crushing France as a preliminary to dealing with the problems of Holland, Belgium, Austria and the naval supremacy of England.

I consider it my duty to warn His Majesty's Government that, in the event of the answer to be given to the enquiries of the French Ambassador not assuring to France more than a continuance of diplomatic support, or of neutrality in the event of a war provoked by Germany, there is serious danger of a complete revulsion of feeling on the part of the French Government and of public opinion in France. The Government would consider that they had been deserted and might, in order to avoid the risks of a war without ally, deem it advisable to make great concessions to Germany outside Morocco in order to obtain liberty of action in that country.

Such concessions might not be very great sacrifices for France, but they might well be very detrimental to the interests of the British Empire, for, in the temper in which France would then be, it could not be expected that she would give them much consideration.

In the event of His Majesty's Government later on being prepared to give an assurance such as is desired by the French Government it would of course be necessary to stipulate that the French Government should take His Majesty's Government entirely into their confidence and take no step likely to cause offence to Germany without consultation with them.

I have the honour, &c.
FRANCIS BERTIE.[14]

The First Sea Lord, Admiral Fisher, apart from an unofficial conversation with the French naval attaché on 2 January 1906, had done nothing since. Sir George Clarke, a key member of the Esher Committee, which had reported in February and March 1904 and made a major contribution to the CID, went to see Fisher on 13 January. He minutes Esher, who was a friend of Fisher and the 'quintessential courtier', [15] that Fisher thought there was no risk of military trouble and war breaking out, a view he held to consistently. He reported, 'He said he would never be a party to military cooperation with the French on French territory.'[16] Fisher's alternative suggestions for a Baltic expedition or a landing on the German North Sea coast were, however, never properly fleshed out, there being little enthusiasm. There was little evidence of a coherent military view emerging in 1906, from either the Army or the Navy. This meant that Grey relied too heavily upon diplomats in the Foreign Office, who had only one answer: commit to a British Expeditionary Force for France.

---

14 *British Docs*, Vol III, p 174.
15 Roy Hattersley, *The Edwardians* (Little, Brown, London: 2004) p 6.
16 R F Mackay, *Fisher of Kilverstone* (Clarendon Press, Oxford: 1973) p 353.

It is too crude an assessment to say Grey fell under the influence of anti-German Foreign Office officials as some have suggested. What those officials, some of whom he knew from his previous time in the Foreign Office, were able to do was to reinforce his inner views and to provide a carapace over his words which carefully stayed within the diplomatic language of an entente rather than an alliance. The documentary record is always correct in that the words do not of themselves make commitments, but the underlying message had the effect of challenging that intention. Albeit slowly, but steadily, a commitment was built up amidst great secrecy amongst key decision makers, until the whole issue was eventually raised in Cabinet in 1911.

In early 1906, Sir Charles Hardinge, who had been Ambassador in St Petersburg, and was very close to the King, became the new Permanent Under-Secretary, taking over from Sanderson and starting a five-year relationship with Grey that Hardinge himself characterised as 'ceaseless sunshine without a shadow'. Yet Hardinge after 1909 never missed an opportunity to repeat his description of Germany as 'the only aggressive Power in Europe'.[17] 'As PUS, Hardinge was ruthless in monopolising decision-making within the Foreign Office' ... 'an overbearing jack-in-office' and nicknamed The Grand Panjandram.[18]

Grey's new private secretary Louis Mallet, as already demonstrated, was a convinced Francophile. This job in the Foreign Office, though names might be suggested to a Foreign Secretary by the Office, has always been a personal choice of the Foreign Secretary and is not an automatic appointment. The new head of what was called in the Foreign Office then the Western Department, Eyre Crowe, was not a political choice. His very important, detailed and long 1907

---

17 Christopher Clark, *The Sleepwalkers: How Europe Went to War in 1914* (Penguin, London: 2013), pp 161, 165.
18 T G Otte, *The Foreign Office. The Making of British Foreign Policy 1865–1914* (Cambridge University Press, Cambridge: 2011) p 258.

Memorandum is described later in this chapter and printed in full in the Appendix. Another significant change which took place later was the replacement of Sir Francis Lascelles in 1908 by Sir Edward Goschen as Ambassador to Berlin, a decision on which after the introduction of the Committee of Selection the Foreign Secretary would be consulted and could oppose, but which was strictly no longer part of his patronage. Sanderson had written to Lascelles in 1902 about how his colleagues in London thought badly of the Germans: 'There is a settled dislike of them and an impression that they are ready to play us a shabby trick.' Yet Goschen was coming to Berlin as a diplomat convinced that Germany was hostile to Britain.

* * *

On 12 January 1906 polling started in the General Election, and in those days it took place over three weeks. Many political leaders including the Prime Minister were campaigning in the country. Grey was exceptional in staying mainly in London. He was declared MP for Berwick on 27 January with his best ever result. It was a sensationally good election result for the Liberal Party. The Liberals, with 397 members, had a majority of 124 over all other parties and could have expected to be joined in most decisions by Labour, with 29 members, some of whom called themselves 'Lib-Labs'. The Unionists won 156 seats and the Irish Nationalists 82. The Liberals won again in 1910 when the Unionist coalition under Balfour had 272 members, a net gain for Balfour of 116. The Liberals had 274 and had the support of Nationalists with 82 members and 40 Labour MPs.

On 15 January Sir Edward Grey wrote to Sir Francis Bertie saying that he had spoken to the Secretary of State for War, Haldane, in Northumberland, where he had been campaigning, and had been authorised by him to say that communications might proceed with the French Military Attaché and Major-General Grierson direct. The Prime Minister Campbell-Bannerman had still not been consulted – see Chapter Three, pp 85–6.

No. 215

Sir Edward Grey to Sir F. Bertie

F.O. 371/70
(No. 33) Very Confidential.

Foreign Office, January 15, 1906.

Sir,

I told M. Cambon to-day that I had communicated to the Prime Minister my account of his conversation with me on the 10th instant. I had heard from the Prime Minister that he could not be in London before the 25th of January, and it would therefore not be possible for me to discuss things with him before then, and the members of the Government would not assemble in London before the 29th. I could therefore give no further answer to-day on the question he had addressed to me. He had spoken to me on the 10th of communications passing between the French Naval Attaché and the Admiralty. I understood that these communications had been with Sir John Fisher. If that was so, it was not necessary for me to do any more; but, with regard to the communications between the French Military Attaché and the War Office, I understood from him that these had taken place through an intermediary. I had therefore taken the opportunity of speaking to Mr Haldane, the Secretary of State for War, who had been taking part in my election contest in Northumberland on Friday, and he had authorised me to say that these communications might proceed between the French Military Attaché and General Grierson direct; but it must be understood that these communications did not commit either government. M[onsieur] Cambon said that the intermediary in question had been a retired Colonel, the Military Correspondent of the 'Times', who, he understood, had been sent from the War Office.

[I am, &c.
E. GREY.][19]

---

19 *British Docs*, Vol III, p 177.

On 16 January Major-General J M Grierson wrote to the Belgian Military Attaché to say he could tell his Chief of Staff that Britain was prepared to put in the field four cavalry brigades, two Army corps and a division of mounted infantry totalling 105,000. This with the caveat that 'Such communications must be solely provisional and non-committal':

No. 217(b)

Major-General J . M . Grierson to Lieutenant-Colonel Barnardiston

W.O. Liaison I/3. Secret. Winchester House,
St. James's Square, S .W.,
January 16, 1906.

My dear Barnardiston,

I have received a letter from Lord Sanderson in which he authorises me, in Sir E. Grey's name, to ask you to consult the Belgian military authorities 'as to the manner in which, in case of need, British assistance could be most effectually afforded to Belgium for the defence of her neutrality. Such communications must be solely provisional and non-committal.' These are his exact words and you must limit yourself strictly to the scope of these instructions. You may tell the Chief of the Staff what we are prepared to put in the field in this case, 4 cavalry brigades, 2 Army Corps, and a division of mounted infantry, and you know from our conversations the general lines on which you should go. The total numbers will be about 105,000 and we shall ferry over to the French coast – Calais, Boulogne, Dieppe, & Havre – railing afterwards if necessary to Belgium, and then, when command of the sea is assured, changing our base to Antwerp.

You should show this letter to Sir E. Phipps, and of course keep him acquainted with all you do or hear, but the fewer people that know what you are doing the better.

I remain

> *Yours very sincerely,*
> *J. M. GRIERSON.*[20]

The first Cambon meeting referred to in 210(a) on p 32 can be usefully compared with Grey's earlier interview with the German Ambassador Count Metternich, recounted at some considerable length below. It is a comparison which is actually suggested by the authors of the collection of *British Documents* as it demonstrated that from the start Grey was in constant communication not only with the French but also with the German Ambassador. The important paragraph is this one:

'But,' I said, 'if things go well at the Morocco Conference, you may be sure of this, that the Anglo-French *entente* will not be used afterwards to prejudice the general interests or the policy of Germany. We desire to see France on good terms with Germany. This is the one thing necessary to complete the comfort of our own friendship with France, and we shall certainly not 'egg on' France at the Conference further than she wishes herself to go. I said this because Count Metternich had told me the other day that he considered that the British Government had been 'more French than the French.' He said he entirely believed now that we were not more French than the French, and that what I had said represented our real attitude. I said that it really was so, and that our diplomacy was perfectly open and frank. We had gone to a certain point in our engagements with France, from which we could not think of receding. We must keep those engagements, but if the keeping of those engagements proved, at the Conference, to be compatible with Germany's view of her own interests, there would be a sensible amelioration immediately in English public opinion.

---

20 *British Docs*, Vol III, p 179.

No. 229

Sir Edward Grey to Sir F. Lascelles

F.O. 371/171
(No. 11)

Foreign Office, January 9, 1906.

Sir,

I told the German Ambassador on the 3rd inst[ant] that since we last had a conversation on the subject I had been giving further attention to the question of Morocco, and that I felt uneasy as to the situation, I had noticed that a little time ago Prince Bülow had described the question as 'très mauvaise'. I had also heard that Lord Lansdowne had said to Count Metternich that, in the event of war between Germany and France, public feeling in England would be such that in his opinion it would be impossible for England to remain neutral. Count Metternich said that Lord Lansdowne said that would be so in the event of an unprovoked attack by Germany on France and that of course the question of what was unprovoked was one of interpretation.

I said that we did not intend to make trouble at the Morocco Conference. We wanted to avoid trouble between Germany and France, because I really thought that if there was trouble we should be involved in it. Public feeling here would be exceedingly strong, not from hostility to Germany, but rather because it had been a great relief and satisfaction to the English public to find themselves on good terms with France, and if France got into difficulties arising out of the very document which had been the foundation of the good feeling between us and France, sympathy with the French would be exceedingly strong.

Count Metternich restated again emphatically the German point of view, which was that we and the French had no right to dispose of the interests of a third party in Morocco; however we might deal with *our own. I said that we had undertaken distinct engagements to give diplomatic support to France for the purposes of the Agreement – the engagements which were published in Article IX. Count Metternich observed that all we had promised was diplomatic support, and that what Germany resented was that public opinion in England spoke as if armed support had been promised. I said that I could only speak on such a matter as a private individual, my opinion being worth no more than that of Lord Lansdowne speaking in the same way, but the opinion was the same. It was not a question of the policy of the Government; what made a nation most likely to take part in war was not policy or interest, but sentiment, and if the circumstances arose, public feeling in England would be so strong that it would be impossible to be neutral.*

Count Metternich said that Germany felt herself too strong a nation and in too strong a position to be overawed by a combination even of two other Great Powers. I said I understood that, but I was speaking frankly now because such a contingency had not arisen, and therefore it was possible now to talk frankly, whereas at a later date, if things became very difficult, he might be much less willing to listen and I might be unable to speak freely. 'But,' I said, 'if things go well at the Morocco Conference, you may be sure of this, that the Anglo-French entente will not be used afterwards to prejudice the general interests or the policy of Germany. We desire to see France on good terms with Germany. This is the one thing necessary to complete the comfort of our own friendship with France, and we shall certainly not 'egg on' France at the Conference further than she wishes herself to go. I said this because Count Metternich had told me the other day that he considered that the British Government had been 'more French than the French'. He said he entirely believed now that we were not more French than the French, and that what I had said represented our real attitude. I said that it really was so, and that our diplomacy was perfectly open and frank. We had gone to a certain point in our engagements with France, from which we could not think of receding. We must keep those engagements, but if the keeping of those engagements proved, at the Conference, to be compatible with Germany's view of her own interests, there would be a sensible amelioration immediately in English public opinion.

We spoke of the tone of the Press both in England and in Germany. Count Metternich complained of a recrudescence of a bad tone in our Press, and its misstatements. I said that we could not control our Press and that we were not inspiring it, and if I were to say anything in public now to promote a better tone I should at once be told by the Press that this was all very well, but that they must wait till the Morocco Conference took place before they could accept my view. On the other hand, if things went well at the Conference, it would be possible afterwards for any one [sic] in my position to speak in a friendly tone with effect.

We had some conversation on the details of the Conference. Count Metternich said that Germany could not content herself simply with guarantees for her economic interests because such guarantees would be worthless if France really had the control of affairs in Morocco. German commerce would then suffer, as foreign commerce had suffered in Tunis and in Madagascar. I said that there were guarantees for the open door in Morocco which did not exist in the cases of Tunis and Madagascar. Count Metternich said that that would not be enough. If French influence was supreme in Morocco, concessions and so forth would be entirely in French hands. I said I understood that there was to be a State Bank for Morocco, and that the French had already agreed to German participation in the Bank, and surely that in itself was a certain guarantee.

Beyond general statements that Germany could not allow France a special position in Morocco, Count Metternich gave me no idea of what the proposals of Germany were likely to be or of her attitude at the Conference.

I am, &c.
EDWARD GREY.[21]

---

21 *British Docs*, Vol III, p 209.

Cambon left the Foreign Secretary with an assurance that whatever conversations had taken place under Lansdowne would now be put on a more formal basis. On 12 January Grey and Haldane discussed the concept together and Haldane authorised a letter to be written from the Director of Military Operations, Grierson, to the French Military Attaché that, interestingly, was required to emphasise that the talks did not commit Britain. By 15 January the initiative over the Military Conversations had been completed and was official, though undeclared, policy.

The Prime Minister, Campbell-Bannerman, was informed on 26 January on his return to London and he agreed that the talks could proceed. (This whole period is analysed politically in greater detail, largely from No. 10, at the start of Chapter Three.) On the 27th, the Prime Minister and Grey were guests of the king at Windsor Castle and he was told about the talks. They were, however, not mentioned at the Cabinet in its first meeting since the General Election, on 31 January. CB's love for France was 'deep and strong'. He had talked the issue through with Ripon whose 'opinion he valued more than any other of his colleagues'. He distrusted Morley's judgement and had been determined not to have him as Foreign Secretary and decided 'to keep the radicals in the dark'.[22]

On 31 January Grey saw Cambon and importantly said an 'assurance' of the kind the Ambassador wanted could be 'nothing short of a solemn undertaking. It was one which I could not give without submitting it to the Cabinet and getting their authority.'

Sir Edward Grey sent a record of his meeting with Cambon to Sir Francis Bertie:

---

22 Wilson, *CB*, p 531.

No. 219

Sir Edward Grey to Sir F. Bertie

F.O. 371/70
(No. 76) Secret.

Foreign Office, January 31, 1906.

Sir,

The French Ambassador asked me again today whether France would be able to count upon the assistance of England in the event of an attack upon her by Germany.

I said that I had spoken on the subject to the Prime Minister and discussed it with him, and that I had three observations to submit.

In the first place, since the Ambassador had spoken to me a good deal of progress had been made. Our military and naval authorities had been in communication with the French, and I assumed that all preparations were ready so that if a crisis arose no time would have been lost for want of a formal engagement.

In the second place, a week or more before M. Cambon had spoken to me, I had taken an opportunity of expressing to Count Metternich my personal opinion, which I understood Lord Lansdowne had also expressed to him as a personal opinion, that, in the event of an attack upon France by Germany, arising out of our Morocco Agreement[,] public feeling in England would be so strong that no British Government could remain neutral. I urged upon M. Cambon that this, which I had reason to know had been correctly reported in Berlin, had produced there the moral effect which M. Cambon had urged upon me as being one of the great securities of peace and the main reason for a formal engagement between England and France with regard to armed co-operation.

In the third place, I pointed out to M. Cambon that at present French policy in Morocco, within the four corners of the Declaration exchanged between us, was absolutely free, that we did not question it, that we suggested no concessions and no alterations in it, that we left France a free hand and gave unreservedly our diplomatic support which she could count on; but that, should our promise extend beyond diplomatic support, and should we take an engagement which might involve us in a war, I was sure my colleagues would say that we must from that time be consulted with regard to French policy in Morocco, and, if need be, be free to press upon the French Government concessions or alterations of their policy which might seem to us desirable to avoid a war.

I asked M. Cambon to weigh these considerations in his mind, and to consider whether the present situation as regards ourselves and France was not so satisfactory that it was unnecessary to alter it by a formal declaration as he desired.

M. Cambon said that in Morocco, if the Conference broke up without favourable result, Germany might place herself behind the Sultan and acquire more and more influence, that trouble might be stirred up on the Algerian frontier, that France might be obliged to take measures to deal with it as she had done before, and that Germany might announce to France, as she had already once done, that an aggression on Morocco would be an attack upon her, and would be replied to accordingly. In such an event war might arise so suddenly that the need for action would be a question not of days, but of minutes, and that if it was necessary for the British Government to consult, and to wait for manifestations of English public opinion, it might be too late to be of use. He eventually repeated his request for some form of assurance which might be given in conversation. I said that an assurance of that kind could be nothing short of a solemn undertaking. It was one which I could not give without submitting it to the Cabinet and getting their authority, and that were I to submit the question to the Cabinet I was sure they would say that this was too serious a matter to be dealt with by a verbal engagement but must be put in writing. As far as their good disposition towards France was concerned, I should have no hesitation in submitting such a question to the present Cabinet. Some of those in the Cabinet who were most *attached to peace were those also who were the best friends of France, but though I had no doubt about the good disposition of the Cabinet I did think there would be difficulties in putting such an undertaking in writing. It could not be given unconditionally, and it would be difficult to describe the conditions. It amounted in fact to this: that if any change was made, it must be to change the "entente" into a defensive alliance. That was a great and formal change, and I again submitted to M. Cambon as to whether the force of circumstances bringing England and France together was not stronger than any assurance in words which could be given at this moment. I said that it might be that the pressure of circumstances – the activity of Germany, for instance – might eventually transform the "entente" into a defensive alliance between ourselves and France, but I did not think that the pressure of circumstances was so great as to demonstrate the necessity of such a change yet. I told him also that should such a defensive alliance be formed, it was too serious a matter to be kept secret from Parliament. The Government could conclude it without the assent of Parliament, but it would have to be published afterwards. No British Government could commit the country to such a serious thing and keep the engagement secret.*

M. Cambon in summing up what I had said, dwelt upon the fact that I had expressed my personal opinion that, in the event of an attack by Germany upon France, no British Government could remain neutral. I said that I had used this expression to Count Metternich first, and not to him, because, supposing it appeared that I had over-estimated the strength of feeling of my countrymen, there could be no disappointment in Germany, but I could not express so decidedly my personal opinion to France because a personal opinion was not a thing upon which, in so serious a matter, a policy could be founded. In speaking to him, therefore, I must keep well within the mark. Much would depend as to the manner in which war broke out between Germany and France. I did not think people in England would be prepared to fight in order to put France in possession of Morocco. They would say that France should wait for opportunities and be content to take time, and that it was unreasonable to hurry matters to the point of war. But if, on the other hand, it appeared that the war was forced upon France by Germany to break up the Anglo-French "entente", public opinion would undoubtedly be very strong on the side of France. At the same time M. Cambon must remember that England at the present moment would be most reluctant to find herself engaged in a great war, and I hesitated to express a decided opinion as to whether the strong feeling of the Press and of public opinion on the side of France would be strong enough to overcome the great reluctance which existed amongst us now to find ourselves involved in war. I asked M. Cambon however to bear in mind that, if the French Government desired it, it would be possible at any time to re-open the conversation. Events might change, but as things were at present I did not think it was necessary to press the question of a defensive alliance.

M. Cambon said the question was very grave and serious, because the German Emperor had given the French Government to understand that they could not rely upon us, and it was very important to them to feel that they could.

[I am, &c.]
E. G.[REY][23]

Lord Sanderson, no longer PUS but just retired, wrote a very important memorandum about his meeting on 2 February with the French Ambassador in his Embassy, held in effect to ensure that there were no misunderstandings and that the message Cambon would convey to his government was what the Foreign Secretary had actually said. As he was now no longer an official he said he could speak freely and wished to make one or two observations on his own personal views. Sanderson then spelt out from long experience in his Memorandum that follows why, 'if the Cabinet were to give a pledge which would morally bind the country to go to

---

23 *British Docs*, Vol III, p 180.

war in certain circumstances, and were not to mention this pledge to Parliament, and if at the expiration of some months the country suddenly found itself pledged to war in consequence of this assurance, the case would be one which would justify impeachment.' A view that has some immediate relevance in the light of the Report in 2014 of the Iraq Inquiry by the Committee of Privy Counsellors chaired by Sir John Chilcot.

No. 220 (b)

Memorandum by Lord Sanderson

F.O. 371/70

Foreign Office, February 2, 1906.

I called on the French Ambassador yesterday afternoon, according to Sir Edward Grey's instructions, in order to hear the account which he had drawn up of his conversation with Sir Edward Grey on the previous day. I took with me a copy, which Sir Edward Grey had given me, of his own account of the conversation.

He had M. Cambon read to me his summary of what had passed. It differed in form from Sir Edward Grey's account, in that it gave a summary of what had been stated on either side instead of putting these statements in the form of consecutive remarks and answers. It also gave some remarks of detail on the part of M. Cambon in the way of illustration of his arguments, which Sir Edward Grey had omitted. But in substance it corresponded with Sir Edward Grey's own account.

I suggested one small alteration, and then produced Sir Edward Grey's statement. M. Cambon after reading this, said that he should like to make some alterations in his report in order to bring out a remark of Sir Edward Grey's that he had felt less hesitation in giving a decided opinion to the German Ambassador, inasmuch as if it proved to be in any way mistaken, that would not entail any disappointment in Germany; but that he felt the need of being more cautious in expressing personal opinion to the French Ambassador, which, if in any way mistaken, might be the cause of serious disappointment in France. M. Cambon had omitted this remark, and said he wished to insert it. He promised that when he had corrected his memorandum he would send a copy of it to Sir Edward Grey.

I then said that as I was no longer an official, I might speak to him quite freely, and that I wished to make to him one or two observations on my own personal views.

In the first place, in the course of my experience, which was a pretty long one, I knew of no instance of any secret Agreement by the British Government which pledged them further than that if a certain policy agreed upon with another Power were in any way menaced, the two Powers should consult as to the course to be taken. That I thought was the limit to which the Government could properly bind itself without in some way making Parliament aware of the obligations that it was incurring.

Secondly, it was a maxim which had been impressed upon me by several statesmen of great eminence that it was not wise to bring before a Cabinet the question of the course to be pursued in hypothetical cases which had not arisen. A discussion of the subject invariably gave rise to divergences of opinion on questions of principle, whereas in a concrete case unanimity would very likely be secured. M. Cambon observed that this view was a perfectly just one.

Thirdly, I told him that I thought that if the Cabinet were to give a pledge which would morally bind the country to go to war in certain circumstances, and were not to mention this pledge to Parliament, and if at the expiration of some months the country suddenly found itself pledged to war in consequence of this assurance, the case would be one which would justify impeachment, and which might even result in that course unless at the time the feeling of the country were very strongly in favour of the course to which the Government was pledged.

M. Cambon thanked me for these remarks and said that he had already told me he did not feel apprehensive personally that war between Germany and France was imminent. He thought it more likely that if the Conference at Algeciras did not come to a satisfactory issue, the Germans would endeavour to obtain a dominant position in Morocco, which might eventually lead to trouble.

I said that no doubt the situation would be one which would require great patience and prudence on the part of France, but that the position of France in Morocco was naturally a stronger one than that of Germany, and that I thought in the long run the advantage must be with her.

M. Cambon said that this might be so, but he was a little apprehensive of the Germans getting into favour with the Sultan and obtaining concessions from him in the manner which they had practised so successfully in Turkey.

I said that there was this difference, that commercial development in Morocco was absolutely impossible without reforms, and that the Germans could not really obtain any great advantages there without such reforms being instituted. They could scarcely really undertake them alone, and they certainly could not do so without rendering themselves distasteful to the Sultan.

M. Cambon paid me some compliments, and seemed to me on the whole satisfied with the results of his interview with Sir Edward Grey.

MINUTE BY KING EDWARD.
Approved. – E .R.[24]

Grey also wrote to the British Ambassador in Paris about a meeting he had had with the German Ambassador, who had expressed concern following an interview with a British general published in a French newspaper, which was subsequently explained in *The Times*. But this was only after Grey had had a very tough denunciation of the interview from CB written on 26 January, concluding, 'For a man to speak in such terms at this moment is little short of criminal' (the full text is quoted in Chapter Three, p 86).

---

24 *British Docs*, Vol III, p 184.

No. 264

Sir Edward Grey to Sir F. Lascelles

F.O. 371/76
(No. 53)

Foreign Office, January 31, 1906.

Sir,

The German Ambassador spoke to me a week ago about an interview with Sir Frederick Maurice which had been published in the French papers. I told His Excellency to-day that I had, in consequence of his reference to it, read the interview and very much disapproved of it, but no doubt he had now got the explanation which had been published in the 'Times'. I said it had occurred to me that some of the information which constantly reached me here in connection with the German Army, their unusual purchases of material for war, and so forth, might account for the way in which Sir Frederick Maurice and others discussed the eventuality of war, but I said that I regarded all information of this kind as indicating on the part of Germany not preparations for war, but precautions, which, in view of the state of feeling which existed six months ago, it was quite natural that Germany should take, and which were not the least inconsistent with the pacific intentions which Count Metternich had assured me were hers. 'Preparations' I used in the sense of an intention to attack; 'precautions', on the other hand, indicated only the intention to defend.

Count Metternich said that France also, according to the statements which Sir Charles Dilke and others had made, had been strengthening her position very much. I said I had no doubt it was true, and that also, in view of the state of feeling which had existed a few months ago, was a perfectly natural precaution for her to take; but I could assure him that as long as I remained at the Foreign Office, or indeed as long as the present Government remained in

*office, whatever we countenanced would be purely precautions in the
sense in which I had used the word, and not aggressive preparations.*
I am, &c.
EDWARD GREY.

MINUTE BY KING EDWARD.
App[rove]d. – E.R.[25]

On 6 September the British Ambassador in Paris wrote to the
Foreign Secretary about a German article in *Deutsche Revue*
inspired by 'a very high if not by the highest authority in Germany
and probably by both', which included criticism of the French
Foreign Minister Delcassé's policies.

No. 437

Sir F. Bertie to Sir Edward Grey

F.O. 371/79
(No. 338)

Paris, D. September 6, 1906.
R. September 8, 1906.

Sir,

*The 'Times' of yesterday gives a summary and the important
points of an article which is to appear in the September number of
the 'Deutsche Revue'.*

*The article which has evidently been inspired by very high if not
by the highest authority in Germany, and probably by both, discusses the recent interview at Friedrichshof between Their Majesties
the King and the German Emperor, the relations between England
and Germany, those between England and France and the attitude*

---

25 *British Docs*, Vol III, p 240.

of France as regards Germany and a rapprochement between the British and German Governments.

The Article states that:–

(a.) A pacific policy in France could not but desire the relations between England and Germany to assume a friendly character. An Anglo-German understanding therefore offers for France the best possible guarantee of peace, for no one in Germany thinks of an aggressive war against France, which even in the event of victory would offer to Germany no advantages. The ambitions attributed to Germany in the French Press being imaginary, the reason for the anxiety shown by French Diplomacy to prevent the rapprochement between Germany and England cannot be the preservation of peace. It must be the hope of British support in case of war and of a war which France intends to bring about, the Delcassé traditions continuing to be the policy of French Diplomacy, viz., to hem in German diplomacy with the help of England, Russia, and other States so closely that the ultimate and inevitable attempt of Germany to break through the circle should end by her defeat diplomatic and military.

(b.) The Article, after referring to the view taken in France that England will hold unswervingly under every Cabinet to the entente with France, and stating that the present Cabinet contains several Germanophile Ministers, chief amongst them the War Minister and the Lord Chancellor, and setting forth what it considers to be your view in regard to the entente and a reconciliation with Russia, and negotiations with Germany in questions affecting the 'Nearer East', states that the kernel of AngloGerman relations therefore lies herein, that you shall not identify yourself with the French interpretations, viz. the Delcassé Policy – that is to say the isolation of Germany – but shall meet her with confidence.

(c.) The question, the Article says, may be summed up as follows:–

'Will the Anglo-French Group close up still more closely as a counterpoise to Germany, which is the object of French Diplomacy, or conscious that it is not strong enough especially in view of the temporary elimination of Russia and of the actual dispositions of her policy, will

*it now strive to expand the understanding to Germany, which, it must
be understood, should not be taken to mean the accession of Germany
to the policy of the Western Powers? Since the meeting at Friedrichshof
we may be justified in assuming that we are travelling, though slowly
and step by step, to a period of* rapprochement. *Germany could argue
with some force, and let us hope not without success, that a peaceful
policy for Great Britain can alone consist in holding out the hand to
Germany, and that peace would thereby be much more effectively
secured than by Congresses and Disarmament Proposals. The relations between England and France would not be thereby imperilled,
since England has irrevocably declared that the entente with France
is a permanent basis of her policy. No doubt could exist on that point
in France, even if England were to woo Germany openly and without
constraint. As for the possibility of a Franco-German* rapprochement
*– that is to say, of more friendly relations of France to Germany –
false hopes and baseless fears would appear still to stand in its way,
and an open relationship of friendliness on the part of England
towards Germany might materially help to remove them. The policy
of* ententes *outside of Germany and against Germany is uncertain
in execution and not without danger in its consequences. This policy
of counterpoises will persist however as long as England, out of fear
of displeasing Paris, continues to treat with coolness the honourable
approaches of Germany. Germany is thereby necessarily compelled to
remain on her guard. Towards Germany England has only the choice
between either the policy, which might easily become disastrous, of an
Anglo-French counterpoise, or that of including Germany within the
circle of her friendships. These logical conclusions can hardly fail to
have carried weight at Friedrichshof and in the British Foreign Office.
Substantial results will only naturally mature slowly.'*

(d.) As to the question of German Naval Expansion and the comments made on it in the English Press, the Article emphasises the
necessity for England of accepting the situation as follows: –

'*England must reconcile herself to the thought of seeing the German
Fleet occupy alongside of the British Fleet a position commanding*

and imposing respect on the sea... A year ago the belief did exist in Germany that our relations with England were in a stage analogous to the relations of Prussia and Austria before 1866, and that in all probability a cordial understanding would have to be preceded by a sharp encounter. The estrangement which rendered such a belief possible, though it may not have justified it, is past. Both nations may feel confident that it will be possible to arrive at a cordial agreement without any previous armed conflict.'

For convenience of reference I have marked with distinguishing letters the various portions of the above-recited Article which relate to different parts of the questions therein dealt with, and I have the honour to submit for your consideration the following comments on the Article, which I believe represent the views held on the several points raised in it by responsible persons in France.

(a) Contrary to the view put forward by the 'Deutsche Revue', the policy of France is one of peace and she desires the relations between England and Germany to be of a nature to obviate a recourse to arms between those two countries; for she feels that, whether her engagements bound her to become a party to such a war or not, she would inevitably be dragged into it either by being attacked by Germany or in defence of her vital interests.

The French do not at all believe that no one in Germany thinks of an aggressive war against France; on the contrary they have the conviction that had it not been that England and France held together in the question of Morocco France would have been either humiliated or attacked by Germany.

The German Government gave out that it was M. Delcassé personally who was the obstacle to good relations between Germany and France. M. Bouvier, who had no experience of foreign affairs, sacrificed M. Delcassé, and took his post as Minister for Foreign Affairs, but he soon realised that the stumbling block was not his late colleague but the good understanding which that Minister had negotiated with England, and that the policy of the German

Government was to impress on France the disadvantage of friend-
ship with England and the benefits to be expected from an agree-
ment with Germany.

Inasmuch as the ambitions attributed to Germany in the French
Press are in great part those announced by prominent German
writers and speakers, and that many of them are very natural for
patriotic Germans to feel, French opinion does not consider them to
be imaginary on the part of the French Press. Provided that a rapprochement *between Germany and England has only for its aim the*
removal of any outstanding Diplomatic difficulties between the two
countries and tends therefore to the preservation of peace, no objec-
tion will be felt in France, for no party in the country desires to bring
about a war with Germany in reliance on British support.

I do not believe that the Delcassé traditions which the Revue alleges
to continue to be the policy of French Diplomacy [sic] was to hem in
Germany diplomatically with the help of England, Russia and other
States so closely that the ultimate and inevitable attempt of Germany
to break through the circle should end by her defeat diplomatic and
military. M. Delcassé was alarmed at the growing strength and dic-
tatorial attitude of Germany and the aim of his policy was by coming
to terms with England to prevent an Anglo-German agreement to
the detriment of French interests, which he knew to be the desire of
the German Emperor and his government, and consequently through
improved relations or an understanding with England to render
France less liable to attack by Germany.

(b.) There is no doubt that German agents, with the view of creat-
ing distrust against England, have propagated the theory that there
is a tendency on the part of some of His Majesty's advisers to favour
an understanding with Germany rather than one with France, and
this may account for the nervous sensitiveness shown by M. Bour-
geois in regard to the possibility of Mr. Haldane, in the course of his
visit to Germany, accepting an invitation to attend ceremonies which
might be connected with the celebration of the great French defeat six
and thirty years ago. I do not think that M. Bourgeois personally is

suspicious of any intention on the part of His Majesty's Government to depart from the spirit of the understanding between the British and French Governments, viz. to consult confidentially and freely and act together so far as possible in all questions affecting the interests of England and France, but he has to count with others who are not sure of the stability of British policy, and to remember that the Nationalist party and many Royalists were formerly in favour of an understanding with Germany and that an agitation for such a policy might easily be started again if the French public were led to suspect that His Majesty's Government contemplated an agreement with Germany, not only on specific questions actually at issue, but on general policy.

(c.) The Revue refers to the possibility of more friendly relations between France and Germany through an open relationship of friendliness on the part of England towards Germany and lays stress on the view that the policy of ententes *outside of Germany and against Germany is certain in execution and not without danger in its consequences.*

The suggestion that England should act the part indicated would certainly entail a great danger to the existing relations between her and France, for it would be taken as an attempt to persuade the mouse to make friends with the cat and be regarded as covering some secret designs arranged with Germany.

It appears to me that our policy as regards relations between France and Germany should be not to create friction as was Prince Bismarck's practice in regard to the relations between France and England; but to do nothing to facilitate an understanding between Germany and France; for it is difficult to conceive how an understanding of any real importance between these two countries could be satisfactory to Germany without being detrimental to our interests.

(d.) With regard to the necessity for England emphasised by the Revue to accept German naval expansion and to reconcile herself to seeing the German fleet occupy alongside the British fleet a position

commanding and imposing respect on the sea, opinion in France is that the reduction in English naval expenditure will not lead to any diminution in German naval preparations to contest the naval supremacy of England in the north of Europe whenever a suitable opportunity may occur, and that it is incumbent upon France and that it will be necessary for England not to relax in their determination to keep up the existing relative strength of their naval forces in proportion to the increases in the German fleet.

I have, &c.

FRANCIS BERTIE[26]

The British Ambassador to France reported on how a nationalist French Senator challenged the French government in the Senate: 'Is there a military convention between France and England? Yes or No?' This caused much fluttering in London where from Grey downwards they realised they were skating on thin ice, and the ice was becoming thinner.

To the historian Trevelyan, it was simple.

> The only thing that was wrong with the Military Conversations was that the Cabinet was not told of them at once. Grey erred in thinking that all others would regard the Conversations as he himself regarded them – as a technical affair of experts without any political implications. But those who blame Grey most for this seldom mention the equal responsibility of the Prime Minister, Campbell-Bannerman, who knew of the Conversations but did not bring them before Cabinet.[27]

Sadly historians, even those of such eminence, have a tendency to slide over the personalities and complexities of politics, but Trevelyan was correct in attributing responsibility to Campbell-Bannerman

---

26 *British Docs*, Vol III, p 385.
27 Trevelyan, *Grey of Fallodon*, p 117.

who in fact bore far greater responsibility for this secrecy up until his death than Grey. See Chapter Three, pp 87–8.

No. 443

Sir F. Bertie to Sir Edward Grey

F.O. 371/74
(No. 463)

Paris; D. November 21, 1906.
R. November 22, 1906.

Sir,

The policy of the Government was yesterday challenged in the Senate by a 'Nationalist' Senator, M. Gaudin de Villaine, who subjected the President of the Council to a certain amount of 'heckling'. He declared that M. Clemenceau's statesmanship consisted of war on the Roman Catholics at home and of an 'English Policy' abroad. On Monsieur Clemenceau retorting that, as to the latter point, it was impossible to answer anything so vague, M. Gaudin de Villaine interrupted him saying: –

'Is there a military convention between France and England? Yes or No.' I have the honour to transmit to you herewith, extracted from the 'Journal Official' M. Clemenceau's reply, in which he said that he had only been at the head of the Ministry for three weeks, but that among the documents laid before him by the Minister for Foreign Affairs concerning such agreements, for instance, as those on the subject of Morocco he had not seen anything of the sort. He protested against questions of that kind being addressed to him, and added that there might be occasions when a Government conscious of its responsibilities ought not to give any reply to them and that it was not right that anything should be said from that Tribune which might 'décourager des amitiés' or 'rompre des accords'. It is stated in the 'Matin' that his replies to M. Gaudin de Villaine were very *cavalier in tone and he concluded with the ironical phrase 'J'ai bien l'honneur de vous saluer.'*

The Senate expressed their confidence in the Government by 213 votes to 32.

I have, &c.
FRANCIS BERTIE.

No. 444

Minutes by Mr. E. Crowe, Sir Charles Hardinge and Sir E. Grey

F.O. 371/74.

Foreign Office, November 24, 1906.

The article tries to justify M. Clemenceau's cryptic utterance respecting the alleged Anglo-French military convention, by urging that it is not fair or wise to discuss whether, on certain contingencies arising, the two countries might not be led to extend their political cooperation by entering into an agreement for assistance of another kind.

This is no doubt a sensible view, but the curious thing is that M. Clemenceau was asked not whether he intended to conclude a military convention, but whether one had already been concluded. To this question the 'Temps' argument is no answer at all.

It remains to be seen whether the question will be taken up in Germany.

E. A. C.

Nov. 24.

Hardly worth sending to Berlin.

E. B.

M. Cambon alluded to this incident yesterday and I pointed out to him that it would be awkward if a similar question were put in

Parliament. There is no doubt that the German Gov[ernmen]t are very anxious for a denial of the existence of a military convention which many Germans (such as C[oun]t Reventlow who states in an article sent home from Munich that such a Convention almost undoubtedly exists) believe to have been concluded. In view of the fact that Conferences took place last spring to concert joint measures of action and that no Convention actually exists it would, I thought, have been best if M. Clemenceau had given a 'démenti'.

M. Cambon was not quite of the same opinion as he regards the myth of the existence of a Convention as a deterrent to Germany.

C. H.

It would have been difficult for M. Clemenceau to deny the existence of a convention without giving the impression that such a Convention was not desired. I shall endeavour to avoid a public denial, if I am asked a question.

E. G.

The British Military was now dealing, eleven months later, directly with the French Military Staff and furthermore it was very clear already that Britain would very likely opt for an expeditionary force. The secrecy, however, was still such that no official letters passed on the subject between the War Office and the Admiralty. In November a memorandum (No. 689) was circulated that shows how far the Military Conversations had gone over five years (quoted in full in Chapter Three, pp 125–9).

1 January 1907 saw the publication by the British Foreign Office of the Memorandum of Mr Eyre Crowe, then the head of the Western Department, on 'The Present State of British Relations with France and Germany'. It was described by Henry Kissinger as a 'classic document' in his book *Diplomacy*. Kissinger also wrote:

True to the tenets of Realpolitik, Crowe argued that structure, not motive, determined stability; Germany's intentions were essentially irrelevant; what mattered were its capabilities ...[28] Though the Crowe Memorandum did not actually go further than to oppose an understanding with Germany, its thrust was clear: if Germany did not abandon its quest for maritime supremacy and moderate its so-called Weltpolitik, Great Britain was certain to join Russia and France in opposing it.

Although the Military Conversations are not directly referred to, the hidden perspectives of British diplomats on the Conversations permeate every line of the Crowe Memorandum. Its coverage of events and its insight into Sir Edward Grey's own mind are invaluable, as are Grey's brief comments on the Memorandum.

MINUTE

Mr. Crowe's Memorandum should go to the Prime Minister, Lord Ripon, Mr. Asquith, Mr. Morley, Mr. Haldane, with my comment upon it. – E. G.

This Memorandum by Mr. Crowe is most valuable. The review of the present situation is both interesting and suggestive, and the connected account of the diplomatic incidents of past years is most helpful as a guide to policy. The whole Memorandum contains information and reflections, which should be carefully studied. The part of our foreign policy with which it is concerned involves the greatest issues, and requires constant attention. – E. GREY. January 28, 1907.

Grey also adds one criticism – that Crowe underestimates the impact of Emperor Wilhelm: 'the whole situation would be changed in a moment if this personal factor were changed ...' This

---

28 Henry Kissinger, *Diplomacy* (Simon & Schuster, New York: 1994) p 193.

is an oft repeated view by Grey over the next few years but not one so strongly endorsed by contemporary historians.

The inclusion of Ripon and Morley on the very limited list of Cabinet Ministers to whom this secret memorandum was sent is very interesting. Ripon, Leader of the Lords, had been involved in the Military Conversations early on by Campbell-Bannerman. Morley, Secretary of State for India, was becoming important to Grey in his main objective for 1907 of tying Russia into the Entente Cordiale in the Triple Entente since Morley was ready to stifle the objections of the Indian Government. The older man admired Grey as a Parliamentarian and Grey had a soft spot for Morley's views on Home Rule as well as reform of the House of Lords.

The complete Memorandum is placed in the Appendix as some readers may want to read it in full, even though to present-day readers some parts appear rather stilted and read in an old-fashioned style.

The immense significance of Eyre Crowe's Memorandum lies in one fact: that after he had read it, it was described by the Foreign Secretary, Edward Grey, as 'most valuable' and 'most helpful as a guide to policy' in the accompanying Minute. Also the fact that Grey specifically asked for it to be sent to the Prime Minister, Campbell-Bannerman, and Lord Ripon, the then Chancellor of the Exchequer, Asquith, also Morley and Haldane. The Memorandum's appearance a year after Grey became Foreign Secretary reflects his by then settled priorities for foreign policy and his embrace of the prevailing 'Foreign Office view'.[29]

There has been a tendency for the Foreign Office to develop from time to time an all-powerful internal zeitgeist among its senior

---

29 T G Otte, *The Foreign Office Mind: The Making of British Foreign Policy, 1865–1914* (Cambridge University Press, Cambridge: 2011) and Valerie Cromwell and Zara S Steiner, 'The Foreign Office before 1914: A Study in Resistance' in Gillian Sutherland (ed.), *Studies in the Growth of Nineteenth-Century Government* (Routledge & Kegan Paul, London: 1972).

diplomats about aspects of foreign policy. This has sometimes enhanced and sometimes damaged its reputation over the last century. This Foreign Office view was there under Grey after 1906 with respect to hostility towards Germany. Then it developed in the late 1930s under the Foreign Secretary Lord Halifax into appeasement of Germany. Interestingly, after Anthony Eden courageously resigned as Foreign Secretary on 20 February 1938, Churchill was quick to sign a round robin in support of Chamberlain's policy in the House of Commons. He told the Chief Whip, David Margesson on 17 March that his Prime Minister's point of view and his were not divergent.[30] Eden's resignation never therefore became a rallying point to remove Chamberlain, and Churchill only unleashed his full invective against Chamberlain on 5 October 1938. Chamberlain was forced out as Prime Minister after much criticism and many abstentions in a debate in the House of Commons in May 1940. Halifax was swayed by Chamberlain and Horace Wilson, who was Chamberlain's influential adviser despite some evidence of having personal doubts on the policy. Chamberlain had cleverly moved Sir Robert Vansittart, the PUS at the Foreign Office, who was fiercely anti-Hitler, into a 'high-sounding innocuous post' as the government Chief Diplomatic Adviser. He then replaced him with the more pliant Sir Alexander Cadogan.[31] Within the Foreign Office opinion was divided, but Rab Butler, then a junior minister under Halifax, was an appeaser, later to become for a short time Foreign Secretary in 1963–4. Another Foreign Office view was critical of the creation of Israel even before the Palestine Mandate in the 1940s under Eden and Bevin; it continues with a longstanding pro-Arabist-leaning group to the present day. A pro-US, Atlanticist 'Foreign Office view' developed momentum with US Secretary of State George Marshall's speech in 1947, and was led by

---

30 David Dutton, *Neville Chamberlain* (Arnold, London: 2001) p 112.
31 David Reynolds, *Summits. Six Meetings that Shaped the Twentieth Century* (Allen Lane, London: 2007) p 42.

Bevin. It still largely survives thanks to PUSs like Antony Acland, John Coles and David Gillmore. Perhaps the most powerful of all Foreign Office views is that of the Europhile lobby, first starting in the 1960s under Macmillan as Prime Minister and heavily influenced by Edward Heath. It was then checked by Wilson, Callaghan, Thatcher and Major, but reemerged from 1997 to 2007 as part of the domination of foreign policy by Prime Minister Blair's EU policy. Such groupings are peculiar to the Diplomatic Service. They are not often found in Civil Service departments, and perhaps have their origins in the fact that their adherents are often serving overseas, and start to feel distanced from domestic opinion. Some diplomats also passionately believe their diplomacy has a special nature distinctive from, and not wholly subject to, political direction.

* * *

Hardinge comments revealingly at the end of Crowe's Memorandum when he gave Lord Sanderson, his predecessor, a copy, that 'to my surprise he has taken up the cudgels for Germany'. Sanderson, though in retirement, provides a fascinating counter from his long experience to the prevailing wisdom in the Foreign Office, demonstrating that the diplomatic 'Foreign Office view' was not universally shared.[32] He challenges Crowe's view that Bismarck was 'guilty of deception' and asserts that Germany had had a long stated interest in Morocco. He sees the French leader, Delcassé, as 'steadily pursuing a series of manoeuvres for the purpose of isolating Germany'. He challenges the view that German colonial policies were acts of 'direct and unmistakable hostility to England.' He claims there is no foundation for the statement that Germany made pressing proposals for England to take sides with the Triple Alliance, puts a different slant on policy towards Samoa, Zanzibar, the Congo and the Transvaal, and says his recollection of the

---

32 *British Docs*, Vol III, pp 420–31.

negotiations over the Anglo-German Agreement of October 1900 does not altogether tally with that given in the Memorandum as 'At that time our relationship with Germany was decidedly friendly and a considerable section of the Cabinet were in favour of an alliance or at least an agreement for joint policy.' He goes on to explain that he had written this note because 'the history of German policy towards this country is not the unchequered record of black deeds which the Memorandum seems to portray.'

Grey's comment on Hardinge's letter, including Sanderson's notes with Crowe's rebuttal alongside them, is terse and dismissive. 'It may all come to rest now. E. G.' A Foreign Secretary who did not share Crowe's views would have been entitled to send the document back to the department for rewriting to reflect Sanderson's and others' criticism before authorising a wider circulation of such a sensitive and secret subject in a named Memorandum.

Crowe has sometimes been called a Germanophobe, but that is too easy a categorisation. He had a German mother and had grown up in Germany, where his father was a British Consul. He even spoke with a slight German accent. His parents had known the eldest son of the German Emperor Wilhelm I and his English wife, who according to Margaret MacMillan 'shared their liberal hopes for Germany'. [33] Crowe had deep affection for Germany and German culture but he deplored what he saw as the triumph of Prussianism with its authoritarianism and stress on military values. He was also highly critical of what he saw as 'the erratic, domineering and often frankly aggressive spirit' which in his opinion animated German public life.

Margaret MacMillan likens the Crowe Memorandum to George Kennan's Long Telegram to Washington at the start of the Cold War with the Soviet Union. This provided the basis for President Truman, George Marshall and Dean Acheson to build their policy

---

33 Margaret MacMillan, *The War That Ended Peace: How Europe Abandoned Peace for the First World War* (Profile Books, London: 2013), p 115.

of containment through NATO. Later came détente, negotiations over nuclear weapons and ideological battles over Soviet Communism. Kennan's long cable was sent to Washington while he was Chargé d'Affaires in Moscow. It was not a State Department document. It came at a time when Truman himself had as yet done nothing to implement his resolution to 'stop babying the Soviets' in the month and a half since his reprimand to Byrnes, his then Secretary of State.[34] President Truman read Kennan's cable, and the Secretary of the Navy, Forrestal, had it reproduced and made required reading 'for hundreds, if not thousands, of higher officers in the armed services.' Crowe's Memorandum, by contrast, was already the policy of the Foreign Secretary and the Secretary for War and in part at least the Prime Minister, Campbell-Bannerman, for over a year. Crowe, like other diplomats, had strongly influenced policy, but Kennan created a policy. The hidden perspective running through the Crowe Memorandum was also not one of containment of Germany, but represented the views of those diplomats and politicians who were resigned to war against Germany. It consolidated their prejudices. It did not stimulate the creation of a realistic policy for holding Germany off war nor a strategy for fighting such a war. It offered military entanglement for Britain but did nothing to bind Europe together.

There is one key passage where Crowe acknowledges that:

the equilibrium established by such a grouping of forces is technically known as the balance of power, and it has become almost an historical truism to identify England's secular policy with the maintenance of this balance by throwing her weight now in this scale and now in that, but ever on the side opposed to the political dictatorship of the strongest single State or group at a given time. If this view of British policy is correct, the opposition into which

---

34 John Lewis Gaddis, *The United States and The Origins of the Cold War, 1941–1947* (Columbia University Press, New York: paperbound edition 1972) p 304.

England must inevitably be driven to any country aspiring to such a dictatorship assumes almost the form of a law of nature.

Crowe's use of the word 'nature' is interesting. 'Nature' implies the use of natural geography, natural forces and natural behaviour. Where Crowe was wrong was that his Memorandum failed to appreciate that the Military Conversations starting in January 1906 were bound to have a profound influence on German behaviour during that year and subsequent years, convincing them that Britain had made its decision to back France. It was also unnatural for Britain to undertake the Military Conversations in the light of its previous military strategy to avoid involvement in continental land battles and to rely on the exercise of maritime power.

The natural military and political response of the French, having been beaten by Germany in 1871 in a land battle, and given that they felt Germany was preparing to attack them again through Belgium, should have been to defend the home base. The natural political response of Great Britain should have encouraged France to build up its home forces at the expense of its overseas forces from 1906, and to do this virtually regardless of cost to ensure their national survival. The other natural military response from Great Britain to the request from France for help should have been to offer to strengthen its military commitment to France by undertaking never to let the German navy be in a position to influence any German-French land battle from the sea. That would not have been a neutralist response but a preventive response. Britain also needed not only to hold the German navy in the North Sea but to develop the capacity of the Royal Navy to intervene against German shipping, to help to force, in the event of war, a negotiated settlement and to bring an end to the sort of protracted land warfare that was being predicted. Under such a twin political and military strategy there should have been no hint that the British would mount an expeditionary force at the request of the French, until at least it was much clearer that this was needed because of

Germany's force levels. Rather Britain should have waited to see whether the French were ready to build up their forces in northern France before taking detailed steps for the deployment of a British Expeditionary Force to France.

Chapter Three

The Cabinet Asserts Itself in 1911

On 14 December 1905 the new Liberal Cabinet was formed. It was 19 strong when it met for the first time. At a mass party rally at the Albert Hall on 21 December, with a General Election in front of them, Campbell-Bannerman was in good spirits, attacking the Balfour Government for departing in a 'midnight flitting' and for having 'run away … in the murky midnight of December'. On foreign affairs he said, 'I wish emphatically to reaffirm my adhesion to the policy of the Entente Cordiale… In the case of Germany also I see no cause whatever of estrangement in any of the interests of either people.'[1]

After the rally MPs moved to their constituencies to fight the General Election, and Cabinet members were much in demand for speaking engagements around the country. Grey, interestingly, stayed over Christmas with his wife at the country estate of Lord Rosebery. If there were still differences over Grey's policy, over the favouring of France in respect of Germany, they were set to one side and the two men were friends again.

In January the business of government continued despite the election, particularly for Sir Edward Grey and the Foreign Office. Sir Edward Clarke, the Secretary of the Committee of Imperial Defence (CID), saw Grey on 9 January 1906 and told him of the

---

1 John Wilson, *CB: A Life of Sir Henry Campbell-Bannerman* (Constable, London: 1973), p 470.

informal discussions of military figures with the French, in particular that of the First Sea Lord, Admiral Fisher, with the French Naval Attaché on 2 January. He also told him the list of questions he had asked the military correspondent of *The Times,* Colonel Charles à Court Repington, to put to the French General Staff through the Military Attaché in London. These covered such sensitive issues as: 'What is the French opinion concerning landings on the German coasts? If we could send 100,000 men for such and assisted France with transports, could she supply another 100,000 men, and in what time and from what ports? ... Would it be possible for France to capture Togoland and the Cameroons, if we captured German E and S.W. Africa and German possessions in the Pacific.'[2]

That all this had gone so far over a month without the specific authority of the new government was a sign that political controls were weak. Clarke even went as far as to say to Grey that he had 'said nothing to the Prime Minister and felt it was better not to do so at this stage'. Grey apparently agreed to say little to CB and in a letter to the Prime Minister on 9 January told him he had promised the French diplomatic support but no more. He furthermore gave no details about the military meetings but did give a clue as to how his mind was moving:

> indications keep trickling in that Germany is preparing for war in the Spring; France is very apprehensive. I do not think there will be a war... But the War Office ought, it seems to me, to be ready to answer the question what could they do, if we had to take part against Germany, if for instance the neutrality of Belgium was violated?[3]

Next day, the 10th, Grey wrote again by hand to CB:

2 Charles à Court Repington, *The First World War, 1914–18* (Constable, London: 1920) p 8.
3 Wilson, *CB*, p 515.

I wrote in innocence last night: this afternoon Cambon put the question to me directly and formally. I enclose the record. Sanderson was present at the whole conversation. I assume you will have a Cabinet directly the elections are over to decide what I am to say. Before that happens I shall be glad of the opportunity to talk it over … I have kept a copy of this conversation: I am leaving it to you to decide to whom it should be circulated & when.[4]

The enclosure describing the meeting was in Grey's own hand, the most sensitive and relevant part of which was:

The French Ambassador asked me today whether in the event of an attack (*une aggression brutale*) by Germany upon France arising out of the Morocco difficulty, France could rely upon the armed support of Britain. I said I could not answer this question: I could not even consult the Prime Minister or the Cabinet during the elections. I was sure there would be a strong sentiment and sympathy on the part of the English public; more than that I could not say and all I could promise was diplomatic support now… . M. Cambon said he would again ask me after the elections were over.

Meanwhile next day in the Foreign Office on 11 January Grey's private secretary Mallet was asking the British Ambassador in Paris without Grey's knowledge to send a tough message about the likely French reaction in order to 'buck up these miserable creatures', and specifically disparaging his political boss Grey: 'he gives no opinion at all himself. In speaking to me he seemed very nervous and said it was a great step to take without Parliament about a secret engagement.' (See Chapter Two, pages 38–9 for the complete text of the letter.) This letter is the smoking gun of the whole of the Military Conversations. It demonstrates Grey was aware of the

---

4 Wilson, *CB*, p 525.

Constitutional impropriety of what he was being asked to embark on and it explains the careful form of words assiduously used by him and the Foreign Office until his moment of truth in the House of Commons on 3 August 1914 (see Chapter Four, p 208) about 'entailing obligations'.

Grey sent a message to the British Ambassador in Paris (see Chapter Two, p 32, Doc. 210(a)) that same day. The original draft of that despatch has a handwritten note by Grey 'Not for print at present'. Copies were also sent to the Prime Minister and Lord Ripon. Since it was only on 18 January that Sir Francis Bertie, Ambassador in Paris, replied, there was definitely some delay in Grey's initial despatch reaching him. On receiving Bertie's reply Grey minuted:

> Nothing is to go to the Cabinet, till I have seen the Prime Minister which I expect to do next week. This despatch ... should go to Lord Ripon (who is in London & whom I hope to see on Monday) as well as to the Prime Minister... they should of course be added to the papers ... to be prepared & considered as a whole by the Cabinet eventually.

To give him credit, Grey, at this stage, was rightly seeing that the Military Conversations was an issue that should go to Cabinet. CB replied on the 21st, 'When would you like to have a Cabinet? Would 30th, 31st, or 1st do? Would you like the answer for the French to be confirmed by a Cabinet before it is given.' To which Grey answered that the date for a Cabinet had better not be fixed till he had talked the matter over with him.[5] Grey spoke to Haldane, who was taking part in his election campaign in Northumberland on that Friday 12 January (see Chapter Two, p 48). The chapter entitled 'The Seeds of War' in Wilson's biography of Sir Henry Campbell-Bannerman is a fascinating account of the political manoeuvring of both Grey

---

5 Wilson, *CB*, pp 528–9.

and Haldane in January 1906. It demonstrates that Haldane's claim in his book before the war to have seen the Prime Minister that January in London, when he had been given authority to hold the talks, is dubious in the extreme. CB was not in London or any-where near it over the weekend of 14 January as he was in Scot-land taking part in the electoral campaign. Haldane's daily letters to his mother make no reference either to any London meeting. So there is no evidence, indeed a lot of contrary evidence, that the 15 January start of the Military Conversations was ever authorised by the Prime Minister and Grey does not mention such authorisation. Thereafter CB was dealing with a likely *fait accompli*. The question for him was whether to risk a row with the two Cabinet Ministers he had least in common with or to roll with the punch and manage the reality that the Conversations had started. Politics is, as the saying goes, 'the art of the possible', and there have been few better or cannier exponents of that art amongst British Prime Ministers than Campbell-Bannerman.

Soon after this, on 26 January, CB fired off the note to Grey about the public interview given by General Sir F. Maurice in France, taken up later in *The Times*, which had resulted in a German protest (see Chapter Two, p 63, Doc. 264). Campbell-Bannerman asked Grey in very blunt terms if he had seen

> … an outrageous interview with Genl. Sir F. Maurice in a French paper, describing all that wd. happen if Germany & France went to war; how we should of course join France, how we would operate from Denmark, not from Schleswig Holstein, & so on.
>
> I have written to Haldane to the effect that in my opinion Genl. Maurice should be severely reprimanded (if he is still in the service) – and if possible that his whole view should be publicly repudiated.
>
> For a man to speak in such terms at this moment is little short of criminal.

This was no minor Prime Ministerial intervention as CB was

experienced in the ways of the military. He had twice been Financial Secretary to the War Office, also to the Admiralty, and Secretary of State for War. He was clearly both very angry and worried.
His political antennae must have been flashing red, well aware that
there would be, if there had not already been, angry protests from
Cabinet members. Lord Ripon, the Leader of the House of Lords
and a friend of CB, appears to have discussed the issue with the
Prime Minister. He also saw the night of the 26th Grey, Haldane
and Sir George Clarke. It was clear that CB reversed his earlier
readiness to go to Cabinet when he told Grey there should be no
Cabinet discussion on the 27th when they were both at Windsor
for the weekend as guests of the King.[6] On 31 January at the fourth
meeting of the Cabinet there was no mention of the military staff
talks.

Why this political panic? CB knew his party very well and he
could sniff an impending row. As described on page 122 later in this
chapter, on 1 November 1911 there actually was a Cabinet revolt,
when Morley led the attack on Grey, not just for never telling the
Cabinet but on the core issue of abandoning traditional neutrality. Most Cabinet members heard then for the first time about the
Military Conversations. The Cabinet split very badly with Prime
Minister Asquith, being forced to find a compromise, there being
15 against Grey and only five in favour. What the balance would
have been in 1906 if CB had decided to put the issue on the Cabinet
agenda is pure conjecture, but it is likely that it would not have
been very different.

'Why look in the crystal ball when you can count the votes?'
is another old political adage. No doubt CB counted the Cabinet
votes in his head in 1906 and found there were not sufficient to
even endorse the Military Conversations, and calculated that a
Cabinet meeting could have led to the forced resignation of Grey
and very possibly Haldane. The strong suspicion must be therefore

6 Wilson, *CB*, p 529.

that it was pure politics not diplomacy or good governance that decided CB's course of action at this time.

By any theory of proper Cabinet government it was a mistake not to tell the Cabinet, a view held rightly by many who have studied the issue, but theory was overtaken by harsh political realities. Politics is a blood sport and decisions often do not follow logic or constitutional precedent; also Cabinet rivalry and differences of view are part of the democratic process. Those members of the Cabinet who had most strongly opposed the Boer War were those most likely to oppose the Military Conversations and they were more strongly represented in the Cabinet of 1906 than in 1911. The Prime Minister judged that he risked a rebellion within a month of taking office from those who felt that the processes likely to follow the Conversations could lead to war. All Prime Ministers zealously guard their right to set the Cabinet agenda and hence it was CB, not Grey, who decided to withhold discussion.

What are the constitutional conventions and guidance for Prime Ministers in this delicate situation? There are few guidelines, mainly it is precedent governing their conduct in Cabinet of meetings. But in 1906 there was no Cabinet guidance on conduct or the procedures to be followed. Nevertheless, at root what this was about was Parliamentary democracy, government of the people, by the people and for the people. While some military matters are too sensitive to bring to Parliament, not bringing them to Cabinet is a very serious matter. Sanderson, the long-serving diplomat, a fount of knowledge about diplomatic and political practice, was correct to tell the French Ambassador Cambon that pledges that bind a country to go to war which are not revealed to Parliament under certain circumstances 'would justify impeachment' (see Chapter Two, pp 59–60).

In 2014, when the Iraq Inquiry will concentrate people's minds on the abuse of Cabinet government and the way in which Prime Minister Blair chose to present to Parliament the case for the Iraq War, it is necessary to remember that Cabinets are an essential part of British democracy where there is no elected President. The Cabinet in the American model is a very different animal to that under the British system. Inevitably, both reflect the personality of the Prime Minister or President. That is inescapable. Even so, the British Cabinet is a mechanism for the sharing of power; a British Prime Minister is not, like a US or French President, Head of State and it is the Queen who is Commander-in-Chief. The Coalition Government of 2010 in Britain, with a fixed five-year Parliament, has demonstrated the transient nature of recent periods of a presidential-style premiership dominated by Prime Ministerial hubris; in the case of Lloyd George 1919–22; of Neville Chamberlain 1937–8; of Margaret Thatcher 1988–90; and Tony Blair 2001–7.[7]

On matters of peace and war there has to be a recognition that some measure of 'needing to know' and restriction of the number of people who do know is the price of victory, and a smaller War Cabinet is therefore essential. Even for lesser conflicts like that over the Falklands in 1982 a War Cabinet is a wise choice. Advice to create one was conveyed by Harold Macmillan to Margaret Thatcher at the start of the fight to retake the Falkland Islands from the Argentinians in 1982. The skill of a good Prime Minister, helped by verbal reports at the top of the agenda routinely made by the Foreign Secretary, is to keep the whole Cabinet well-informed and abreast of all the key issues, particularly during long periods of international tension. The best Prime Ministers are not afraid of Cabinet debate and recognise that there can develop a collective wisdom.

In July and August 1914 there was no question that the Cabinet was fully consulted, and agreed by a large majority reluctantly to go to war. The ultimate authority to declare war lay with Asquith as Prime Minister. The same pattern of consultation was followed to a lesser extent in 1939 by Chamberlain. To a greater extent it was followed by Attlee in 1950 over the Korean War, which involved

---

7 David Owen, *In Sickness and In Power: Illness in Heads of Government During the Last 100 Years* (Methuen, London: revised edition, 2011).

the authority of the UN Security Council. Eden in 1956 did reveal to the Cabinet the clandestine nature and involvement of Israel in the invasion of Egypt at the Suez Canal. In 1991 John Major could easily have gone to Parliament over the war with Iraq following its invasion of Kuwait, but judged it more helpful to maintaining cross-party unity not to put the issue to the vote and have some Opposition MPs voting against. In 2003 there was all too little real debate in Cabinet but there was a vote in Parliament. That might well have established a precedent, however Gordon Brown, who wanted to change his Prime Ministerial prerogative to declare war, found that it was difficult to devise another mechanism and it has not been formally changed. It is hard to see a way that it can be if the necessity in some circumstances for speed and secrecy of action is to be preserved.

The two votes of the House of Commons on 30 August 2013 demonstrated that a majority saw military action targeted on Syria in retaliation for the use of gas as counter-productive, and David Cameron, the Prime Minister, recognised this as soon as the key vote, with a large number of abstentions, was announced. This vote had important and beneficial immediate consequences as it led to President Obama referring the US action to Congress for its approval, who were reluctant to approve it. This gave time for a much-needed dialogue between Russia and the US, leading to the destruction and removal of all chemical weapons from Syria under international supervision agreed by the UN Security Council – the first positive action over Syria in a deadlocked Security Council for three years. It is difficult to say after 2013 that the House of Commons and the democratic process has no impact any longer on international affairs. So far the chemical weapon eradication programme in Syria is being implemented on the approved schedule and the stand-off in the UN Security Council with Russia and China has been ended.

Cabinet government is a complex mechanism, because its effective working depends on individual behaviour. James Callaghan is the only British Prime Minister to date to have served in all four of the great offices of state. (Churchill was at the Exchequer and the Home Office, but not the Foreign Office.) Callaghan's rule of thumb was a wise one – those four key Cabinet Ministers should not disagree around the Cabinet table unless they had previously tried to sort out their differences. After that they were fully entitled to challenge the Prime Minister in Cabinet. In 1906, though the Foreign Secretary and the Secretary of State for War knew about the Military Conversations, Asquith as Chancellor of the Exchequer was not in the loop, though Lord Ripon, the Leader of the House of Lords, was. The First Lord of the Admiralty was not consulted but he probably soon came to know of the Conversations through other channels such as the CID or through communications within the Admiralty. Grey has been unfairly attacked as being solely responsible for withholding the facts about the Military Conversations from the Cabinet in 1906, when the decision was the Prime Minister's. Grey's sin of omission was not to tell Asquith when he became Prime Minister in 1908 and to leave doing so until April 1911 as is discussed on page 100 of this chapter.

The Prime Minister became increasingly concerned about the Military Conversations, and wrote to Lord Ripon on 2 February: 'I do not like the stress laid upon joint preparations. It comes very close to an honourable undertaking and it will become known on both sides of the Rhine.' He was correct on both counts. It was in effect 'an honourable undertaking' and it became more so over the next few years. Also, the Germans did, in fact, soon know about these Conversations from a secret agent but chose not to tell their embassy in London. Some have implied that withholding such information meant they were not sure it was true. It is not unusual, however, when dealing with highly sensitive intelligence, to restrict circulation to the home capital for fear of revealing what may in this case have been a very sensitive source. Particularly since those in England who were judged to need to know were at this time very strictly limited. The source likely to be less highly placed might have been in France.[8]

On 7 April 1907 the Prime Minister travelled to Paris to meet the French Prime Minister Clemenceau privately at the British Embassy. The Ambassador Bertie was not present – a significant exclusion. This was no accidental exchange, this was CB determined to send a political, not Foreign Office, message to France. Expecting to find him committed to come to the aid of France, Clemenceau was shocked to find that CB did not regard himself in any way committed. It was 'a douche of cold water'. Fortunately for the historic record, Admiral Maxse's daughter Lady Edward Cecil, who later married Lord Milner, wrote up her dinner on 10 April 1907 with Clemenceau that same evening. She described Clemenceau calling the British Prime Minister '*Quel père imbécil, quel idiot* … It comes to this,' Clemenceau said, 'in the event of your supporting us against Germany are you ready to abide by the plans agreed upon between our War Offices and to land 110,000 men on the coast while Italy marches with us in the ranks?' Then from Campbell-Bannerman came the crowning touch: 'The sentiments of the English people would be totally averse to any troops being landed by England on the Continent under any circumstances.' Clemenceau, she went on to write, was 'knocked over by the combination of waste and imbecility'. Clemenceau had every right to be angry, but at least CB had the courage and honesty to disown Grey's policy directly to Clemenceau, not leave it to fester, and when the Foreign Office and French protests followed CB gave little ground. He knew that his message had hit home.

In the period 1906 to 1914 the two Prime Ministers, Campbell-Bannerman and Asquith, were very different in age, experience, temperament and style. CB chose to have no reference to the Military Conversations made in discussion or in papers for the two years of his premiership. Asquith's attitude to and knowledge is

---

8 Wilson, *CB*, p 530.

discussed later in this chapter. There were in those days no formal Cabinet minutes, but the Prime Minister wrote a personal hand-written account for the King. In the case of CB these notes were short, sometimes very short, and he considered writing them a chore. Asquith wrote two to three pages; nevertheless the King preferred CB as a man to deal with, seeing Asquith, in Roy Jenkins's words in his biography of Asquith, as 'something of a political parvenu'. The letters to the King were copied by hand by the Principal Private Secretary and kept as the only government record. All this means that constructing what actually happened in the political world as distinct from the diplomatic world with their carefully calibrated dispatches and telegrams is very difficult.

It is also worth recalling that there was no Ministry of Defence or Chief of the Defence Staff in the first part of the 20th century. The Army and the Navy went head to head for resources and in 1908 both Lloyd George as Chancellor and Winston Churchill as Home Secretary were ready to champion cuts in defence expenditure. All through this period the constants in pushing the Military Conversations were Grey and Haldane, and Grey was already seen by A G Gardiner, then editor of the *Daily News,* in less than flattering terms for a Liberal-supporting newspaper:

> The inflexibility of his mind, unqualified by larger knowledge, swift apprehension of events of urgent passion for humanity, constitutes a peril for the future. His aims are high, his honour stainless; but the slow movement of his mind and his unquestioning faith in the honesty of those on whom he has to rely render it easy for him to drift into courses which a more imaginative sense and a swifter instinct would lead those to question and repudiate.

A summing up which is cited in Niall Ferguson's book as a judgement that has largely stuck.[9]

---

9 Niall Ferguson, *The Pity of War* (Allen Lane, London: 1998), p 567.

The First Sea Lord, Fisher, expressed his view of the defence decision-making and structure of the CID in a private letter to Lord Esher, its first chairman, later published in Fisher's rather bizarre autobiography – the book starts with a preamble, the opening sentence of which is, 'There is no plan or sequence!' On 12 September 1907, a few months after the British Prime Minister had spoken his mind to the French Prime Minister, Fisher wrote:

> My unalterable conviction is that the Committee of Imperial Defence is tending rapidly to become a sort of Aulic Council and the man who talks glibly, utterly irresponsibly, will usurp the functions of the two men who must be the 'Masters of the War', the First Sea Lord and the Chief of the General Staff. Make no mistake, I don't mean those two men are to be dictators, but the Government says 'Do so and so!' – these are two *executive officers* ... In regard to the 'Invasion Bogey' about which I am now writing to you, how curious it is that from the German Emperor downwards their hearts were stricken with fear that *we* were going to attack *them*.[10]

Examination of the records of the CID shows that on 19 December 1905 and 6, 12 and 19 January 1906 issues surrounding the Military Conversations were discussed in some detail. At the last meeting a plan was outlined and agreed. Thereafter there was nothing recorded until July 1907 when the War Office revised the plan and it was signed off by Grey, not CB. It is impossible to come to any other conclusion but that Campbell-Bannerman had deliberately distanced himself from the Military Conversations. To try to pretend he was not well aware of what the Foreign Office and his Foreign Secretary were up to is absurd. Prime Ministers do not travel to France privately to see their opposite number and exclude a diplomat of the seniority of Bertie without due thought

---

10 John Arbuthnot Fisher, *Memories, By Admiral of the Fleet, Lord Fisher* (Hodder & Stoughton, London: 1919) pp 181–2.

and deliberation. He had a message which he felt honour-bound to deliver to Clemenceau and he delivered it in plain English.

Asquith became Prime Minister on 1 April 1908 after CB had become ill, suffering a series of heart attacks. Campbell-Bannerman died after being invited by Asquith to continue to stay in No. 10 Downing Street on 22 April. On 28 April 1908 Clemenceau came to London and saw Grey whose note of the meeting is published in his autobiography. 'He dwelt with great emphasis upon the certainty that we should have to intervene on the Continent of Europe against any Power which attained a position of domination there, just as we had had to do in the time of Napoleon.' Presumably the French had decided that after CB had met Clemenceau in Paris they would have to wait until he died before progress could be made and this explains Grey's rather odd inclusion of his minute as an Appendix.[11]

Asquith was aware of the revised War Office Plan but surprisingly not the Military Conversations. He referred the Plan to a sub-committee of the CID on the Military Needs of the Empire, which met three times on 3 and 17 December 1908 and 23 March 1909. On 3 December the CID sub-committee according to Fisher held a 'furious meeting' although there is nothing of it in the official record. Prior to the meeting Fisher had decided against pressing any longer for an amphibious operation to be launched against German territory in the Baltic and he found there was no support for trying to occupy Zealand. In Fisher's own written reconstruction of the meeting, written much later, Asquith said to Fisher,

'Sir John, we've not heard you say anything?'
    Fisher: 'No, it's a purely military matter!' [military meaning Army]
    Asquith: 'But you've something on your mind – say it.'
    Fisher: 'If I were the German Emperor I should tell my millions

---

11 Edward Grey of Fallodon, *Twenty-Five Years, 1892 1916* (Hodder & Stoughton, London: 1925) p 289.

to fight neither with small or great but fight only with the 160,000 English and decimate them and massacre them.' [In fact the BEF at that time was planned to be 110,000.]

Fisher commented after 'massacre them' and indeed Mons came near to it.[12] (Fisher was referring to the Battle of Mons on 23 August 1914 when to hold the line just under 36,000 British troops fought and 1,600 were killed or wounded and had lost ground so Sir John French ordered the BEF to retreat. This was the first clash of arms on the European Continent since Wellington fought at Waterloo in 1815)[13]. Grey did not attend the sub-committee which was presided over by Prime Minister Asquith, who was still not fully aware of the Military Conversations. Among the other Ministers attending were Haldane, McKenna, First Lord of the Admiralty, Fisher, and Hardinge, the Permanent Under-Secretary at the Foreign Office, who said that the only grounds upon which the French could base any hopes of military assistance were the semi-official conversations that had taken place between the French Military Attaché and the British General Staff, an indirect reference, and not one that Asquith would have necessarily taken up as having great significance.

Already 'Fisher's sands at the Admiralty were running out',[14] and he soon was due to step down. The revised Plan was adopted at the 23 March 1909 meeting, the following being its conclusion:

(a) In the event of an attack on France by Germany, the expediency of sending a military force abroad, or relying on naval means only, is a matter of policy which can only be determined, when the occasion arises, by the Government of the day.

---

12 R F Mackay, *Fisher of Kilverstone* (Clarendon Press, Oxford: 1973) p 406.
13 Martin Gilbert, *First World War* (Weidenfeld & Nicolson, London: 1994) pp 57–9.
14 Mackay, *Fisher of Kilverstone*, p 408.

(b) In view, however, of the possibility of a decision by the Cabinet to use military force, the Committee have examined the plans of the General Staff, and are of opinion that in the initial stages of a war betwen France and Germany, in which the British Government decided to assist France, the plan to which preference is given by the General Staff is a valuable one, and the General Staff should accordingly work out all the necessary details.[15]

There is, however, recognition in the proceedings of the meeting that an economic blockade was a strategic option. Sadly that option was never fully studied or planned for. The proceedings also contained a passage stating that in the event of an attack on France by Germany, the expediency of sending a military force abroad, or of relying on naval means only was a matter of policy which could only be determined when the occasion arose by the Government of the day; hardly a ringing endorsement for an expeditionary force, yet accepted by planners as being the official go-ahead.

The sub-committee reported its conclusion to the Committee of Imperial Defence on 24 July 1909, and in its report the sub-committee remarked that it would be possible in the course of a few months to strengthen the British Expeditionary Force of four divisions and one cavalry division by two remaining divisions, thus bringing the force up to 160,000 men. The sub-committee also explained that in accordance with the conclusion arrived at by the General Staff they had continued to elaborate the scheme, certain alterations being made from time to time in the ports of embarkation and disembarkation in conformity with variations in the naval situation and in the French plans of military concentration.

In April 1909, when a recurrence of tension between France and Germany seemed to some as not improbable, in the CID meeting

the possibility of at once despatching six instead of four Divisions

---

15 See Doc No. 689 on pp 125–9.

beside the Cavalry Division came under consideration, and revised tables of the larger force with accelerated dates of mobilization were worked out. The tables for movements by rail, embarkation, sea transport, and disembarkation were similarly revised. This enlarged scheme was drawn up not in supersession of, but as an alternative to, the original scheme, from which it only differed in contemplating the immediate despatch of the two additional Divisions instead of in the course of a few months. As the greater includes the less, it is obvious that arrangements made for the despatch of a larger force would *a fortiori* provide for the despatch of a smaller force. It was recognised by the General Staff that the alternative scheme would have to be referred to the Committee of Imperial Defence for consideration.[16]

On 23 August 1909, the Prime Minister presiding and Grey, Lloyd George, Haldane, McKenna, Winston Churchill, and the First Sea Lord being present, even though doubt was expressed by some as to the prudence of adopting this alternative scheme, more particularly in connection with the requirements of home defence, no changes were made and it was formally adopted.

Throughout 1909, Grey, seeing the economic arguments about increasing defence expenditure in Cabinet gaining traction, did try to assuage German fears about encirclement. The King's visit to Berlin on 9 February 1909 went ahead, but Grey ruled out accompanying the royal party. The Cabinet insisted, however, that a responsible minister should go. A communiqué following the visit referred to the two governments' 'identity of view' on the Bosnian crisis. Grey around this time rejected French and other attempts to try and detach any of Germany's partners from the Triple Alliance. 'Italy is best left as she is – an ally of Germany by Treaty, with a strong leaning to friendship with us and France.' He kept a certain distance from Russia for much the same reason. Over the

---

16 Doc No. 689 on pp 125–9.

Baghdad railway Grey put pressure on the Turks as a way of getting the Germans to negotiate. This was sensible and well-judged. Then when, after the resignation of Bülow in July, the new German Chancellor Bethmann-Hollweg launched a major diplomatic initiative, Grey was bound to accept a negotiation. For a brief moment it appeared that a new phase was opening up in Grey's foreign policy over a naval understanding with Germany, and on 1 September the Cabinet approved a statement of the British position, and the anxieties of Grey and the Foreign Office 'that the ententes should not be imperilled was recognised with the eagerness of the radicals to take up the German offer.' That offer was a 'relaxation of the tempo' of construction over the next three years. By April 1910 Grey had reverted to language which his PUS Hardinge had used a year before to the German Foreign Minister Kiderlen. Grey demanded significant concessions and saw no merit in embarking on a course of gradual step-by-step negotiations. He put both Persia and the Baghdad railway into the negotiations, crudely overloading the agenda, as always persuaded that nothing should upset France or Russia.[17]

Roy Jenkins in his biography of Asquith questioned the widely held assumption up until then that Asquith was told about the Military Conversations in 1908 on becoming Prime Minister, claiming that there was no evidence that he was told of the position even when he succeeded to the Premiership. He asserts that in April 1911, when it seemed likely that the French would ask for further conversations, Grey wrote to Asquith with a brief account of what had occurred in 1906 in terms that suggest he was telling him for the first time:

---

17 D W Sweet, Chapter 11, 'Great Britain and Germany, 1905–1911', in F H Hinsley (ed.), *British Foreign Policy Under Sir Edward Grey* (Cambridge University Press, Cambridge: 1977) pp 225–32.

Letter to Asquith from Sir Edward Grey

April 16, 1911.

MY DEAR ASQUITH, – *Please look at Bertie's despatch of April 13. I have marked it for you, Morley, or Haldane, and I would suggest, as soon as Haldane returns, that you and Morley should have a talk with him.*

Early in 1906 the French said to us, 'Will you help us if there is war with Germany?'

We said, 'We can't promise, our hands must be free.'

The French then urged that the military authorities should be allowed to exchange views, ours to say what they could do, the French to say how they would like it done, if we did side with France. Otherwise, as the French urged, even if we decided to support France, on the outbreak of war we shouldn't be able to do it effectively. We agreed to this. Up to this point C-B., R. B. H., and I were cognisant of what took place – the rest of you were scattered in the Election.

The military experts then conversed. What they settled I never knew – the position being that the Government was quite free, but that the military people knew what to do, if the word was given.

Unless French war plans have changed, there should be no need of anything further, but it is clear we are going to be asked something.

Yours sincerely,

E. G.[18]

It is as clear as can be that Jenkins is correct and Grey's letter above of 16 April to Asquith and the accompanying enclosure of 11 April 1911 were the first intimation to Asquith of what happened in 1906 on the Military Conversations. It is also a very limited portrayal by Grey even in such a short letter of what had actually happened. To write to the Prime Minister, a close friend, in this way, on a matter

---

18 Grey, *Twenty-Five Years*, Vol I, pp 94, 95.

on which Grey had not briefed Asquith when he became Prime Minister in 1908, was to compress events in a way designed to minimise their importance. He makes no mention of the fact that he himself had initially expected, as had Campbell-Bannerman, to go to Cabinet after the election on 31 January 1906 (see Chapter Two, p 39). Asquith needed to be told by a political colleague why this matter had been withheld for over five years from him and the Cabinet, not just have it brushed aside as if it were a matter of no democratic importance.

As for writing of the military, 'what they settled I never knew', this stretches credulity to breaking point. Grey, since taking office, had often been invited to attend meetings of the CID and as described on page 99 in this chapter actually signed off the 'battle plan' in 1907. Even if he did not attend all the meetings, the lengthy proceedings were circulated. Grey was also a close friend of Neville Lyttelton, whom he had met in India in 1887 and who had become Chief of the General Staff in 1904, and Grey's biographer records, 'Grey, who knew next to nothing about military matters, would find Neville an excellent sounding board in the years to come.'[19] Indeed, if there is any truth in Grey's claim that he did not know what the military were up to, this can only be yet one more sign that this was a Foreign Secretary whose grasp of the core strategic questions facing Great Britain was damagingly defective throughout his period of office.

The despatch from the Ambassador to France to which Grey refers is not identified in his memoirs, where he writes that it 'should be in the official archives of the Foreign Office but a search there has not been able to identify it'. The explanation appears to be that Grey is referring to a short letter from Bertie enclosing Report No. 460 to him from Colonel Fairholme, the Military Attaché in the Embassy, received in the Foreign Office on 11 April, not 13

---

19 Michael Waterhouse, *Edwardian Requiem: A Life of Sir Edward Grey* (Biteback Publishing, London: 2013), p 17.

April. This is attached below and in an undated minute Grey said it should be sent to the Prime Minister, Morley and Haldane. The choice of Morley, who Grey must have suspected as a likely critic of the Military Conversations, is interesting. The key elements in the French general's viewpoint are referred to below for case of reference and underlined in the long enclosure.

> It will by no means suffice that a decision to co-operate should be arrived at after war has been declared, or even on the eve of rupture.
>
> The most acceptable and the only really effective form which British help could take would be the dispatch of the strongest possible expeditionary force, in time to take part, side by side with the French armies, in the decisive battle or battles between the main forces.

No. 460

Sir F. Bertie to Sir Edward Grey

F.O. *13392/13392/11/17*
(No. 168) Confidential

Paris, D. April 9, 1911
R. April 11, 1911

Sir,

I have the honour to transmit to you herewith, a despatch which I have received from Colonel Fairholme, the Military Attaché to this Embassy, reporting a conversation with General Foch, Commandant of the Staff College, on international politics.

I have, &c
FRANCIS BERTIE

Enclosure in No. 460

Colonel Fairholme to Sir F. Bertie

(No. 4) Confidential.

Paris, April 8, 1911

Sir,

I have the honour to submit to your Excellency the following state-ment of some views expressed by a prominent French general, in the course of a conversation which I had with him yesterday.

The officer in question is General Foch, Commandant of the Staff College, and he is in the closest touch with the French General Staff, and with its chief, General Laffon de Ladebat, so that his views may, I think, be taken as representative of the best-informed military opinion in this country,

The general expressed himself as profoundly impressed by the astuteness, activity, and continuity of German policy all over the world, and he lamented the fact that he was unable to detect those qualities, at least in the same measure, in the foreign policies of France, England and Russia.

The last-named Power, he said, is being fooled by Germany, and indeed, unmindful of recent Manchurian experiences, to weaken herself by embarking on fresh adventures, in Persia, which will infal-libly result in ultimate discontent at home, and in consequent revolu-tionary outbreaks which will tend to immobilise the Russian armies. This he considers to be the inward meaning of the recent Potsdam meeting.

He alluded to the outwitting of M. Isvolsky by Count Aehranthal, and it may interest your Excellency to learn that he spoke of the new Russian Ambassador as notoriously under German influence here in Paris.

General Foch dwelt on the flattering manner in which the German Emperor lavishes personal attentions and favours on all Russian *missions and officers who visit Germany, a policy which is not without its effect on the Russian army, and against which republican France is unfortunately not in a position to compete.*

Similarly, he continued, by fostering Moslem hostility against England, in Turkey and Egypt, Germany is preparing difficulties for the former Power, which will hamper her action on the continent of Europe when the day for action comes.

Germany is daily extending her influence over the minor European States, Belgium, Switzerland, Holland, &c., as well as in the near and Far East, in all of which regions there is a corresponding decline of British prestige.

'Germany,' the general went on to say, 'will never declare war against us, she will go on her way, gradually encroaching in all directions, always armed to the teeth and ready to fight if her pretensions should be challenged, until one day, at a moment when Russia and England have their hands full elsewhere, she will bring about a situation in which the ententé *Powers will find themselves confronted with the choice of making war on her or of suffering injury to vital interests. They will then have to decide between war at an unfavourable moment and effacement in the future.'*

It is thus that General Foch considers that war with Germany will come, and his forecast is that big events may be expected 'à partir de 1912.'

To remedy this state of affairs the general is of opinion that it behoves France and England to pursue a more active policy towards the minor European States, with a view to encouraging them to resist German influence and to oppose German incursion in case of war.

If Belgium, for instance, could be induced to contemplate a resolute defence of her frontier, with her 120,000 men, on the line of the Meuse, instead of a useless concentration back in Antwerp, the German advance would find itself seriously hampered. Similarly with Switzerland and Holland.

None of these States have any special love for Germany, but they fear her and naturally want to be on the winning side. They have constant evidence of Germany power and self-assertion, which are not counterbalanced by corresponding activity on the part of England and French diplomacy.

The general further considers that the French and British Governments ought to settle beforehand exactly what they are prepared to concede, and what to resist, in the many political questions of the moment, so that they may not be perpetually faced by fresh minor encroachments of German policy all over the world, which become faits accomplis *before a joint decision has been arrived at to resist them.*

But, above all, General Foch is firmly convinced of the urgent necessity for an understanding between His Majesty's Government and that of the republic regarding the form which joint action should take in the event of war between France and Germany.

It will by no means suffice that a decision to co-operate should be arrived at after war has been declared, or even on the eve of a rupture.

The most acceptable and the only really effective form which British help could take would be the dispatch of the strongest possible expeditionary force, in time to take part, side by side with the French armies, in the decisive battle or battles between the main forces of France and Germany [my emphasis], where it would help materially to neutralise the considerable numerical superiority of the German army, and where its early arrival and subsequent presence would enormously enhance the confidence, and hence the fighting value, of the French troops, who are always particularly susceptible to moral influences.

The collision may be expected to take place any time after the thirteenth day of the French and German mobilisation, when the main opposing forces will probably meet on a front of some 190 miles, extending from Namur on the north to about Epinal on the south.

In order that the British expeditionary force should be in its place by that date, it would have to be mobilised simultaneously with the French army, and it would have to be transported to the continent, and railed to the front without a moment's delay.

It must be evident to anybody in the least familiar with the complicated mechanism of modern war, aptly described by General Foch as

*de l'horlogerie,' [i.e. as intricate as that of a watchmaker] that an oper-
ation on such a scale could only be undertaken, with the slightest hope
of success, if the whole plan had been worked out beforehand on both
sides of the channel in its minu[t]est details, down to the sequence and
composition of the hundreds of troop-trains, as well as the exact hours
and minutes of their respective departures from the selected ports of
debarkation and of their arrival at their ultimate destinations.*

*The preparation of such a scheme offers no special difficulties to
the British and French general staffs, and it is obviously their function and duty to study and work out beforehand the military problems connected with any course of action which their respective
Governments may be expected to adopt under any reasonably probable circumstances.*

*But General Foch points out that, however fully such a scheme
might be prepared beforehand by the two general staffs, the French
Government, when the time came, could not possibly afford to
earmark railway lines and rolling-stock for such a purpose at a
moment when all its resources must be so urgently required, unless
indeed it had received a previous assurance that it could count with
certainty on the arrival of the British contingent.*

*Hence the absolute necessity for a clear previous understanding
between the two Governments. Upon its existence may depend the
result of the war and, consequently, the fate of Europe.*

*A British contingent dispatched at a later moment than as above
might probably just as well stay away.*

*General Foch observed that no doubt there might be insuperable
difficulties in the way of getting a majority in the British Parliament
to vote for such an agreement at the present moment, but he pointed
out that the Anglo-Japanese Alliance had been arranged without the
previous consent of Parliament having been obtained.*

I have, &c.
W. E. FAIRHOLME,
Military Attaché

MINUTES.

General Foch's remarks are worthy of the most serious attention. He sums up the situation in the paragraph marked on page 2, and his forecast agrees with that of many shrewd observers. The General however does not tell us how we are to stimulate Belgium, Denmark, Holland, etc., against Germany. What possible chance have these little States against an army whose peace strength is about to be raised to 5 millions.

The question of a definite military Convention with France is one fraught with such immense consequences that it can hardly be considered in a departmental minute.

War Office in original.

G. H. V.

11/4/11

I think that General Foch's description of German policy is accurate, and that the danger he depicts is both real and urgent. Germany's immediate efforts are at present concentrated on –

1. *Ostentatiously seeking British friendship;*
2. *Doing everything to create friction between Great Britain and other States, by action in Russia, in France, in Turkey and elsewhere; with a view to the levy of political blackmail;*
3. *Being absolutely prepared for a war when it comes;*
4. *Encouraging the pacifist movement in England – so diametrically opposed to all German principle of policy – in order to prevent Great Britain from taking any serious measures for combining with France and Russia to resist the German attack.*

It looks as if Germany were meeting with success in all these endeavours.

E. A. O.

Ap. 11

Colonel [sic] Foch's diagnosis is probably correct but nothing that we may say will persuade the small Powers to show a bold front to Germany if they think, and they probably do think, that on land at least she has the big battalions and that a day of reckoning will come for them in which their independence will be jeopardised.

W. L.

This is too wide a question to discuss by minutes. Should it not go to the Cabinet Committee?

A. N.

Prime Minister
Lord Morley
Lord Haldane
  in first instance.

E. G.

Sir E. Grey thinks this circulation sufficient.

W. T.[20]

On 1 July 1911 a German gunboat, the *Panther*, arrived at the port of Agadir on the Moroccan coast and a few days later a German light cruiser, the *Berlin*, sailed in as well. It was a deliberate challenge to France but because of the Military Conversations and the Triple Entente it began to be seen in London as a challenge to Great Britain as well. Some feared a more intense re-run of the 1904–5 crisis over Morocco. The British expert opinion was that France had not lived up to the terms of the 1906 Treaty of Algeciras. In the words of Margaret MacMillan, 'the Quai d'Orsay had flouted both the Treaty's spirit and its provisions by trying to establish political and economic dominance over the country and its feckless sultan.'[21]

---

20 *British Docs*, Vol. VI, p 617.
21 Margaret MacMillan, *The War That Ended Peace: How Europe Abandoned Peace for the First World War* (Profile Books, London: 2013) p 414.

Nevertheless, in Germany the new Chancellor, Bethmann-Holl-weg, who had very few personal problems with Britain, having sent his son to Oxford, seemed determined to court public opinion and to take a stand against French policy. His Foreign Minister Kiderlen, an uncouth addition to the conduct of foreign affairs, had created the crisis by sending in the *Panther*. His French oppo-site number then asked him outright at a meeting in July what he wanted and Kiderlen asked for a map and pointed to the whole of the French Congo. In London, Eyre Crowe saw the French readi-ness to make concessions as meaning not loss of interests or loss of prestige, but defeat, with all its inevitable consequences. On 4 July, Berlin was told that Great Britain had interests in any Moroccan negotiations. On 21 July the Foreign Office decided, having had no reply, to tell Germany that Britain would not accept any settlement over Morocco in which it did not participate, hoping to steady the negotiating process.

Surprisingly, that evening the Chancellor of the Exchequer, Lloyd George, in part at least as a party political positioning move, suddenly decided to speak on Morocco at the Lord Mayor of Lon-don's Mansion House. Grey, as demanded by protocol, approved the speech that he gave and it did not go to the Prime Minister. Lloyd George spoke in trenchant terms.

I believe it essential in the highest interests of not merely this country, but of the world, that Britain should at all hazards main-tain her place and her prestige amongst the Great Powers of the world. Her potent influence has been, many a time in the past and may yet be in the future, invaluable to the cause of human liberty. It has more than once in the past redeemed continental nations who are sometimes too apt to forget that service from overwhelming disaster and even from national extinction. I would make great sacrifices to preserve peace. I conceive that nothing could justify a disturbance of international goodwill except questions of the gravest international moment. But if a situation were to be forced on us in which peace could only be preserved by the surrender of the great and beneficent position Britain has won by centuries of heroism and achievement, by allowing Britain to be treated where her interests were vitally affected, as if she were of no account in the Cabinet of Nations then I say, I say emphatically, that peace at that price would be a humiliation intolerable for a great country like ours to endure. National honour is no party question. The security of our great international trade is no party question. The peace of the world is much more likely to be secured if all nations realise fully what the condition of peace must be.[22]

The speech made the German Foreign Minister Kiderlen pause as was intended. It also laid the foundation for the 'Welsh Wizard' to push out Asquith in 1916 because Conservatives began to revise their opinion of Lloyd George and his foreign policy positions. The Agadir speech had the dramatic effect of pushing Lloyd George up into the highest ranks of the Liberal Government: no longer was he just a social reformer; now he was seen as the coming man with global views, in the process shedding his public image as an anti-Boer War pacifist.

On 29 August Bertie sent another report with an enclosure from Colonel Fairholme, reporting on a meeting with the newly appointed French Chief of the General Staff, General Joffre. The key section gives Joffre's views (underlined for ease of reference on p 113) on both a German attack through Belgium, in which case the French would aim to hold them in check on that flank, and an attack on Alsace and Lorraine on the other flank, where he was certain the population would rise up in support of France.

---

22 David Lloyd George, *War Memoirs of David Lloyd George* (Odhams Press, London: 1938) Vol 1, p 44.

No. 475

Sir F. Bertie to Sir Edward Grey

F.O. 34109/34109/11/17
(No. 377.) Secret.

Paris, D. August 25, 1911
R. August 29, 1911

Sir,

I have the honour to transmit to you herewith a despatch as marked in the margin which I have received from Colonel Fairholme, Military Attaché to this Embassy reporting a conversation with General Joffre, Chief of the French General Staff, respecting strategical problems which would arise in a war between Germany and France and other matters.

I have, &c
FRANCIS BERTIE

Enclosure in No. 475

Colonel Fairholme to Sir F. Bertie

(No. 12) Confidential

Paris, August 24, 1911

Sir,

I have the honour to report to Your Excellency that I was to-day received by General Joffre, the newly appointed Chief of the French General Staff, who, under the recent reorganisation of the High Command, occupies the position of supreme head of the main French Armies in Peace and War.

General Joffre, who took part in the defence of Paris as a

Sub-Lieutenant in the Siege Artillery, and was transferred to the Engineers after the war, has seen service in several Colonial Expeditions, including Tonkin, in all of which he rendered eminent services. He commanded the IInd Army Corps (Amiens) up to last year, when he was appointed a member of the Supreme Council of War.

I was favourably impressed by the personality of the new Chief, who is a big, square-built man, quiet in manner, but with an unmistakable air of confidence and resolution. He is 59 years of age.

I found the General extremely well-disposed towards England, and anxious to maintain the cordial and intimate relations which have existed of late between the two Armies. He expressed his intention of affording all possible facilities for the interchange of information, and of visits by French and British officers, with a view to mutual improvement and understanding.

When the first reserve had worn off, he became more communicative than most French Generals in responsible positions, and it may interest Your Excellency to know what he said about the present political and military situation.

General Joffre considers that, though relations with Germany are undoubtedly very strained, ('très tendues'), the principal danger of the protracted negotiations lies in the possibility of incidents occurring which might inflame public opinion on either side.

The French Military Attaché in Berlin, who was formerly Chief Staff Officer to General Joffre, had, in letters to his late commander, for some time past predicted the present difficulties with regard to Morocco, but, in his opinion, Germany does not want war at the present moment. He thinks it probable that an unsatisfactory agreement, wanting in finality, will be patched up. He writes, however, that the German General Staff is very busy just now with war preparations.

On the French side, General Joffre said that he and his Staff have been, and are still, hard at work settling the details of their plans of campaign, which, he stated, will be ready in every particular in a few days' time.

The General then went on to discuss the strategical problem.

The one unknown factor is whether the Germans mean to come through Belgium or not. 'I wish I knew that,' he observed, 'and I wish I knew that they intend doing so; it would be better for us. It would greatly hamper our dispositions if we did not know their intentions in this respect by about the fourth day of mobilisation, as it would be difficult to get back any considerable force in time for employment in the main theatre of operations which had been originally sent to oppose an advance through Belgium. Recent German preparations, construction of railways and detraining platforms, &c., point to an intention to move considerable bodies of troops in these regions.'

The new Chief attaches the very greatest importance to the co-operation of a British expeditionary force, which concentrating somewhere between Douai and Cambrai, and falling on the right flank of the German advance, might produce great, and even decisive, results. But it would have to be sent early in the day; its intervention, for instance, on the 18th day of the French mobilisation, might not prove a bit too soon. As regards the provision by the French authorities of the requisite railway transport to convey the British Contingent to the points of concentration which might ultimately be fixed on, he anticipates no difficulty, even should all the six British Infantry Divisions be dispatched.

He stated that arrangements have recently been made by which the carrying powers of the French railways in War have been considerably increased.

'In any case,' he said, 'Germany must pour a large force into Alsace and Lorraine, as if they allowed us to gain a footing there the populations of both provinces would rise. This we know for certain. And then every possible difficulty would be created for their transport, &c.'

I gathered that, if the Germans should advance in force via Belgium, the French plan would be to hold them in check on that flank, and to attack vigorously on Alsace and Lorraine.

General Joffre remarked that if the Germans did not attack in *force through Belgium, the front of contact between the two armies would become very restricted for such large forces.*

I ventured to suggest that such a contingency might not prove disadvantageous to France in view of the notorious superiority of the German forces in numbers.

'That superiority,' General Joffre replied, 'does not trouble me very much. It would only amount to two or three Army Corps. Against the German Reserve Corps we have our Reserve Divisions, and we can count on the active intervention of the Russian army, which would be on the move certainly before the 30th day of our mobilisation. But we should very much like to know what Austria would do.'

On my mentioning Italy, the General said very positively, 'Italy will make no move. Her interests lie on our side, not on that of Germany and Austria.'

Speaking of the abandonment of the French Army Manoeuvres, which has now been definitely decided on, General Joffre said that this is due to the prevalence of foot-and-mouth disease in the North of France; from his manner, and from the details he gave me, I am satisfied that this, and not the possibility of war, is the true reason for the change of plans.

He informed me that the manoeuvres of the VIIth Army Corps, (Besançon), which, like the VIth, is a frontier corps of three Infantry Divisions, will be transformed into Army Manoeuvres, but on a smaller scale than those originally contemplated, and that the Foreign Officers will be invited to witness these instead of those which have now been cancelled.

I have, &c.
W. E. FAIRHOLME Colonel
Military Attaché[23]

Asquith's patience over the Military Conversations appeared to be running out by 5 September 1911; when he realised how detailed they were he wrote a strong letter to Grey about the conversations

---

23 *British Docs*, Vol. VI, p 642.

'between General Joffre and Col. Fairholme as they seemed to him to be rather dangerous; especially the part which refers to possible British assistance. The French ought not to be encouraged in present circumstances to make their plans on any assumption of this kind.' Grey replied on 8 September, 'It would create consternation if we forbade our military experts to converse with the French. No doubt these conversations and our speeches have given an expectation of support. I do not see how that can be helped.'[24]

Grey's explanation in his memoirs that his words 'expectation of support' here concerned only the Agadir crisis is nonsense: he knew very well that the expectation in Paris was that there would be support at any time Germany looked hostile, and General Joffre specifically states in the conversation with Fairholme that, in his opinion, with regard to Morocco, Germany did not want war.

Asquith also seemed to sense that planning in the Admiralty was defective in many respects, not least over any blockade. Haldane had expressed a wish to become First Lord of the Admiralty instead of McKenna, but the Prime Minister decided to appoint Churchill that autumn, using the excuse to his friend Haldane, who by then was sitting in the Lords, that with Naval matters controversial within their Party and between the Parties, he needed the First Lord to be in the Commons. In so doing Asquith may have expected to detach Churchill from that element, which included Lloyd George, which had been cutting back on Naval expenditure.

Asquith's health, which in office had hitherto been pretty good, was now deteriorating. He had had a near collapse on 2 April 1911, when he complained of having felt giddy for three weeks, and appeared exhausted, having been dealing over many long hours with the first national coal strike. His doctor diagnosed hypertension and warned him to substantially reduce his alcohol intake, which was mainly in the form of wine and brandy at dinner. It is

---

24 Keith Robbins, *Sir Edward Grey: A Biography of Lord Grey of Fallodon* (Cassell, London: 1971), p 246.

claimed that henceforward 'he seems to have taken a firm hold on his alcohol consumption'.[25] But that claim is not sustainable, as two later accounts reveal Asquith still drinking during his wartime premiership. Field Marshal Sir Douglas Haig had also remarked on his drinking when he wrote to his wife after Asquith visited his HQ in France:

> The PM seemed to like our old brandy. He had a couple of glasses (big sherry glass size!) before I left the table at 9.30 and apparently he had several more before I saw him again. By that time his legs were unsteady, but his head was quite clear and he was able to read the map and discuss the situation with me.

In another episode, after having lunch with Asquith, Constance Battersea, an old friend, wrote to her sister: 'The PM kind, extremely cordial, but how he is changed! Red and bloated – quite different from what he used to be. He gave me a shock. They all talk of his overeating and drinking too much. I am afraid there is no doubt about it.'

By modern diagnostic standards, Asquith became an alcoholic while Prime Minister.[26] He also had a bizarre relationship with Venetia Stanley, the youngest daughter of Lord Sheffield. It began in 1910 when she was 25, and he was 58. He wrote to her regularly and with increased volume into and throughout his life as war leader, sometimes many times a day, and even during Cabinet meetings.[27] 'The relationship was certainly emotional (although probably never physical) and conducted with a charming candour.'[28]

25 Colin Clifford, *The Asquiths* (John Murray, London: 2002) pp 192–3.
26 David Owen and Jonathan Davidson, 'Hubris syndrome: An acquired personality disorder? A study of US Presidents and UK Prime Ministers over the last 100 years', *Brain*, Vol 132, Issue 5 (February 2009), pp 1396–1406.
27 Michael and Eleanor Brock (eds.) *H H Asquith: Letters to Venetia Stanley* (Oxford University Press, Oxford: 1982).
28 Roy Hattersley, *The Edwardians* (Little Brown, London: 2004) p 50.

While neither his drinking nor this relationship was solely responsible, there was in the House of Commons and in the country a certain loss of esteem for Asquith. He was not the first senior minister to indulge himself, and nor would he be the last. It was becoming evident, however, that crucial support was starting to drift away. Lloyd George had put down a marker over Agadir and it was now obvious that he was gathering political momentum in Parliament. This was apart from the Marconi Scandal, which involved Lloyd George and began on 7 March 1912 ending in effect in Parliament on 19 June 1913. Thereafter, he continued to rise in public esteem until he imposed in Keynes's words a 'Carthaginian peace at the 1919 Paris negotiations'. Looking back, comparisons between Lloyd George and Asquith are notoriously difficult. Roy Jenkins, speaking about Asquith in 1987 and reflecting on the biography he had written in 1964, tried hard to be fair: 'I think he was in office too long and his style was unsuited to the demands of wartime leadership.'[29] Whereas Lloyd George's style was well suited to the role of Prime Minister until he acquired hubris syndrome in around 1920. In 1915 he was ready to become Minister of Munitions in the new coalition, and since this meant giving up the great office of Chancellor of the Exchequer, some saw it as a demotion. But he judged wisely that it would allow him to be identified more than as Chancellor with the civilian war effort. He subsequently became Secretary of State for War after Kitchener was drowned at sea when HMS *Hampshire* struck a mine on 5 June 1916.

On 6 December 1916, Lloyd George became Prime Minister of the Coalition government. In a complicated manoeuvre, he and a significant number of Conservative members of the wartime coalition had for some time been pressurising Asquith to accept a revised form of War Cabinet, which Asquith did on 3 December but then rejected on the 4th, causing a rift within the government

---

29 Roy Jenkins, *Portraits and Miniatures* (London: Macmillan, 1993), pp 126–7.

and leading him to resign. The Conservative Opposition leader Bonar Law had a belief in Lloyd George and when Balfour agreed to serve under Lloyd George it was inevitable that Asquith and many Asquithians decided not to continue in government. Lloyd George, besides having Bonar Law as Chancellor of the Exchequer, managed to keep Arthur Henderson, Leader of the Labour Party, but a schism within the Liberal Party was created, the residues of which can still be detected today amongst Liberal Democrats.

* * *

This book is not the place for an account of Lloyd George's premiership, but it is important to start to gauge the personality of the man who was destined to play from 1911 to 1922 an ever greater role in the governance of Great Britain. He did not play an active part in the Cabinet row over the Military Conversations in 1911, but was crucial in the Cabinet discussion in July-August 1914. He was then the key player from December 1916 as Prime Minister in the First World War and its aftermath. His appointment as Prime Minister came as a tonic for the British public. By the third year of the war, the German submarine threat was starting to imperil the Merchant Navy and the nation's crucial supply lines. Victory seemed far off, defeat possible.

Unlike Winston Churchill's coalition in 1940, where Churchill, by then a member of the Conservative Party, had the majority of MPs, the Lloyd George coalition was dependent on Conservative MPs' support and he could not rely on half of his own Liberal MPs nor on the Irish National Party. In essence, the war-time coalition had its origins in Lloyd George's positioning of himself over the Agadir speech, which made him acceptable to Conservatives like Bonar Law. Bonar Law had made it possible for Lloyd George to become Prime Minister by agreeing to be Chancellor of the Exchequer and encouraging Balfour to agree to serve as Foreign Secretary. Yet in 1922 it was Bonar Law, who had left government on grounds of ill health in 1920, who went to the Carlton Club meeting on 19 October. He was one of the 185 Conservatives who voted against Lloyd George continuing and it was he who became Prime Minister while Balfour stood by Lloyd George.

Lloyd George introduced what the Conservatives wanted, a small War Cabinet. The surprise was that of its five members, he was the only Liberal. The other members were Andrew Bonar Law, the Conservative leader, who as well as Chancellor of the Excheq-uer became Leader of the House; Arthur Henderson, the Labour leader; and two Conservative peers, Earl Curzon and Viscount Milner, who were not very party political, proconsuls and proven administrators of the empire, who were brought in as ministers without portfolio.

The Prime Minister, in effect, by this arrangement, wisely con-tained his own mercurial personality. It worked because virtually every day after breakfast Lloyd George would walk along the con-necting passage from 10 to 11 Downing Street and spend around an hour with Bonar Law reviewing the day's business and submitting his own imaginative ideas to Bonar Law's practical, critical mind.[30] Stanley Baldwin called this arrangement the most perfect partner-ship in political history. In this way potentially the most hubristic British Prime Minister in the last century constrained for two years that side of his personality, allowing his charismatic and creative personality to provide formidable leadership. Only in July 1919 did he start to acquire hubris syndrome.[31]

It was a Cabinet structure that contributed massively to his success. Lloyd George's biographer, John Grigg, wrote that his power over the War Cabinet was due to force of talent and per-sonality rather than inherent strength of position, and that while he was bold, positive and decisive, he was not autocratic and 'set

---

30 John Grigg, *Lloyd George: War Leader, 1916–1918* (Allen Lane, London: 2002), pp 11–13.

31 Owen, *In Sickness and in Power* (revised edition, 2011) pp 13–19.

much store by conciliation and liked, if possible, to carry people with him.' Lloyd George's two most significant interventions were to force the Admiralty to accept the convoy system in 1916, and in 1918 to insist on meeting the Ludendorff offensive with an attack by fresh troops from Britain and to persuade the Americans to commit troops.[32]

When at eleven o'clock on the eleventh day of the eleventh month in 1918 the war ended, with the announcement of the armistice terms, it was appropriate that Lloyd George was widely acclaimed as 'The Man Who Won the War'.

What this forward look makes clear to us, then, is that from the summer of 1911 in Lloyd George Britain had in place a Prime Minister designate. He had by then begun to focus his activity on achieving that role, widening his political horizons. And he was also tailoring his views to put himself in a position to do so. There is nothing reprehensible in this. Democracy thrives on competition for the top job; sometimes the consequences of that competition are damaging, but in the main they are beneficial.

As Asquith's control over policy slipped, Lloyd George moved to make his presence felt more widely. It was now clear, as he wrote to Churchill, that 'The thunderclouds are gathering'. He was 'not at all satisfied that we are prepared or that we are preparing'. A sort of peace, however, was reached between France and Germany on 4 November 1911, when Germany obtained 100,000 square miles of Central Africa from the French, an indirect outcome of the Agadir Crisis and a sign that Germany was still interested in building up its overseas empire.

Lloyd George's relations with Churchill had to change when the latter became First Lord of the Admiralty in October 1911; when Churchill had been President of the Board of Trade, the two had been partners in reducing Naval expenditure, now Lloyd George accepted they would be partners in increasing it. Yet Lloyd George

---

32 Hugh Purcell, *Lloyd George* (Haus, London: 2006) p 142.

would ensure that Churchill never outflanked him on the issue of patriotism. As will be seen in Chapter Four, page 205, at a critical stage in the days immediately leading up to war in 1914, Churchill would choose to remind Lloyd George of what he had said over Agadir three years earlier.

Meanwhile, on 23 August 1911 in London, discussion on the Military Conversations agenda returned at another meeting of a CID sub-committee, and in addition to the Prime Minister attending, Grey and Lloyd George were invited. The Naval position had hardened considerably and they were now refusing to convey the Army's expeditionary force to France because their resources were better deployed, they felt, against the German navy. Admiral Sir Arthur Wilson, the new First Sea Lord, referred to Wilhelmshaven in the Baltic Sea as one of the largest German naval bases, and the fact that the Kiel Canal now enabled German ships to sail into the North Sea without having to go around the tip of Denmark, since the canal had been widened and was big enough to take the new type of super-battleship, the Dreadnought. At this meeting, with the Navy and Army seriously at odds and Naval opposition supported by the First Lord of the Admiralty, McKenna, it could have been a moment for a change of strategy. But Asquith intervened; the Naval opposition to the planned deployment of the BEF was, he said, 'puerile' and 'wholly impracticable'. It was McKenna's last meeting.

The British Expeditionary Force planning Max Hastings describes as the 'manifestation of a huge, historic British folly, repeated over many centuries including the 21st: the adoption of gesture strategy, committing small forces as an earnest of good intentions, heedless of their gross inadequacy for the unitary purpose at hand.'[33] This view was to be stated just as clearly by Kitchener on 5 August 1914 (see Chapter Four, pp 216–211).

---

33 Max Hastings, *Catastrophe: Europe Goes to War 1914* (William Collins, London: 2013) pp 37–40.

Brigadier Henry Wilson, the Director of Military Intelligence, who had revised his plans for the expeditionary force upwards, now maintained that Britain sending six infantry divisions and one cavalry would make the difference between victory and defeat. The Army, better organised with its Imperial General Staff, had the support of both Haldane and Grey, and this was reinforced by Haldane threatening to resign if the War Office plan was not accepted. While Churchill, interestingly, and some others were of the view that the French army unassisted could hope to withstand a German attack, the clear majority was for the War Office.[34] Wilson had written in his diary just before the meeting that he was not impressed by Grey and Haldane's grasp of the situation, Grey 'being much the most ignorant and careless of the two, he not only had no idea of what war means but he struck me as not wanting to know … an ignorant, vain and weak man quite unfit to be the Foreign Minister of any country larger than Portugal.' The feelings of the politicians about Wilson were expressed by Asquith to Venetia Stanley, as 'that poisonous clever ruffian'.

On 1 November 1911, the Cabinet met to discuss the controversial Military Conversations for the first time. Grey's previous wooing of Morley had achieved little, since he denounced the secret Military Conversations in no uncertain terms and the Cabinet meeting broke up without reaching a conclusion. Asquith reported as follows to the King:

Lord Morley raised the question of the inexpediency of communications being held or allowed between the General Staff at the War Office and the General Staff of foreign states, such as France in regard to possible military and naval cooperation, without the previous knowledge and direction of the Cabinet. Lord Haldane explained what had actually been done, the communications in question having been initiated as far back as 1906 with Sir Henry Campbell-Bannerman's

---

34 Niall Ferguson, *Pity of War* (Allen Lane, London: 1998) pp 65–6.

sanction and resumed in the Spring and Summer of the present year. The Prime Minister pointed out that all questions of policy have been and must be reserved for the decision of the Cabinet, and that it is quite outside the function of military or naval officers to prejudge such questions. He added that he believed (and Sir Edward Grey concurred) that this was fully recognised by the French Government. Considerable discussion ensued, and no conclusion was come to, the matter being adjourned for further consideration later on.[35]

The row in Cabinet was an unpleasant experience for Asquith. Pressed by Loreburn as to why they had not been informed, Asquith went as white as a sheet. Loreburn told Scott, the editor of the *Manchester Guardian*, that Grey's policy 'was rotten to the core.' Haldane felt in no way hampered regarding discussions in the War Office, but given Asquith's summing up, it was wrong in every political sense. More than a warning note had been sounded: a split of 15 against the Military Conversations and five in favour was a very substantial democratic reverse. Nor should that have been so surprising. One did not need to be a military expert to sense immense potential dangers in sending the planned expeditionary force to France. Lewis Harcourt, who had succeeded Lord Crewe as Colonial Secretary in 1910, one of the plan's critics, said such an expeditionary force was 'criminal folly'. Harcourt had been the MP for Rossendale since March 1904, and like his father, Sir William, stood against the inexorable rise in naval and military expenditure and opposed the Boer War. He left office when Asquith, a friend, resigned in 1916.

In retrospect, those who saw the dangers then facing an expeditionary force were correct. It is amazing that those dangers had to be actually demonstrated at Dunkirk in 1940 by the evacuation, what Churchill called 'a miracle of deliverance'. Churchill's War Cabinet of six people had met nine times on the 26, 27 and 28 May 1940

---

35 *Asquith Papers*, Cabinet Letters to the King for 1 November 1911, in Dep. Asquith 6, ff. 76.

to consider the Foreign Secretary Lord Halifax's wish to respond to a peace initiative brought to him by the Italian Ambassador on Saturday 25 May. It was critical for Churchill to win round Chamberlain, his immediate predecessor as Prime Minister, to reject opening negotiations, which he eventually did. The actual evacuation of the British Expeditionary Force from the beaches around Dunkirk started on the 27 May but not until the War Cabinet had determined its line, which was to support Churchill against Halifax over opening negotiations, did the miracle of the evacuation become clear. Some 7,000 men were taken off the beaches on 27 May, a further 17,000 the next day and 50,000 a day from 29 May to 1 June. Still on the 28 May Chamberlain was reasoning 'that we might get better terms [from Hitler] before France went out of the war and our aircraft factories were bombed, than we might get in three months' time.'[36] Anyone who doubts the value of Cabinet government and democratic debate at a time of maximum peril should read those Cabinet minutes in their entirety. They are the ultimate vindication of Cabinet government.

* * *

Churchill's first day in the Admiralty was 25 October 1911. Before leaving the Home Office he wrote to Admiral Lord Fisher, 'I want to see you very much'. On 18 October they drove by car to Reigate together and en route Fisher poured out his ideas. Later that month, when ensconced in the Admiralty, Churchill wrote about Fisher, 'The power of the man was deeply borne in upon me and I had almost made up my mind to do what I did three years later and place him again at the head of the Naval Service'. But Churchill was anxious about 'the poise of mind at 71'.[37]

---

36 Niall Ferguson, "A Miracle of Deliverance?" *The New York Review of Books*, 30 November 2006, pp 26–29.
37 Mackay, *Fisher of Kilverstone*, pp 432–3.

On 6 November 1911 a memorandum was circulated by Brig-adier-General Sir G N Baron Nicholson that shows how far the Military Conversations had progressed over the past five years. The British Military was now dealing directly with the French Military Staff, and furthermore it was very clear already that Britain would opt for an expeditionary force. The secrecy, however, was still such that no official letters passed on the subject between the War Office and the Admiralty. Much of the relevant material in Document No. 689 has already been highlighted in this chapter but for complete-ness it is reiterated as part of the whole.

No. 689

Memorandum by Brigadier General Sir G N [Baron] Nicholson

Action taken by the General Staff since 1906 in preparing a plan for rendering military assistance to France in the event of an unprovoked attack on that Power by Germany.

W.O. Liaison I/6. Secret.

War Office, November 6, 1911.

In January 1906, when French and German relations were strained in connexion [sic] with Morocco, the General Staff with the approval of the Ministers of State concerned began to consider what steps could be taken to render military assistance to France in the event of an unprovoked attack on that Power by Germany, should His Majesty's Government in such an event decide to render such assistance.

The problem was treated as being of a secret and hypotheti-cal nature, and all that was done at first was to estimate the force which could be made available and the period within which it could be mobilised at the stations where the several units composing the force were quartered. After due consideration, and having taken into account the requirements of home defence, the General Staff were of opinion that our military resources would admit of the formation of an expeditionary force for the purpose in view, consisting of four Divisions and a Cavalry Division. But if the scheme were to be of any value should the occasion arise for carrying it into effect, it was necessary to go further and to collect and formulate information regarding the ports of embarkation and railway transport thereto, transport by sea across the Channel[,] the ports of disembarkation, and railway transport therefrom to the assumed area of operations.

The consideration of some of these questions obviously involved secret and unofficial communication with one or more members of the French General Staff and reference was made to the Foreign Office on the subject. In reply Lord Sanderson informed General Grierson, then Director of Military Operations, on the 15th January, 1906, that Sir Edward Grey in concurrence with the Secretary of State for War agreed to communications being entered into with Colonel Huguet, the French Military Attaché, for the purpose of obtaining such information as might be required, it being understood that the communications must be solely provisional and non-committal.

Colonel Huguet was accordingly consulted, and a preliminary scheme was drawn up with the assistance of the Admiralty in regard to the ports of embarkation and disembarkation and the arrangements for sea transport across the Channel. As secrecy was essential, no official letters passed on the subject between the War Office and the Admiralty.

Meanwhile the tension between France and Germany began to relax, and hopes were entertained, which were afterwards realised, that the dispute about Morocco might be capable of amicable settlement, at any rate for the time being.

In October, 1906, General Ewart succeeded General Grierson as Director of Military Operations, and found that the original scheme needed revision on account of changes in the organisation of the Home Army. Intimation had also been received of certain changes in the French plans of mobilisation and concentration, which affected the ports of disembarkation and the railway transport therefrom. A revised scheme was therefore prepared, but before communicating it to Colonel Huguet Sir Neville Lyttelton, then Chief of the General Staff, approached the Foreign Office and on July 26th, 1907, submitted a covering memorandum indicating the action which it was proposed to take. In this memorandum it was clearly laid down that the scheme was not binding on the British Government, but merely showed how the plans made in view of the situation in 1906 would be modified by the changes made in the organisation of the Home Army in 1907. The memorandum with a few verbal amendments was approved by Sir Edward Grey, and Colonel Huguet was informed accordingly.

At the same time the Admiralty were unofficially acquainted with the changes in the scheme so far as that Department was concerned, and Lord Fisher, then First Sea Lord, authorised General Ewart to settle details with Sir Charles Ottley, then Director of Naval Intelligence, and the Director of Naval Transport.

The scheme was then further elaborated, and on December 3rd, 1908 it was laid before a Sub-Committee of the Committee of Imperial Defence appointed by the Prime Minister to consider the Military Needs of the Empire. This Sub-Committee was presided over by the Prime Minister and included among its members the Marquess of Crewe, Viscount Haldane, Mr McKenna, Lord [Sir C.] Hardinge, and Lord [Sir J] Fisher. The question of rendering naval assistance to France in the event of an unprovoked attack on that Power by Germany was considered at a second meeting of the Sub-Committee on December 17th, 1908; and at a third meeting on March 23rd, 1909, the question of rendering military assistance was further discussed, the following conclusion being unanimously arrived at:

> *(a) In the event of an attack on France by Germany, the expediency of sending a military force abroad, or relying on naval means only, is a matter of policy which can only be determined, when the occasion arises, by the Government of the day.*
> *(b) In view, however, of the possibility of a decision by the*

Cabinet to use military force, the Committee have examined the plans of the General Staff, and are of the opinion that in the initial stages of a war between France and Germany, in which the British Government decided to assist France, the plan to which preference is given by the General Staff is a valuable one, and the General Staff should accordingly work out all the necessary details.

The Sub-Committee reported this conclusion to the Committee of Imperial Defence on July 24th, 1909. In their Report the Sub-Committee remarked that it would be possible in the course of a few months to strengthen the British Expeditionary Force of four Divisions and one Cavalry Division by two remaining Divisions, thus bringing the force up to 160,000 men.

In accordance with the conclusion arrived at the General Staff continued to elaborate the scheme, certain alterations being made from time to time in the ports of embarkation and disembarkation in conformity with variations in the naval situation and in the French plans of military concentration,

In April last, when the recurrence of tension between France and Germany seemed not improbable, the possibility of at once despatching six instead of four Divisions beside the Cavalry Division came under consideration, and revised tables of the larger force with accelerated dates of mobilisation were worked out. The tables for movements by rail, embarkation, sea transport, and disembarkation were similarly revised. This enlarged scheme was drawn up not in supersession of, but as an alternative to, the original scheme, from which it only differed in contemplating the immediate despatch of the two additional Divisions instead of in the course of a few months. As the greater includes the less, it is obvious that arrangements made for the despatch of a larger force would a fortiori provide for the despatch of a smaller force. It was recognised by the General Staff that the alternative scheme would have to be referred to the Committee of Imperial Defence for consideration, and it was submitted and explained in detail to the Committee on the 23rd August last, the Prime Minister presiding and Sir Edward Grey, Mr Lloyd George, Lord Haldane, Mr McKenna, Mr Winston Churchill, and the First Sea Lord being present with other members. At the meeting doubt was expressed by some of those present as to the prudence of adopting the alternative scheme, more particularly in connection with the requirements of home defence, but no conclusions were arrived at.

It may be added that the greatest care has been taken throughout by the General Staff to treat the plans for rendering military assistance to France, should His Majesty's Government determine to render such assistance on occasion arising, as being secret, hypothetical, and non-committal. Personally I have never spoken on the subject to any French officer, not even to Colonel Huguet. It has been unavoidable for the Director of Military Operations to consult Colonel Huguet and a few experts of the French General Staff whom he has interviewed on technical matters at Colonel Huguet's request; but that the non-committal proviso has been rigidly adhered to is evident from a note which was made in French of a conversation which took place on July 20th, 1911. This note is prefaced by a statement which may be translated as follows – 'First and foremost, it is placed on record that these communications are devoid of any official significance, and are in no way binding on the British and French governments.'

(Sd.) W. G. N.
War Office
6–11–11

[ED NOTE – The difference between the military and naval points of view, and a summary of Admiral Sir Arthur Wilson's opinion as expressed at the meeting of the Committee of Imperial Defence of August 23, are in Churchill's *The World Crisis*, pp 58–9. The result of this disagreement was shown in Lord Haldane's demand for an Admiralty Board to work in full harmony with the War Office plans. W. Churchill, *The World Crisis, 1911–4*, p 59; Asquith, *Genesis of the War* (1923), p 96; and Haldane, *Autobiography* (1929), pp 225–34]

Inevitably, on 15 November 1911, the full Cabinet returned to the subject of the Military Conversations. It required a masterly assertion of Prime Ministerial skill over two meetings to reach some form of words and the final result was reported by Asquith to the King. It was in some senses an assertion of Cabinet government, but Grey's hidden perspective remained. Asquith wrote:

> A prolonged and animated discussion. Sir E. Grey made it clear that at no stage of our intercourse with France since January 1906 had we either by diplomatic or military engagements compromised our freedom of decision or action in the event of a war between France and Germany. On the other hand there was a prevailing feeling in the Cabinet that there was a danger that communications of the kind referred to might give rise to expectations, and that they should not, if they related to the possibility of concerted action, be entered into or carried on without the sanction of the Cabinet. In the result, at the suggestion of the Prime Minister, unanimous approval was given to two propositions:
>
> 1. That no communications should take place between the General Staff here and the Staffs of other countries which can, directly or indirectly, commit this country to military or naval intervention.
>
> 2. That such communications, if they relate to concerted action by land or sea, should not be entered into without the previous approval of the Cabinet.[38]

The underlying fact was that the majority of the Cabinet had decided that Grey had for nearly six years compromised their freedom of decision. It would have been a better outcome of their assertion of democratic control if Grey had resigned after the Cabinet meeting.

---

38 Asquith Papers, Cabinet Letters to the King for 15 November 1911, in Dep. Asquith 6, ff. 79–80.

The Military Conversations had been comprehensively called into question by a clear Cabinet majority. The government as a whole would have had the opportunity, stemming from Grey's resignation, to rethink its whole geo-political strategy. It was, however, never likely he would resign and, given their personal relations, for Asquith it was virtually impossible to give any hint to Grey that his resignation was required, even if he had desired it.

There were too many links of friendship and loyalty between the two men, but a particularly telling one was when in the House of Commons Asquith was howled down for 30 minutes during the Parliament Bill on 24 July 1911. He remained on his feet, unable to be heard, and Opposition MPs shouted 'Divide! Divide!' even the words 'Traitor' and 'Squiffy', a reference to Asquith's penchant for alcohol could be heard. Grey, prompted by a note from the Prime Minister's wife, Margot Asquith, in the gallery, 'For God's sake, defend him from the cats and cads!' rose to intervene and a hush fell. 'If arguments are not to be listened to from the Prime Minister there is not one of us who will attempt to take his place.' Grey, flushed and angry, had confronted and silenced the Conservatives. Such courageous acts in political life are not lightly undertaken or forgotten and Asquith did not forget this one. Margot Asquith met Grey 'for a moment afterwards alone, and when I pressed my lips to his hand, his eyes filled with tears.' [39]

Asquith, however, had already shown a certain alarm at the implications of the Military Conversations. In the circumstances, Grey should have instinctively known that resignation was the path of duty. He had noted on Asquith's draft for the King, 'I think the last paragraph is a little tight.' He subsequently crossed this out and it is not clear whether Asquith had seen it and ignored it; either way the draft was sent unaltered to the King.

Contemplating and threatening resignation was something Grey

---

39 Robbins, *Sir Edward Grey*, pp 232–3; Margot Asquith, *Autobiography* (Thornton Butterworth, London: 1920), Vol I, p 148.

had done on many other issues, for example, before the Cabinet in October 1910, and after the Cabinet in December 1911.[40] There was an obdurateness to Grey's character, and actually, resigning was not in the nature of the man; it was always he who was correct, rarely, if ever, his critics. There was one clear exception. Grey wrote in his memoirs, published in 1925:

> I have always regretted, however, that the military conversations were not brought before the Cabinet at once: this would have avoided unnecessary suspicion. But it has also been a great satisfaction to me that they did come before the Cabinet some two years before we were called upon to face the outbreak of war. The Cabinet were wise in having the understanding put into writing. Cambon and the French Government, with their own record of diplomatic conversations before them, would never have disputed the point; but to have it in writing and signed on both sides made it quite clear for public opinion in Britain and in the outside world when the crisis came in 1914.[41]

There was another aspect to the 1911 Cabinet split: Lloyd George not only did nothing rash to exploit it but started to work on improving his relations with Grey. This was reciprocated. In November, Lloyd George publicly stated his readiness to make an amendment to an adult suffrage bill (which was under discussion) in favour of women. Grey at once aligned himself with the Chancellor of the Exchequer.[42] Britain was still not a proper democracy with women excluded from voting.

Instead of rethinking after the Cabinet asserted its authority over the Military Conversations, the government went on with the most unsatisfactory stance of neither disowning the Conversations, nor

---

40 Ferguson, *Pity of War*, p 63.
41 Grey, *Twenty-Five Years*, p 99.
42 Robbins, *Sir Edward Grey*, p 247.

putting something else in their place. In Roy Jenkins's phrase, if there was deceit it was self-deceit over the interpretation put on paragraphs 1 and 2 of Asquith's letter to the King cited earlier. When in 1912 the French asked for further naval co-operation the Cabinet discussed the matter four times. The Military Conversations continued to shape the debate, but now it was at least a democratic debate. The Cabinet's decisions in 1914 about going to war were admittedly weighed down by the decision in 1906, but they could have insisted that a British Expeditionary Force was no longer a given of British policy in 1911. The reality was that they did not do so.

There was no one among the Cabinet members at CID meetings either who was ready to question the premise and argue against its central planning priority for an expeditionary force. Nor was there any real discussion of how the German military were – though they would not admit it – worried about encirclement from the Triple Entente as Russian military strength and militancy grew. It was neither necessary nor would it have been in British interests to argue the case for a strictly neutralist stance – that could be left anyhow to Cabinet members such as Morley. The way was certainly open to argue that the British commitment if Belgium were attacked would be purely naval and deprive Germany of the use of their navy in support of a Continental war or the use of their merchant ships to sustain such a war. Clear and precise. Whatever Lloyd George said after 1918 there is no evidence that he ever expressed the view in Cabinet or in the CID prior to the end of July 1914 that an attack on Belgium was a *casus belli* for the Liberal government.

What was lacking was a strategy for keeping the peace in Europe. The balance of power, as Lord Salisbury demonstrated, was never founded on neutralism, but on realism. Great Britain's overriding interest was in demonstrating to Germany that it would win any maritime war and that it was also preparing for a maritime blockade of Germany to bring any war that did start on the Continent to a speedy end. Such a strategy was not neutralism for in any continental war Germany would be deprived by British Naval power of access to all the Channel ports. The CID, which did not settle 'large questions',[43] discussed the Netherlands and Belgium as of immense importance, and concluded that if they were neutral and accorded full rights as neutrals, Britain should be unable to bring any offensive pressure upon them and that it was essential that Britain should do so. The key questions about Belgium had also been specifically mentioned by General Joffre to Colonel Fairholme (see p 113). The legal position was long known and is described in Chapter One, p 17.

In January 1912, the Lord Chancellor, Earl Loreburn, raised a fundamental point, that if war came a British Expeditionary Force could not prevent France from being overrun and that Britain would need to send not 150,000 men but at least half a million to do any good. A comment that was to be reiterated by Kitchener as Minister for War on 5 August 1914. See Chapter Four, p 211. A prescient forecast.

By the autumn of 1917, the British Expeditionary Force was 354,700 strong and the American Expeditionary Force in France 61,531. By 21 March 1918 American troops in France numbered 300,000.[44] By the end of May 1918 the total number of American troops in France and Britain was nearly half a million, most of them brought over in British ships. From this mass of Americans 290,000 or so had been formed into 11 combat divisions.[45] It was a blessing for Britain and France that America came in at a point when it could and did offset the decline and fall of the contribution to the Triple Entente from the Russian military. The backlash in America to shouldering the commitments involved in the League of Nations and the fact that the US did not enter the Second World

43 Mackintosh, *The British Cabinet*, p 322.
44 Lloyd George, *War Memoirs*, Vol II, pp 1792, 1811.
45 Grigg, *Lloyd George, War Leader*, p 531.

War until attacked by the Japanese at Pearl Harbor were signs that President Wilson's policies were deeply contentious. Otto von Bismarck once said, 'God has a special providence for fools, drunks, and the United States of America.' In 2001 *Special Providence*, a book by Walter Russell Mead on American foreign policy and how it changed the world, was acclaimed by the diplomat Richard Holbrooke as offering a highly original way of looking at American foreign policy far beyond the conventional wisdom of realists vs. idealists. It describes four schools of thought shaping American foreign policy rooted in domestic policy – the Hamiltonian: the protection of commerce; the Jeffersonian: the maintenance of the democratic system; the Jacksonian: populist values and military might; and the Wilsonian: moral principle. Not surprisingly, some of that book will have to be adjusted to what followed 9/11, the war in Afghanistan and the Iraq War of 2003, after it was written in March 2001. History has to reflect such large experiences, but it is so far true that for no such period of change has it taken longer for the realities and tensions to be learnt than the war of 1914–18, still sometimes unfortunately called by the name The Great War.

The evidence, such as it is, from comparing the levels of armed forces from 1904 to 1914 is that France had scope for increasing its military numbers in Europe yet only increased them significantly in 1913. It is very difficult to find accurate comparative figures showing the size of the competing armies in Europe, as distinct from those being held overseas, whether in the build-up over the years immediately preceding the start of the war in 1914 or through the differences in spending. The following Tables 1 and 2, from *The Arming of Europe and the Making of the First World War* by David G Herrmann, give some indication.[46]

---

46 David G Herrmann, *The Arming of Europe and the Making of the First World War* (Princeton University Press, Princeton: 1996).

Table 1: Peacetime Strength of the European Armies, 1904–1913[47]

	Russia*	Germany	France	Austria-Hungary	Italy	Great Britain
1904	1,900,000+	606,866	575,000	361,770	221,085	209,460
1905	1,9000,000	609,552	595,000	361,770	220,834	213,780
1906	1,000,000	614,353	590,000	362,398	249,816	196,600
1907	1,000,000	616,838	602,492	366,578	249,917	179,209
1908	1,000,000	619,006	610,923	365,742	~247,000	183,280
1909	1,209,000	610,196	567,484	369,203	~247,000	181,900
1910	1,303,000	610,083	574,342	370,510	238,617	182,350
1911	1,345,000	612,557	593,556	353,017	253,786	182,700
1911	1,332,000	646,321	611,709	391,297	256,000	192,590
1913	1,300,000	782,344	~700,000	n.a	256,000	192,144

Based on Gerhard von Pelet-Narbonne, ed., *Von Löbells Jahresherichte über die Veränderungen und Fortschritte im Militärwesen*, Berlin, 1904–13. The numbers listed as approximate for France and Italy in 1908, 1909 and 1913 are interpolations made when the *Jahresherichte* do not list the number of officers for the year. Since the bulk of the forces were enlisted and the number of officers did not fluctuate very much, the variation is not likely to be significant.
* The figures for the Russian army between 1904 and 1908 cover only troops stationed in European Russia and the Caucasus; thereafter the entire empire is included.

Table 2: Army Expenditures of the European Powers, 1904–1914[48]

	Russia[a]	Germany[b]	France[c]	Austria-Hungary[d]	Italy[e]	Great Britain[f]
1904	38,135,105	31,655,076	26,811,890	17,568,152	8,165,153	40,292,214
1905	38,800,726	34,544,958	27,149,037	17,005,860	11,337,958	32,227,365
1906	39,841,721	36,369,819	28,491,214	16,903,416	11,496,531	29,806,589
1907	41,093,773	39,171,776	30,921,155	18,381,998	11,853,320	29,077,038
1908	50,440,315	41,897,734	30,916,754	18,303,948	11,837,463	27,403,495
1909	56,956,710	39,820,279	31,709,611	19,446,159	11,948,464	27,024,192
1910	56,101,091	39,558,815	34,574,847	19,958,399	12,958,149	27,256,162
1911	56,161,071	39,955,932	37,191,744	21,060,797	14,147,445	27,579,826
1911	59,504,479	47,302,090	36,491,522	22,394,923	16,751,706	28,033,305

---

47 Herrmann, *The Arming of Europe*, Appendix A: 'Peacetime Strength of the European Armies', p 234. Reprinted by permission of Princeton University Press.
48 Hermann, *The Arming of Europe*, Appendix B: 'Army Expenditures of the European Powers', 1904–1914, p 237. Reprinted by permission of Princeton University Press.

	Russia[a]	Germany[b]	France[c]	Austria-Hungary[d]	Italy[e]	Great Britain[f]
1913	67,751,868	80,938,522	37,194,227	24,130,138	n.a.	28,242,320
1914	n.a.	68,534,435	47,716,936	n.a.	n.a.	28,532,992

Note: Amounts converted to sterling according to exchange rates listed in the *Statesman's Yearbook*, London, 1904–14. These did not fluctuate significantly in the period.
a 'Nouvelles Miitaires,' *Revue militaire des armées étrangéres*, Paris, 1904–14.
b 'Einnahmen und Ausgaben des Deutschen Reiches.' *Statistisches Jahrbuch für das Deutsche Reich*, Berlin, 1904–16.
c Assemblée Nationale, *Journal official de la République Française: Lois et Décrets*, Paris, 1903–July 1914. Supplementary credits voted during each year have been included.
d Pelet-Narbonne, *Von Löbells Jahresheriche über die Veränderungen und Fortschritte im Militärwesen*, Berlin, 1904–13.
e Ibid., 1904–13. Expenditures voted by fiscal rather than calendar year (e.g. 1903–14).
f PRO W033/536, 550, 554, 586, 631, War Office, *Reports on the Account of Army Expenditure*, London 1904–14. Expenditures voted by fiscal rather than calendar year.

The figures show that French army levels fluctuated between 1904 and 1912 but only increased significantly in 1914. Germany's started to increase in 1912 and 1913. Russia, the largest army, varied throughout, as did Great Britain's after a fallback in numbers in 1905 as a result of a winding down after the Boer War. There was an increase in Austria-Hungary's forces in 1912 but little change in Italy.

It seems reasonable to conclude that France, which from 1905 to 1912 was constantly 'crying wolf' and warning Great Britain that Germany was preparing for immediate war over Morocco, took no significant steps to build up its own land forces in response to the perceived threat. The size of the French army actually fell from its 1908 level of 610,923 to 593,556 in 1911. This calls into question the extent to which from 1906 the French were deliberately exaggerating the threat in order to extract from Great Britain a commitment to send an expeditionary force in the event of France being attacked.

By 1912 Churchill was steadily concentrating the Royal Navy in home waters. In 1914 mobilisation took place in continental Europe for all those who had a record of recent service. In Britain, by contrast, with the smallest army in Europe of the major powers, conscription did not begin until 1916. That did not stop Kitchener bringing into the European theatre troops from India and elsewhere. Another explanation for the French failure to build up their numbers before 1914 lies in the failure to increase the population generally. In 1911 Jacques Bertillon wrote a bestselling work on 'How to prevent France from disappearing? How to maintain the French race on earth?'.[49] France's population had increased by only 2 million over the last 30 years, while Germany's had increased by 18 million and Great Britain's by 10 million. Thus, a higher proportion of the French male population was required to serve in the military to achieve parity of numbers with the German army.[50]

Army expenditures increased rapidly from 1904–1914 in Germany, less so in France but, tellingly, Russia, fearing Germany and Japan, increased its expenditure considerably more than France. There was a slight increase in Austria-Hungary and Italy and no significant rise in Army expenditure in Great Britain. Where Britain had a considerable advantage was in the huge stock of accumulated overseas capital which it was building up.

Yet if Great Britain was to have the capacity to develop a fleet capable of blockading Germany by sea, if the latter threatened any Entente partner, Britain had to spend more on its Navy. But not just on Dreadnought battleships; more expenditure was needed on submarine warfare. Even the CID, when it came to war in 1914, despite the earlier economic objectives laid down in the War Plan, found it had failed to plan for a successful blockade and acknowledged that it had proved impossible to make full and immediate use of British naval power to deny the enemy the supplies of raw materials and food it was by then accustomed to import by

---

49 *La Dépopulation de la France* (Librairie Félix Alcan, Paris: 1911).
50 Florian Illies, trans Shaun Whiteside, *1913: The Year Before the Storm* (Clerkenwell Press, London: 2013).

sea.[51] The situation improved by 1916, but for a blockade to be a strategy for preventing war the Germans had to fear it well before any hostilities broke out. At no stage, it appears, did Germany fear Great Britain's capacity quickly and effectively to implement this strategy. A reason for this ambivalence was that the British government was not ready to curb the City of London, which was financing the booming German foreign trade, running the only free market in gold and insuring the German merchant marine. The CID had analysed this and was aghast at the weakness it revealed were any maritime blockade to be imposed.[52] Yet the politicians who were aware of this – Asquith, Grey, Lloyd George, Churchill and Haldane – did nothing substantive about it.

A wise government discovering in 1911 these alarming facts would have acted openly to reduce this vulnerability. It would have meant overruling the Treasury, which was opposed to building up gold stocks, preferring to trade them. Stopping the financing of German maritime trade or at least greatly reducing it, and stopping or reducing insuring German shipping. These actions would have sent a very powerful warning shot at the German government's military strategists. Namely, Great Britain was preparing a Naval blockade that would bite if Germany attacked France or Russia on land.

---

51 Arthur Marsden, Chapter 29, 'The Blockade', in F H Hinsley (ed), *British Foreign Policy Under Sir Edward Grey* (Cambridge University Press, Cambridge: 1977), p 488.
52 Paul Kennedy, *Strategy and Diplomacy, 1870–1945* (Fontana, London: 1984), pp 58, 94–7.

Chapter Four

Last Chances for Peace – the Haldane and Tyrrell Missions

In February 1912 the Secretary of State for War, Lord Haldane, went to Germany for new discussions regarding a British-German agreement. The optimists intended to stop the Germans increasing their naval resources, thus giving Britain naval superiority. The realists were ready to settle for an appreciable slowing. In return Britain was to try to facilitate some of Germany's colonial territory-building demands. The core aim was to avert war. Had by then a preventative strategy for war breaking out or for negotiating a ceasefire through maritime blockades by the Royal Navy been in place, the Germans would likely have been more flexible in the talks. Although apprehensive about the process, Grey had accepted that a fresh attempt should be made to reach an agreement with Germany but, sadly, according to Robbins, 'As a diplomatic exercise it was to prove a vindication of Grey's linguistic intransigence and cultural insularity'.[1]

The background to the Haldane Mission is that Harcourt, the Colonial Secretary, had written in September 1911, 'The idea of war is monstrous and inconceivable – and if it took place it would involve the whole of Europe.' By December, a proposal for further

---

1 Keith Robbins, *Sir Edward Grey: A Biography of Lord Grey of Fallodon* (Cassell, London: 1971), pp 256–60.

discussions with Germany had begun to take shape and privately Harcourt was stating that Anglo-German relations could be permanently improved if there were conversations concerning territory, which might give Germany what Asquith called in the House of Commons 'a place in the sun', without injury to Britain's colonial or imperial interests. If anything, Harcourt thought that a deal should be to the definite advantage of Germany.

Harcourt's search for a solution was premised on the belief that pushing Germany to reduce naval expenditure was not enough, there had to be a political carrot; and he saw an opportunity over Portugal. Great Britain's position on Portugal was defined by two secret agreements, one made with Germany in 1898 and one with Portugal in 1899. The former regulated the partition of Portuguese colonies in the event that Portugal collapsed economically and/or politically; the latter confirmed Portugal as the oldest ally of Great Britain and committed Britain to defend its colonies: an inconsistency that would become immediately obvious if the agreements were ever to become public.[2]

In late December 1911, Grey wrote privately from Fallodon to Sir Edward Goschen, the British Ambassador in Berlin. As was often the case with Grey, the analysis was excellent and he did not pull any punches over the Portuguese colonies, but the inner steel to take risks was still lacking. To make a deal with Germany it was necessary to put a check on the dominant relationship with France and put economic and moral pressure on Portugal to sell some of its colonies to Germany, and to find other areas, particularly financial help, where Great Britain could ease the political problems for Portugal. This is what Grey wrote to Goschen:

> As to the future, it is clear to me from what Metternich [the German

---

2 Richard Langhorne, 'Anglo-German Negotiations Concerning the Future of the Portuguese Colonies, 1911–1914', *Historical Journal*, Vol 16, No 2 (June 1973), pp 361–87.

Ambassador] has already said that the Germans would like a division of the Portuguese Colonies to take place as soon as possible. So should I. These colonies are worse than derelict so long as Portugal has them; they are sinks of iniquity … the Union of South Africa will never rest so long as she (Portugal) has Delagoa Bay: on every ground, material, moral and even Portuguese, it would be better that Portugal should at once sell her colonies. *But* how can we of all people put pressure on Portugal to sell: we who are bound by an alliance to protect and preserve her colonies for Portugal – an alliance renewed secretly for value received during the Boer War? And Portugal won't part with her colonies … for when nations have gone downhill until they are at their last gasp, their pride remains undiminished if indeed it is not increased. It clings to them as Tacitus says the love of dissimulation clung to Tiberius at his last gasp.

However, I am to meet Harcourt next month and study the map with him in a pro-German spirit: then the Cabinet will review the situation. For a real bargain about naval expenditure in which Germany gave up the attempt to challenge our naval superiority we might give something substantial, but the difficulty is that cession of territory can hardly from the German point of view be *in pari material* with a naval arrangement.[3]

The published document was cut short for reasons of international courtesy and this meant removing the reference to Portuguese colonies as 'sinks of iniquity'.[4]

Meanwhile, Sir Francis Bertie had by January 1912 discovered that the agreement he had so much disapproved of involving Portugal in 1898 was again under discussion, and he wrote from

---

3 Sir Edward Grey to Sir E Goschen, 29 December 1911; Grey Papers, FO 800/61. The version in *British Documents*, Vol X, Part II, p 266
4 Robbins, *Sir Edward Grey*, p 270.

Paris to protest.[5] Grey wrote back as always reassuring him. To put pressure on Portugal to sell would, Grey replied, be 'an even greater scandal than the retention of the colonies, and their government, or rather misgovernment by Portugal'.[6] The Francophiles in the Foreign Office were relieved when they recognised that Grey would not be wooed by Metternich's 'satanic invitation'. They emphasised their case against a revised agreement at length. Portugal was necessary to British security, and the alliance with it constituted a necessary obligation. If Germany gained at the expense of Portugal, Belgium would believe that Britain was encouraging a similar division of the Belgian Congo and that would also upset the French. Even before embarking with Harcourt on discussions with Germany Grey was showing his persistent unwillingness to contemplate any action that would upset the French.

Around the same time, Sir Arthur Nicolson, now the senior diplomat as PUS at the Foreign Office, wrote to Lord Hardinge – his predecessor as Head of the Foreign Office and now Viceroy of India – perhaps hoping he would use his excellent contacts with the King, warning him that the British government was contemplating publishing the secret agreements with Portugal of 1898 as well as the renewal of the treaty with Portugal in 1899.

> I hear that Metternich has received instructions to lay some proposals before us, and I have little doubt that they are connected with this question of the Portuguese Colonies. I shall await the result with some anxiety and apprehension as to how these proposals will be received by our government. I sincerely trust we shall keep our backs very stiff in the matter.[7]

---

5 Sir Francis Bertie to Sir Edward Grey, 21 December 1911, *British Docs*, Vol X, Part II, p 265.
6 Sir Edward Grey to Sir Francis Bertie, 2 January 1912, *British Docs*, Vol X, Part II, p 267.
7 Lord Nicolson to Lord Hardinge, 1 February 1912, University of Cambridge, Hardinge Papers, Vol 92, I, f 204.

The more austere and aloof Nicolson never established the close rapport with Grey that Hardinge had.[8] He was of Hiberno-Scottish descent and married to the daughter of an Ulster Landowner. He had little sympathy for Asquith's renewed embrace of Home Rule for Ireland. His younger son Harold, when second secretary in Constantinople, feared at that stage that his father might resign over policy differences with Grey, so there was a tension in the relationship not helped by his offensive remarks about the 'Radical-Socialist Cabinet' in an outburst to Cambon, the French Ambassador in London.[9]

The Cabinet first discussed who might go to Germany on 2 February. The request from the German government had been that it should be Grey and the First Sea Lord, but as usual Grey did not want to go; according to his biographer Trevelyan, he felt his presence would frighten the French. Instead, he suggested that Richard Haldane should represent Britain. The Cabinet instruction was to feel the way in the direction of a more definite understanding. There was always a deliberate ambiguity about the status of Haldane's visit to Berlin. He was not sent formally as Secretary for War but under the guise of an educational visit as chairman of a Royal Commission seeking to widen knowledge of German education. He had, as spelt out in guidance sent to the German government, no authority to make any agreement or to bind any of his colleagues.

Haldane was in Berlin between 8 and 11 February and reported to the Cabinet on the Mission to Germany on 20 February. According to Robbins, 'Haldane resisted [Chancellor] Bethmann-Hollweg's plea for an unqualified pledge of British neutrality[,] and the final "sketch of a conceivable formula" was suggested.'[10] The

---

8 T G Otte, *The Foreign Office Mind: The Making of British Foreign Policy 1865–1914* (Cambridge University Press, Cambridge: 2011) p 322.
9 Cambon to Poincaré, 18 April 1912 DDF (2) ii, no. 363.
10 Robbins, *Sir Edward Grey*, p 25.

agreement, outlined in the *European Diplomatic History*, was to be such that 'If either of the high contracting parties (i.e. Britain and Germany) becomes entangled in a war in which it cannot be said to be the aggressor, the other will at least observe toward the Power so entangled a benevolent neutrality.'[11] Haldane was delighted with his enterprise and impressed by the Chancellor, to whom he spoke in German one-to-one for an hour, describing him in his book *Before the War* [12] as 'sincerely desirous of avoiding war as was myself'. Writing to his mother in the train on the way back from Berlin, he assured her that the prospect for the moment was very good. But he saw Tirpitz as a strong and difficult man – a typical Prussian – and he and they fought, as Haldane described it, stiffly. The Emperor, he felt, had been delightful and wanted peace.

After the Cabinet meeting, according to Robbins, Grey and Haldane went to see the German Ambassador to clarify certain points, in particular recruitment to the German navy. When the Kaiser was told of this query he was furious, whether genuine or contrived, claiming it was an attempt to get them to abandon Germany's new Naval Law and that he must reject out of hand such a monstrosity. Fortunately, Chancellor Bethmann-Hollweg hit back at the Kaiser, and offered to resign as Chancellor, countering, 'but to cause a war ourselves so long as our honour and our vital interests are not involved, that I would regard as a sin against Germany even if we could expect victory. But that too is not the case, at least on sea.' Somewhat unexpectedly, Robbins records that 'The Kaiser retreated, agreed to respect Bethmann-Hollweg's office and promised changes in the Navy Law.'[13]

On 29 February, Harcourt wrote that as a follow-up to the

---

11 Raymond Sontag, *European Diplomatic History 1871–1932* (McGraw-Hill, New York: 1995) p 169.
12 Viscount Haldane, *Before the War* (London and New York: Funk & Wagnalls Co, 1920).
13 Robbins, *Sir Edward Grey*, p 258.

Cabinet he was to join Grey and Metternich in discussions,[14] and on 9 March these began at the Foreign Office. The discussions were held in relation to Portugal in the spirit of Grey's letter to Goschen of December rather than reflecting on Crowe's anxieties about needing permission for publication. Harcourt pointed out that, if there was to be publication of a revised agreement, the earlier agreement would have to be brought out too, for the sake of British public opinion. Not surprisingly, Metternich had demurred somewhat at this. Harcourt went for a big settlement, saying he understood that Germany would like to have that part of Portugal's provinces reserved for them in the 1898 agreement, but that in exchange for that large area he felt Great Britain should be compensated with a large area of Mozambique in eastern Africa. Harcourt, who had already been talking around this for some time with his counterpart as Colonial Secretary in Germany, Dr Wilhelm Solf,[15] was being ambitious because he, unlike Grey, believed that linking territorial gains to a cut in German naval expansion was essential. Metternich, not a party to some of the discussions, replied by talking of Harcourt's 'extravagance', to which Grey responded that Harcourt was that *rara avis*, a Colonial Secretary who was a willing seller.

Then Haldane on 12 March was suddenly asked to go to the German Ambassador in London. He was told that 'if the British Government would offer a suitable political formula the proposed Fleet Law as it stood would be withdrawn'. Lord Haldane wrote a memorandum recording his meeting with Count Metternich:

---

14 Lord Harcourt, 29 February 1912, Oxford: Bodleian Library, Papers of Lewis Harcourt, 1st Viscount Harcourt, 1890–1923 (hereafter Harcourt Papers), MS D D Harcourt c 578, Box 14.

15 P H S Hatton, 'Harcourt and Solf, The Search for an Anglo-German Understanding through Africa, 1912–1914', *European Studies Review*, Vol 1, No. 2 (1971).

No. 533

Memorandum by Lord Haldane of a conversation with Count Metternich

Very Secret

Tuesday March 12, 1912

This evening I received a note from Count Metternich expressing a wish to see me immediately, as he had 'something of importance and urgency to tell me.' I saw him at the German Embassy at 10.45. He informed me that he had a communication from the Chancellor in reply to his report that serious exception was taken here to the magnitude of the changes contemplated by the New Fleet Law, and especially to the large increase of perso[n]nel. What he had learned he wished in the first place to tell me quite privately and informally. He gathered from Berlin that if the British Government would offer a suitable political formula the proposed Fleet Law as it stood would be withdrawn. Some Fleet Law there must be, but one of less magnitude would be introduced. I asked him whether he could tell me the extent of the reduction. He replied that he gathered that it would be considerable, but that he was not in a position to define it. I gathered that he thought it extended to perso[n]nel. I asked whether he wished this communication to be treated as merely between him and me. He said no, he was officially instructed, but he had wanted to see me in the first place to say that time pressed, as a statement would have to be made almost at once in the Reichstag about the Fleet Law, and the Chancellor wished to be provided with the offer of a formula from us as a reason for not proceeding with the original proposals. I asked whether the formula need go beyond the declaimer or aggressive intentions and combinations. He indicated that he thought it need not. He added that he was instructed to say that if, having offered the formula, we were dissatisfied with the naval reductions when they came out we were to be regarded as quite free to withdraw it, in other

147

words it was to be conditional on our being satisfied in this respect.
I said I would see Sir Edward Grey at once.

H of C[16]

This was followed next day by a letter from Nicolson to Goschen in Berlin, who had sent him an account of the Kaiser's outburst. Nicolson rebutted the 'unfounded' assumption by the Germans of what Haldane said. He also indicated he was aware of the inflammatory nature of Churchill's speech but showed no wish or inclination to have its tone changed. It is also evident from Nicolson's memorandum that conversations were on-going with France and Russia about a wider alliance with Italy and Turkey.

No. 534

Sir A. Nicolson to Sir E. Goschen

Private

Foreign Office, March 13, 1912

My Dear Goschen,
I am much obliged to you for the two letters which I received by last Messenger.[17] The story you relate as to the Emperor's indiscretion, I agree with you that it was a studied indiscretion, is very interesting and significant. I shall treat your letter in regard to it as one which can be shown to the King and Haldane, as I think it is desirable that the latter especially should be cognisant of the remarks which have

---

16 *British Docs*, Vol. VI, p 710.
17 Not reproduced. The story referred to in the next sentence relates to a statement said to have been made by the Emperor in a private conversation at dinner. The Emperor was reported to have said that he had 'no confidence' in England, 'and that no reliance could ever be placed on her. "For instance," he continued, "I don't mind telling you that when Lord Haldane was here his references to France were not at all friendly."'

been made in respect to his alleged statements. Needless to say they are quite unfounded, as he never intimated, even in the most indirect manner, any unfriendliness towards France. On the contrary, as you know, he made it as clear as he possibly could that any understanding or arrangement to which he might come with Germany must in no wise impair the friendly relations which at present existed between us and France and Russia. All the documents which record the conversations which have taken place during the last two or three days are being sent to you by to-night's messenger and will give you a full account of the latest German proposals and moves, and, I may add, of their misrepresentations which, to my mind, surpass anything that can well be imagined. I need not further comment upon them, as you will be able to draw your own conclusions in respect to them.

I am going to draw up a rough draft of our reply to the German memorandum, which, of course, will have to be submitted to the Cabinet, and which I am prepared should be continually modified, if necessary, by them. I am, on the whole, glad the Germans have shown their hands in the way which they have done. I will not touch further on this question as I should only take up your time unnecessarily, and you will be kept fully informed as to any further developments which may take place.

In regard to other European questions, I do not think that anything of much interest has taken place during the last week, and I am glad to say that no very startling events occurred as I was away on holiday, and have returned very much refreshed by it.

You will see that we and the French have agreed to follow the procedure suggested by Sazonoff [Russian Foreign Minister] in respect to making enquiries at Rome in the first place. I am still of [the] opinion that the French proposal was the more reasonable of the two, and that we should have made simultaneous enquiries both at Constantinople and Rome. We are perfectly well aware what the Italian reply will be, and I do not quite see how the five Powers can carry it in their hands to Constantinople, as whatever may be said, the Turks will undoubtedly consider that in the mere fact of the Powers being the channel for such communication a certain amount of indirect pressure is being brought to bear upon them to accept it. At the same time I have certain doubts as to whether we shall be able to secure unanimity among the Powers for acting in this manner, and I expect that the whole effort to mediate will consequently be once more shelved to a future date.

The very latest communication which was made last night by Metternich and a copy of which will be forwarded to you today, is a somewhat extraordinary step to have taken. I am waiting to see Haldane and have a talk with him on the subject, as Grey, unfortunately, is entirely absorbed in these Coal Conferences and has no time to attend to foreign affairs except intermittently, so I shall do my utmost to find a formula we may submit which will be of as non-committal a character as possible, and also one which will not bind our hands in regard to any eventualities which may possibly arise in the future.

Churchill intends to make a very full and clear statement on Monday next week in introducing his naval budget. I should advise you to read it carefully. I think from the summary which he gave me verbally yesterday it will be made very clear that we intend to maintain preponderance in naval construction at all costs, and I trust that this will show the Germans that it is useless for them continuing this naval competition.

I have just seen Haldane and I had a long talk with him, and I think that the formula which has been drawn up is a perfectly innocent and clear statement, and one to which neither France nor Russia can take the slightest objection. I cannot send you a copy of it as it is to be submitted to the Cabinet, and it is just possible that they may modify it in some respects, but I sincerely trust they will not.

[A. Nicolson][18]

Also that same day, 13 March, Sir Edward Grey wrote to Nicolson,

---

18 *British Docs*, Vol. VI, p 711.

saying Haldane would come to a meeting with him, and commenting 'This German move is very extraordinary'. But not so extraordinary that he should not attend the coal conference.

No. 535

Sir Edward Grey to Sir A. Nicolson

Private

3 Queen Anne's Gate, SW, March 13, 1912

My dear Nicolson,

This German move is very extraordinary. Please read Haldane's pencil memo[random] and consider my pencil draft of a formula which I will discuss with you today when I get time: I must submit a formula to the Cabinet tomorrow (Thursday). I have told Haldane to come to see you this morning. I shall be at the coal conference.

Yours sincerely
E.GREY[19]

You can show it all to Mallet [Grey's private secretary] also.

In his account of the Haldane Mission, the historian Clark highlights the disruptive influence of the Foreign Office, writing that the person 'entrusted with providing Haldane with documentation and advice during the talks was none other than Sir Arthur Nicolson, a man who had always believed that any concession to Germany risked antagonising the Russians, whose benevolence was essential to British security.'[20] Nicolson, as we see in his letter to the British Ambassador in Berlin quoted above (No. 534), made

---

19 *British Docs*, Vol. VI, p 712.
20 Christopher Clark, *The Sleepwalkers: How Europe Went to War in 1914* (Allen Lane, London: 2012), pp 319–20.

no secret of his intention to draw up a 'perfectly innocent and clear statement' to the 'extraordinary' response. Nicolson was seeking to do his utmost to find a formula which would be as non-committal in character as possible, and also one which would not bind Britain's hands in regard to any eventualities which may possibly arise in the future. 'One to which neither France nor Russia can take the slightest exception.'

He had also told Sir Francis Bertie, the British Ambassador to Paris, in February 1912, 'I do not myself see why we should abandon the excellent position in which we have been placed ...' Not surprisingly Bertie agreed and described the Haldane Mission as a 'foolish move', something undertaken merely to silence the 'Grey-must-go radicals'.[21]

At a Cabinet meeting on 13 March Harcourt, according to his later pencil annotation on his papers, read out this statement in which he refers to Richard von Kühlmann, Metternich's deputy in the German Embassy.

I ought also to say that on the evening before I met Count Metternich and Sir E. Grey, I had a conversation at the Court (on the night of the 8th) with Herr von Kühlmann, who had been my confidant in the autumn, in which I told him that I was distressed & disturbed at the German answer about the Fleet Law received that day from Berlin, and that I began to despair of that 'accord' which I knew that he and I so much desired.

He told me that he was going to Berlin for a few days in the week of the 11th of March; that he would do all in his power to attain our mutual object, and wished to see me immediately on his return.

He added that he thought we found Zanzibar and Pemba the most difficult part of the interchange of courtesies and Territories. I said I thought this might prove to be so, and he then begged me to believe that they were not in his view essential to the political

---

21 Clark, *The Sleepwalkers*, p 320.

arrangement, or to the other amicable exchanges and adjustments but that the German interest was mainly in Angola.

I bore this hint in mind during my conversation of today with Sir Edward Grey and Count Metternich.

L. H.

9.3.12[22]

Metternich made it very clear that the formula would not be found to be sufficient in Germany, but the Cabinet, it appears, were given no impression by Grey, and as far as can be judged by Haldane, that it was likely to be rejected. There should have been a major discussion at Cabinet and voices raised by the majority who were known to be sympathetic to reaching an agreement with Germany. Between 1911 and 1914 a mixed bag of imperialists and radicals, Haldane, Harcourt, Lloyd George, Crewe, Runciman, Church-ill, Loreburn, Simon, Morley, Burns, Beauchamp, Pease, Samuel, McKinnon Wood and probably McKenna were all at some stage in favour of an 'understanding' with Germany.[23] Yet the radicals among them never seemed to mobilise their full potential during the Haldane Mission, a political stance that was to become a feature of the run up to war over the next two and a half years. The so-called 'Radicals' were not radical in any true sense of the word when it came to the championing of peace and challenging the dominance of Grey. There was one exception, Harcourt. Sir Edward Grey then wrote to Britain's Ambassador in Berlin enclosing the new formula drafted by himself and unwisely agreed by the Cabinet.

---

22 Lord Harcourt, handwritten notes, 9 March 2012, Harcourt Papers, MS 442, fos 215–17.

23 Hatton, 'Harcourt and Solf', p 142.

No. 537

Sir Edward Grey to Sir E Goschen

Secret

Foreign Office, March 14, 1912

Sir,

Count Metternich, in conversation today, reminded me that the German Chancellor had already invited the proposal of a formula from us, and had emphasised the point that a formula and naval expenditure were inter-dependent questions.

Count Metternich went on to say that, if we came forward with a formula, matters would proceed with regard to negotiations respecting the German naval programme. He had no authority to say that the Novelle [amended naval agreement] would be changed, but he said that any proposal of a formula made by us would be without prejudice and not binding unless we were satisfied that our wishes were met on the naval question.

On this understanding I gave Count Metternich a copy of a draft formula which had been approved by the Cabinet.

I am, &c

E.GREY[24]

Enclosure in No. 537

*Copy of Draft Formula given by Sir Edward
Grey to Count Metternich*

England will make no unprovoked attack upon Germany and pursue no aggressive policy towards her.

Aggression upon Germany is not the subject and forms no part of

---

24 *British Docs*, Vol. VI, p 713.

any Treaty understanding or combination to which England is now a party nor will she become a party to anything that has such an object.

Perhaps not realising that the Cabinet-agreed draft formula had already been passed on to the German government, Haldane and Harcourt, sensing that this British wording would not be enough for Germany, decided to ask Grey to allow the word 'neutrality' to appear somewhere in the formula as it had already been in the 'sketch of a conceivable formula'.

Just prior to seeing Grey, Harcourt had an interview with Herr von Kühlmann between 6.46 and 7.45 pm on 14 March. He made comprehensive notes of this meeting that are extremely valuable because they demonstrate the crucial importance of the British government backing Chancellor Bethmann-Hollweg against Admiral Tirpitz and tell us that Kühlmann had spent four hours with the Chancellor when he had been in Berlin the day before. It also demonstrates that Harcourt had used his position as Colonial Secretary to put a worthwhile territorial offer to the German government in Africa.

Handwritten notes pages 1–18, Harcourt Papers

14 March 1912

Situation Berlin critical. Emperor goes Sat. 23rd to Corfu with Adm. Tirpitz. Death struggle between Bethmann[-]Hol[1]weg and Tirpitz. If Hol[1]weg gets satisfactory formula Emperor will side with him and Tirpitz will go.
If not, Hol[1]weg will go and Tirpitz become Chancellor (with __full__ new Naval Law.)
Kühlmann seen our formula of today. (He spent 4 hours with Hol[1] weg before he left Berlin yesterday).
Says our formula good but wants some additions:

1. *(desirable – but not essential) Haldane's own draft of a 'conceivable formula'.*
'the High contracting Powers assure each other mutually of their desire for peace and friendship'.

2&3. our formula of today.

4. (Haldane's cl. 3 of 'conceivable formula')

This Kühlmann regards as <u>essential</u> to enable Hol[1]weg to secure the Emperor and to shed Tirpitz at once (the chief of the Naval Cabinet will remain and support Hol[1]weg)

'If either of the high contracting parties becomes entangled in a war in which it cannot be said to be the aggressor, the other will at least observe towards the Power so entangled a benevolent neutrality [and use its utmost endeavour for the localisation of the conflict]' (last sentence not essential)

Hol[1]weg not to be asked for details of Naval Law reductions <u>in advance</u>.

But formula not to be definitely given or published until we are satisfied with naval reductions he will make as soon as Tirpitz goes.

If we [are] dissatisfied formula to be torn up.

Formulae to be reciprocal.

I said w[oul]d it be helpful if I indicated to K. what naval reductions might be satisfactory to us.

K. s[ai]d yes.
I s[ai]d 'limit your increase of personnel strictly to what is required

to man your third squadron for training purposes and abandon your third ship in alternate years in your Novelle'

K. said 'when Tirpitz has gone and the row has begun in Germany, Hol[1]weg must have <u>some</u> Novelle for his own defence, as Tirpitz – seeing what was coming – has divulged what was his programme.

K. thinks Hol[1]weg c[oul]d limit the personnel to the 3rd squadron and put off the 3rd ships till 1915–<u>17</u>–19 – giving a much longer period of rest before increase begins.

We turned to territory.

K. s[ai]d Metternich thought I had been very 'exigeant' [exigent]. I said German note of Friday 8th misrepresented Haldane's attitude at Berlin: K admitted this and said it was fully understood all Haldane's conversations were ad referendum.

K. agreed that the idea that Zanzibar and Pemba had been offered for the omission of Timor was ridiculous.

We dealt with

1. Secret Treaty

He accepted the inclusion of St. Thomé and Principé as a set off to Timor as being satisfactory.

He asked whether we might not include a deal over other Islands such as the Azores.

I said 'no, in my view quite impossible – these were not African, but Atlantic – we should confine ourselves mainly to African territory (except Timor & Solomons) in dealing with secret treaty. Public opinion here w[oul]d much resent German acquisition of Atlantic islands – we should then have to consider Madeira where I knew by experience there was not & never could be a harbour.'

K. s[ai]d 'I assumed that you would eventually "take" the Cape Verde Islands.'

I repeated all this was out of the question and he said he was glad to know my view and that if I held this so strongly he could assure me the Islands w[oul]d not be raised.

He s[ai]d Germany wants all Angola but does not like to give as much as I proposed from Portuguese E. Africa.

German Govt. much object to the strip along Lake Nyassa on the E. side and don't like to come up to parallel 10° above the Zambesi. He suggested drawing a line from the S. of Lake Chiuta to the then source of the Luchulingo River and down then to [the] sea – all S.W. of this line to become British. He also suggested more of the eastern-most part of Angola to remain British – viz everything east of 20 deg. longitude from the Okavango R[iver] on the S. to sea where degree 20 crosses the Kassai River on the N. (this w[oul]d include a consider-able portion of the projected Katanga-Lobeto Railway).

We both thought that if this was done the frontier might eventu-ally be delimited by agreement so as not to follow the line of latitude but to diverge to both sides of it in order to follow a natural frontier of rivers or watersheds.

He said that if in any private document we disinterested ourselves in the main part of the Belgian Congo (which Grey has already done publicly) Germany w[ould] recognise our superior claims to all that part of Belgian Congo south of parallel 10° (which includes Katanga).

He believes the German Govt will surrender the Caprivi Tassel and all territory in German W. Africa E of latitude 20° in exchange for Seal & Penguin Islands at Angra Pequena, but the Cape Govt should give the boundary of the Orange River (against Namaqua land) in the talweg and not on the N. Bantu.

In the rearrangement of the Secret Treaty K. suggested that the new only and <u>not the old one</u> should be published. I said it was essen-tial to us for public opinion here that the <u>old</u> should be published as well – without this we could never make our people understand what we had been doing and the limitations under which we had been working.

K. wants with the Secret Treaty, our recognition to the German right of pre-emption of Rio Muni (Spanish Congo) which they have recently acquired from the French and recognition of an older right of pre-emption (also acquired from the French) of Fernando Po.

Zanzibar and Pemba

I s[ai]d it would be much more convenient if these c[oul]d be omitted.

K. said he was mistaken when he told me at the Court on the 8th that this c[oul]d be done.

He found that B. Hol[l]weg attached much importance to them – not for intrinsic value – but as a set off for Baghdad R[ai]1 [wa]y and Persian Gulf, and said that in the row with Tirpitz they would be a 'nice buttonhole'.

I s[ai]d I must have some floral decoration 'en revanche': that I could not exchange territory for rights: that I had suggested the N.W. corner of German East Africa between the Lakes and this had seemed to shock Metternich: he felt that it w[oul]d stop through transit in a possible future from German E to German W. Africa through the Belgian Congo.

K. s[ai]d this was so. I replied that I had no arrière pensée and would he suggest some alternative: he said he w[oul]d do more than that, he w[oul]d ask Berlin to do so.

I mentioned also the Isle of Bouka & Bougainville in the Solomon Group which might be thrown into the deal by Germany and he promised to consider this.[25]

There are some quite startling suggestions regarding in particular Portuguese colonial territories which can be identified in the map that follows. It provided a more far-reaching political agenda than many people who have commented on Haldane's Mission seem to have realised. Given that Grey had appeared to back Harcourt then much of it was deliverable. To make it all possible it would probably have been necessary to include the Portuguese government formally in a treaty with financial support coming to Portugal from both Germany and Britain.

---

25 Lord Harcourt, handwritten notes, 6:45–7:45, 14/03/12, Harcourt Papers, MS 442, fos 196–210.

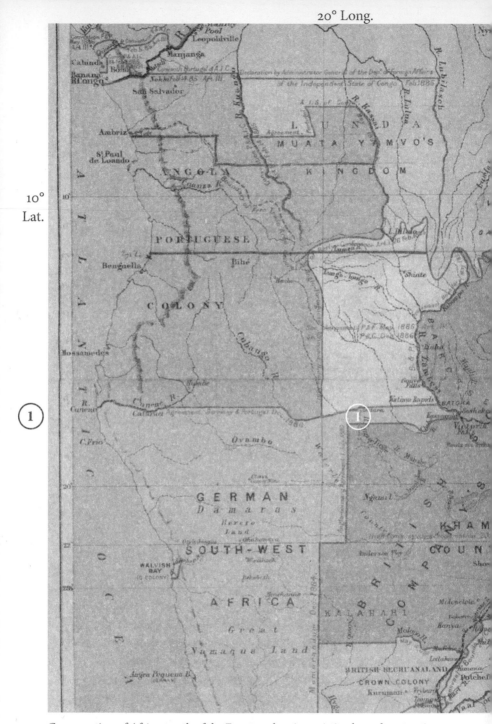

Cross-section of Africa, south of the Equator, showing existing boundary treaties, by George Cawson. Strictly secret as it refers to two separate agreements, one made with Germany in 1898 and one with Portugal in 1899.

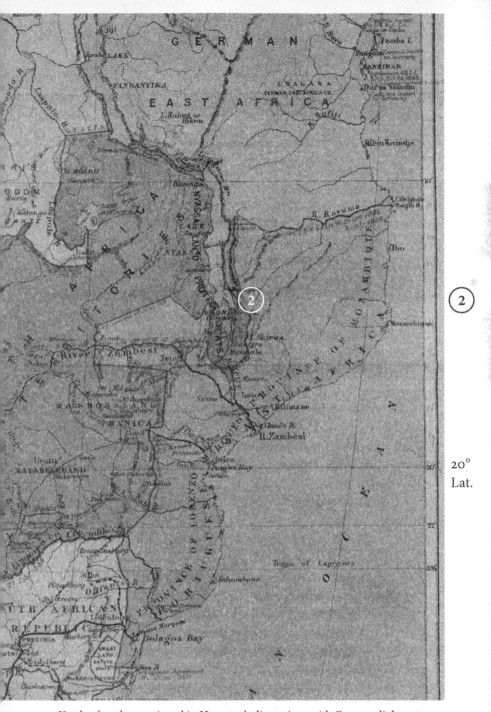

20°
Lat.

Key landmarks mentioned in Harcourt's discussions with German diplomat
Kühlmann pp. 155–9
1. Okavango River and Caprivi Tassel
2. Luchulingo River and Lake Chiuta

Harcourt went to see Haldane at Queen Anne's Gate at 11.00 pm. Afterwards the two met Grey, at 12.15am on 15 March. Harcourt's notes read: 'Grey very stiff: evidently afraid of losing French *entente*'. Importantly, Harcourt also related that a great row had taken place between Metternich and Kühlmann at the Foreign Office that afternoon when Metternich came to see Grey. Metternich discovered Kühlmann talking to Tyrrell, Grey's private secretary, and separated the two forcibly. This and the tone of what Metternich said at meetings leads one to suspect that he was far less keen on a deal than Kühlmann, who was obviously closer to Bethmann-Hollweg.

When Grey and Metternich met the following day, 16 March, to examine possible formulae for dealing with neutrality, they discussed the Balkans in view of the approaching end of the First Balkan War. Grey also commented that the Chancellor 'had inspired the greatest confidence' in Lord Haldane and himself, and that 'as long as he remained German Chancellor, he might rely upon our co-operating with him to preserve the peace of Europe, each of us not only abstaining from aggression upon the other, but each also using what influence we had with others to prevent war'. In fact Grey's refusal to move towards Bethmann-Hollweg's position had left him much weakened for a while in Berlin. At no time did Grey show an appreciation of the political importance of the German Chancellor being ready to challenge Tirpitz over the estimates. This was the political opening which Grey utterly failed to exploit.

On the formula, Grey reported to Sir Edward Goschen. There was, as he must have expected from Metternich, no sign of Germany accepting his minor changes. The letter to Goschen reads as follows:

No. 544

Sir Edward Grey to Sir E. Goschen

F.O. 11712/5569/12/18
(No. 62) Secret.

Foreign Office, March 16, 1912

Sir,

I told Count Metternich today that we had considered his suggestions as to the formula. There could be no objection to a preface, which would make the beginning less abrupt; and we might say: 'The two Powers being mutually desirous of securing peace and friendship between them, England declares that she...' I then explained to Count Metternich my apprehension that, if we used the word 'neutrality', it would convey an impression that more was meant than was said; and I suggested that the substance of what we wished would be obtained and most accurately expressed by saying, instead of the words 'will make no unprovoked attack,' 'will neither make nor join in any unprovoked attack.'

Count Metternich said he feared that unless the word 'neutrality' was used it would be impossible to secure reduction in the Novelle.

Bearing in mind what he had said to me yesterday, I told him that we had been given the impression that some change of 'personnel' in Berlin was possibly impending. I could not see how words used in our formula could have any effect upon the position of the German Chancellor personally, as there was no dispute between him and Admiral von Tirpitz about the Novelle, to which the Chancellor had been a consenting party before Lord Haldane went to Berlin; which [German naval increases] he proposed to cut down only if he obtained from us what he considered to be satisfactory; and which, it was therefore to be assumed, he was free to go on with if what we said did not satisfy him. It would not be useful for us to exchange a formula if a naval increase was impending, because the naval increase would destroy the good effect produced by the formula. But, if public opinion had been excited by the naval increase, we might afterwards consider the territorial questions, and exchange some formula which would have a calming effect.

I went on to tell Count Metternich that, as far as Herr von Beth-mann-Hollweg personally was concerned, I wished to say that he had inspired the greatest confidence in Lord Haldane, who knew him personally, and in myself. We believed genuinely that he wished to pursue a straightforward policy of peace; and, as long as he remained German Chancellor, he might rely upon our co-operating with him to preserve the peace of Europe, each of us not only abstaining from aggression upon the other, but each also using what influence we had with others to prevent war. If this was likely to be of use in personal questions now pending in Berlin, Count Metternich might certainly report it.

I observed that a formula could not be personal. For instance, if we were to exchange with Germany now a formula which made rela-tions between us and any other country more distant, we could have no security that Herr von Bethmann-Hollweg might not be over-thrown a month or two hence: when we should be in the position of having gained nothing as regards the policy of Germany, and we should have lost something elsewhere.

Our conversation was most friendly, and Count Metternich did not show any of the anxiety which there was in his manner yesterday.

In the course of conversations, he referred to the feeling which had been aroused in Germany by the impression that we might attack her.

I said that we were helpless with regard to an impression of this sort, unless the German Press Bureau could take some action to prevent things like Captain Faber's speech from being used in the way they had been used. As long as the question of Morocco was not settled, I understood that it gave occasion for those people who desired to circulate unfavourable reports as to our policy and inten-tions with regards to Germany; but I hoped that these occasions would disappear when the question of Morocco was settled.

I went on to tell Count Metternich, that since the beginning of this year, when the question of mediation between Turkey and Italy had been discussed, I had stipulated that all five Powers, including Germany, should be in agreement before any action was taken. I had stipulated for this in Vienna and in St. Petersburg, when approached on the subject. Similarly, with regard to the questions which might arise in connection with the Balkans, I had said to the Representatives of other Powers: 'Do not let us fall into two groups over these Balkan questions. Let us keep in touch with one another.' It was true that I should be glad to see Russia and Austria come to an agreement which would prevent their getting into a war with each other about the Balkans: a war which would be very inconvenient to their allies and friends. But such an agreement would not make separate groups, for it would bring together two Powers which belonged to different groups. In time this line of policy, if it was given a fair chance, would have a good influence.

Count Metternich asked for the words of alteration in the formula and I wrote them out and gave them to him.

[I am, &c.]
E. G[REY].[26]

Sir Edward Grey and Count Metternich met again on 19 March, when Metternich made it clear that attitudes in Berlin had changed after Haldane had spoken of neutrality and then they discovered that 'the ground on which Lord Haldane took his stand in Berlin was abandoned'. Grey replied that he was 'surprised that the German Chancellor estimated our draft formula at so low a value … What the Chancellor now asked [for] amounted to an agreement of absolute neutrality, which was more than conditional neutrality.' This by any standard of objectivity was not an accurate description of the German Chancellor's negotiating position or that of Haldane's (underlined in the text on p 168). But Grey's interpretation

---

26 *British Docs*, Vol. VI, p 718.

accorded with Metternich's words that in fact the Chancellor had not mentioned 'absolute, but in effect his wish amounted to that.' Yet it is questionable whether Kühlmann, closer to the German Chancellor, would have used anything like the same words. Once again Grey's reluctance to visit Berlin and himself negotiate with the German Chancellor is shown up as a limiting factor. Also, a caution is necessary on these reports; most would have been initially drafted by Grey's private secretary Mallet and his objectivity has already been called into question. Grey was assiduous but he could not have read every one of the despatches in his name. Nevertheless Metternich advised the German Chancellor to persist with diplomacy towards Britain. Grey's record of the meeting is as follows:

No. 545

Sir Edward Grey to Sir. E Goschen

F.O. 12081/5569/12/18
(No 66.) Secret.

Foreign Office, March 19, 1912.

Sir,
Count Metternich informed me today of the following communication from the German Chancellor:

The Chancellor said that our promise not to make or join in an unprovoked attack upon Germany was so elastic as to be valueless: it even left room for the idea that, hitherto, such an attack had been a thing with which Germany had to reckon. The German measures for expenditure on armaments were already known, and the German Government were asked to abandon them for our proposed formula, without getting the necessary guarantee against an attack. In the opinion of the German Naval

Authorities, the German measures of armament were necessary to maintain an efficient defence against the combined fleets of the Triple Entente. In the English calculations, account had been taken of the possibility of a future change in German policy. But, if an agreement were come to, German policy would be bound, no less than English policy, for a considerable period. Though we, on the one hand, might apprehend that, in consequence of a future change in German policy, we might lose the friendship of France: Germany, on the other hand, had to consider that a future change in English policy might have Germany, who had renounced the Novelle by her agreement with us, in maritime inferiority to the Powers of the Triple Entente. Quite apart from this, the person of the German Emperor was a guarantee that German policy would be conducted on friendly lines, and in the peaceful path which had never been abandoned during the time of the Emperor's government. What we offered now could, therefore, not be a basis for serious negotiations. Count Metternich was instructed to make it quite clear that the German Chancellor could recommend the Emperor to give up the essential parts of the Novelle, and justify this action to the public opinion of Germany, only if we could conclude an agreement guaranteeing neutrality of a far-reaching character, and leaving no doubt as to any interpretation.

Count Metternich then went on to say, speaking personally on his own account, that he was afraid that, when the ground on which Lord Haldane took his stand in Berlin was abandoned, what we proposed could not be useful. Lord Haldane had spoken of neutrality, and of large ships only; but, when he had brought the Novelle to us, we had found that there were things in it much larger than Lord Haldane had known in Berlin. When Count Metternich had asked us to specify what reductions in the Novelle would be satisfactory to us, Mr. Churchill had said that we should prefer no increases in the German Navy Law, and that we could not say that we liked any part of any increase.

Count Metternich added that he was afraid that what Mr.

Churchill had said in the House of Commons yesterday, as to our having now a One-Power Standard instead of our previous Two-Power Standard, would not have a soothing effect.

I said that Mr. Churchill's speech represented only actual facts, which had often been put forward in discussion between the German Government and ourselves; and I thought that his reference to the One-Power Standard should rather be taken as a compliment to the great strength which the German Navy had attained, as compared with that of other Powers.

I told Count Metternich that I was surprised that the German Chancellor estimated our draft formula at so low a value. I could not help thinking that the exchange of it would have a favourable effect. No doubt it was true that we had never meditated an unprovoked attack on Germany: but German public opinion thought otherwise. What the Chancellor now asked amounted to an agreement of absolute neutrality, which was more than conditional neutrality.

Count Metternich said that the Chancellor had not used the word 'absolute,' but in effect his wish amounted to that.

I said that I would refer the communication to the Prime Minister and my Colleagues, but I was still in some doubt as to the exact extent of its meaning. I understood the Chancellor to mean that, failing a guarantee of absolute neutrality, the Novelle must proceed.

Count Metternich confirmed this.

I went on to say that I understood clearly this, and the German point of view with regard to it; but, if the Chancellor meant to infer that, failing a guarantee of absolute neutrality, the relations between the two Powers could not be cordial or satisfactory, I thought that such an idea would be unreasonable. In effect, the Chancellor was asking us for an agreement which went much further than anything which we had with any other country except the Japanese alliance and our ancient Treaties with Portugal: it went further than anything we had with France or Russia.

Count Metternich said that we had not had with France or Russia the acute differences which we had had with Germany.

I replied that, at the end of last century and the beginning of this, we had been more than once on the brink of a war with France or with Russia: yet our relations with these two countries had improved, without any agreement so far-reaching as the Chancellor now suggested that we should have with Germany. If the Novelle must proceed, I thought that it should be possible, after public opinion had been stirred by it, to negotiate something which would have a calming influence. In any case, I was ready to continue to discuss from a friendly point of view all the questions which arose between the two Governments; and I saw no reason why this readiness should not be reciprocated by the German Government. In the interests of good relations between us, I would much rather have the Novelle proceeded with, and the Morocco question out of the way, than have no Novelle and the Morocco question still between us.

I added that, as far as we were concerned, we were prepared to continue the territorial discussions surveyed with Mr. Harcourt the other day, if the German Government desired to do so.

Count Metternich said that the Chancellor had not made any reference to these.

Finally, I repeated that I would report the Chancellor's communication to the Prime Minister and my Colleagues.

[I am, &c.]
E. G[REY].[27]

Then, on 21 March, a memorandum was sent to Berlin to be communicated to the Chancellor, drafted in part by Lord Haldane. It represented a triumph for the Foreign Office's French-supporting diplomats and a finessing away of Haldane's agreed form of words with the Germans. Considering Haldane was a longstanding friend of Grey, it was a considerable diminution of his authority within Whitehall to have acquiesced in this Memorandum, as in effect he now had abdicated from his own mission. It demonstrates what

---

27 *British Docs*, Vol. VI, p 719.

a mistake Campbell-Bannerman had made in December 1905 in putting the three Relugas 'plotters', Asquith, Grey and Haldane, in such powerful positions in his government. Albeit he had wanted Cromer as Foreign Secretary. Asquith was to drop Haldane in 1915 and his relationship with Grey by 1916 had also become very strained.

Enclosure in No. 547

Memorandum

His Majesty's Government received on the 6th instant a Memorandum which the Imperial German Government were so good as to communicate through the hands of Count Metternich. His Majesty's Government are in complete accordance with the desire of the Imperial German Government to continue the discussion of a basis for good relations between the two countries in a friendly spirit and with perfect frankness on both sides. They will therefore, with the intention of preventing any misapprehension of their own view of what has up till now taken place, make a few comments on certain phrases which occur in the Memorandum.

Lord Haldane proceeded to Berlin in response to an intimation through an unofficial channel that it would not be otherwise than agreeable if a British Minister were to come there, in the first instance for the purpose of a private and unofficial interchange of views. Although his visit was private, he was received with the greatest friendliness by high personages of the German Government, and the suggestion made by him that the conversations, just because they were to be informal, should take place with complete openness and freedom from reserve, was acted on without difficulty on either side. He began by stating that, while in Berlin with the full approval of the King and of his Colleagues in the Cabinet, and while, as he thought, he was pretty intimately acquainted with their feelings and intentions as regards the topics which might come under discussion, he had no authority to bind them or to make any agreement. His purpose was, if this should prove agreeable to the German Government, to explore the ground as completely as was possible at this stage, with a view to ascertaining what ideas and purposes were common to both Governments, and thus getting the conception of a possible basis for more formal and authoritative discussion. He would state in a very open fashion where he thought there were possibilities of differences as well as of agreement. The informal character of his visit rendered this the more easily possible, and his impressions he would take back to his Colleagues. As he was not come to bind them, all would be ad referendum, and similarly those with whom he was speaking would presumably feel no more bound than he should feel. On this footing the conversations, which were very free and unrestrained, and were conducted in the most agreeable spirit, proceeded. Nothing was excluded.

Lord Haldane indicated that the various questions which might arise could not be considered in isolation, but should be looked on as part of a general negotiation. His Colleagues would have to satisfy Parliament and the British public about the outcome of such a negotiation. There was an excellent spirit, of which his Government would gladly avail themselves; but he ought to say that he thought naval prospects would very materially affect the question of how much was practicable.

As to naval matters, Lord Haldane was only cognisant of the plans of the Imperial Government for a third squadron for training purposes, and for three new battleships. The latter, he said, seemed to him as a civilian to present more difficulty than the former. The desire of Germany to provide for the better training of her recruits was not a matter on which he should venture to make any observation. Broadly speaking, what would cause concern here would be any plan which would impose on England the necessity of further increasing her fleet, and the three new battleships would certainly do this to a substantial extent. But he said that the question was of too technical a character for him to discuss in detail. The Imperial Government most courteously presented Lord Haldane, shortly before he left, with a full copy of the Novelle. It was not suggested that *he should examine it on the spot. He had of course neither the expert knowledge nor the time requisite for such an examination, and it was not until his return and its examination by the Admiralty in London that the increases in 'personnel' and in small craft, which the Novelle contemplated, were realised. As to the three battleships, however, he was fully informed, and it was this information which caused him to express at Berlin some apprehension of difficulty.*

These observations are made because it is not quite clear from some phrases in the Memorandum communicated on March 6th that Lord Haldane's general attitude has been quite correctly defined in these phrases. Against the increase in 'personnel' he is stated to have had no objection to make. He made no comment only because, through no fault either of his own or of those with whom he was conversing, he had no knowledge of its nature or extent. Again, he is said to have declared that the British Government were willing to support such plans for the acquisition of the Portuguese Colony of Angola, as well as of parts of the Congo State, as it might eventually be the policy of Germany to entertain. While expressing his opinion that the British Government would be glad, in the event of the Secret Agreement of 1898 becoming operative, to make arrangements under which Germany might obtain a part of Angola which was not marked out as hers under that Agreement, and also, if Belgium became willing to part with some of the Congo, portions of that State, Lord Haldane referred to the fact that the relations of England to Portugal and Belgium were friendly, and that England could put no pressure on Portugal or Belgium to part with anything if they were unwilling to do so Moreover, he referred to the circumstance that France had certain rights of pre-emption as regards the Congo State. Again, he did not make an unconditional, or for that matter any, offer to cede Zanzibar and Pemba. What he intimated was that these appeared to be very suitable assets to be considered for the purposes of a general settlement extending over all the topics of conversation. He and the high personages with whom he was conversing were discussing all these topics in the most open and informal fashion, with a view to ascertaining their mutual views as to practical possibilities. The questions of the Baghdad Railway, the Island of Timor, the conceivable shapes of a political formula, and the possibilities of diminution of the naval programme on the part of both Governments were all treated in the same spirit, and Lord Haldane no more regarded the Imperial Government as making formal offers, or as actually negotiating a Treaty, than he so regarded himself. Both were in his view on a voyage of discovery, the field of which was to be surveyed as a whole, as a preliminary step to more formal negotiation. It may be pointed out in particular that, in discussing the practicability of a neutrality formula, Lord Haldane drew attention to the immense difficulties to both countries which would result from an unconditional formula. He understood that these difficulties were appreciated.

The British Government therefore hope that, in the light of what has been above stated, the Imperial German Government will see that there has been no desire to shift the basis on which the conversations were conducted at Berlin. They take the opportunity of repeating their assurance of good feeling and of desire for the best relations between the two countries. Finally, they reciprocate with pleasure the friendly expression with which the Memorandum communicated on March 6th concludes.[28]

This was followed by Sir Edward Grey writing to Berlin on 22 March (No. 548) and, with that, the dialogue was in effect over, confirmed in a message (No. 550) from Sir Edward Grey to Britain's Ambassador to Paris of the same date in which Grey distorts the offer on the table from the Germans, writing about remaining neutral 'in all circumstances', which was never what was envisaged. Grey stated that 'even a promise of conditional neutrality might give the impression that we would under all circumstances stand aside.' Again something not contemplated and expressly ruled out by the terms offered by the German Chancellor.

---

28 *British Docs*, Vol. VI, p 722.

No. 548

Sir Edward Grey to Sir E. Goschen

F.O. *12528/5569/12/18.*
(No. 71) Secret

Foreign Office, March 22, 1912

Sir,

Count Metternich told me today that he had reported our last conversation to the Chancellor, and had heard from him that the difficulty between us was not the question of the continuation of the confidential relations established by Lord Haldane in Berlin, for the Chancellor of course wished to continue these; the difficulty was the question of armaments and the naval budget. The Chancellor could deal with this difficulty only if there was an agreement about neutrality of a far-reaching character, and leaving no room for doubt. Such an agreement would not be simply a present from Germany to us: it would have equal advantages for both sides. The Chancellor said that the situation had not been made easier by Mr. Churchill's speech, but the Chancellor did not relinquish hope. Mr. Churchill had spoken of limiting only German armaments, while reserving freedom for England. In fact, Germany, though she was situated between France and Russia, which had an Alliance, was not to increase her Navy: even without getting a promise from England to remain neutral.

Count Metternich reminded me that he had, in previous conversations, told me that there were very important internal questions in Berlin, depending upon our answer.

He added, with reference to rumours, which he believed were current in French circles, to the effect that Germany meant to attack France in the Spring, that he could give me the most absolute assurance that there was no such intention, nor anything which could serve as a basis for such reports. He asked whether I had heard these reports.

I said that I had heard reports from several quarters that in Germany war was expected in the Spring, and I had heard that a similar rumour was current in French circles. In Germany, as far as I could make out, the rumour was in some cases based upon the belief that we intended to attack Germany as soon as she announced her intention to increase her naval expenditure. In French circles, on the other hand, it seemed to be feared that Germany intended to attack France. I had never believed that any of these things were likely to happen and we of course had no intention of making war.

I expressed satisfaction at the Chancellor's desire to maintain confidential relations with us. This desire gave one a feeling of comfort and pleasure.

I explained to Count Metternich that, as the Cabinet was very much occupied by the crisis in the Coal Trade, I could not at the moment say more than that Lord Haldane had already pointed out, when he was in Berlin, the difficulty which there was in the way of either Germany or ourselves promising to remain neutral under all circumstances. I observed that, when Count Metternich was speaking to me the other day about neutrality of a far-reaching character, he had said, in reply to remarks of mine, that though the word 'absolute' was not used it represented in effect the sort of neutrality for which the Chancellor was asking.

Count Metternich again confirmed this.

[I am, &c.]
E. G[REY].[29]

---

29 *British Docs*, Vol. VI, p 724.

No. 550

Sir Edward Grey to Sir. F. Bertie

F.O. 12529/5569/12/18
(No. 148.) Secret.

Foreign Office, March 22, 1912

Sir,

I told M. Cambon today that, while he had been in Paris, the German Government had informed me that the formula which we had suggested was insufficient and that they must have a declaration of neutrality if there was to be any arrangement for the diminution of naval expenditure.

I had pointed out, as Lord Haldane had already done in Berlin, the difficulty there was in the way of either Germany or ourselves promising to remain neutral under all circumstances; and I explained that even a promise of conditional neutrality might give the impression that we would under all circumstances stand aside. I had, however, said that we were prepared to amplify our formula by saying not only that we would not make but also that we would not join in any unprovoked attack upon Germany. But this was insufficient, in the view of the German Government, to justify their coming to a naval arrangement with us; and for the time being the matter was in suspense, though the question of exchanging a formula such as I had suggested, or the question of territorial arrangements in South Africa, might be revived at any time.

M. Cambon appeared quite satisfied with the information, which I told him was for himself and M. Poincare, confidentially.

[I am, &c.]
E. G[REY].[30]

---

30 *British Docs*, Vol. VI, p 726.

Asquith then wrote on 10 April doubting the wisdom of prolonging discussions with Germany. Instead of finding a way of changing the Cabinet's flawed formula, by for example chairing a small group of key Cabinet Ministers – Grey, Haldane, Harcourt, Lloyd George and Churchill – he adopted his oft-repeated stance, 'wait and see'.

The Haldane Mission undoubtedly offered the best opportunity to avoid war with Germany during Asquith's premiership. Only the Prime Minister could have resolved the different views of Harcourt and Grey. Even to try he had to be prepared to risk the resignation of Grey, and tragically he was not ready to do so. Harcourt, whom he liked, could have stepped in as Foreign Secretary, but Asquith was not prepared to promote a potential challenger in Lloyd George or move Churchill from the Admiralty. He was never going to appoint Morley, who was also now too old.

True to form, the key Foreign Office diplomats, Nicolson, Bertie and Crowe, were delighted, having been appalled that the Cabinet should have ever contemplated concessions, as they saw them, to Germany. Such an approach went against their perspective of British policy, namely continued support for the understanding that underpinned the Military Conversations of six years before. On the night of 14/15 April 1912 the liner *Titanic* sank with the loss of 1,500 lives and the world's press had other things to write about than the chance of peace between Germany and England.

No fresh attempt was made to save the Haldane Mission. The territorial negotiations in Africa somewhat surprisingly continued, with no naval element to make for difficulties. A lesser agreement than envisaged by Harcourt was initialled on 13 August 1913, but was never brought into being with Foreign Office officials pedantically still questioning the wording days before war was declared in 1914.

Diplomacy often hinges on wording, and many times in history long frustrating hours and days have been spent with the parties shuffling between each other, mired in detail and in designing a form of words. That sort of diplomacy, hands-on, nitty-gritty, face-to-face and detailed, was never Grey's style. Had Haldane's wording of 'benevolent neutrality' been stuck to by Grey, an agreement was feasible. Yet nothing can really disguise one simple fact: to get an agreement you have to want agreement, and Grey did not want an agreement with Germany. To do so in 1912 would have upset the French, indeed there was no worthwhile agreement that would not have upset the French. He described his own sticking point revealingly as 'where our hands are tied'. But peace agreements often require tying the hands of both sides. It was also never correct to describe in Haldane's deal with Bethmann-Hollweg settling for 'benevolent neutrality' as 'unqualified neutrality'.

In June 1912 Haldane succeeded Lord Loreburn as Lord Chancellor, his record as a reforming War Minister unmatched. His role of peacemaker had been stymied by Grey, but their friendship was either too strong or Haldane's character was too weak for him to embarrass or challenge Grey's position.

The really sad part of Grey's memoirs is Chapter XIX, Volume II, 'Could War Have Been Prevented?' First, it is only a mere 15 pages, of which four and a half pages deal with his fading eyesight. He writes of how after the war he would lie awake until about four o'clock in the morning and would try one hypothesis after another, as to whether the war could have been prevented by anything he could have done in the preceding years.[31]

> The one I dwelt upon most was this. Suppose that, after the London Conference of 1912–13, I had gone to Berlin; had there pointed to the success of the Conference in tiding over a European crisis; had urged upon the Germans the value, even the necessity, of a general agreement between the Triple Alliance and the *Entente* to put the

31 Edward Grey of Fallodon, *Twenty-Five Years, 1892–1916* (Hodder & Stoughton, London: 1925), Vol II, p 47.

same Conference machinery in motion and use it directly a new crisis came!

He sadly concludes 'it would have come to nothing',[32] and constructs as the only alternative if Britain had built up a large British continental Army as well as a Supreme Fleet. This should have been started after Germany attacked France in the years after 1870. He judged, however, 'The war would have anticipated such an event; it would have come when conscription and a large Army ceased to be politically impossible in Britain',[33] and Germany would have attacked in order to pre-empt.

That Grey could believe that the informal meeting of ambassadors that he chaired, which began its work regarding the division of territories following the end of the First Balkan War on 17 December 1912 and ended when he submitted a draft treaty on 27 May 1913, was of such critical importance is odd to say the least. The treaty was signed in London three days after he issued an ultimatum to the ambassadors, to sign or leave. Grey wanted to wind the conference up, fearing that there was a growing tendency on the part of Foreign Ministers in Europe to throw on to the Ambassadors' Conference in London the burden of settling each and every new question as it arose. Before the ambassadors could settle such questions war broke out again on 29–30 June when Bulgaria attacked her former Greek and Serbian allies. To highlight this ambassadorial gathering and ignore the Haldane Mission is, even allowing for Grey's advancing years, extraordinary.

The Balkans features throughout much of Grey's tenure as Foreign Secretary, in particular in October 1908 when Bulgaria declared itself a sovereign state and the Austrians annexed Bosnia-Herzegovina. The Russian Foreign Minister Isvolsky came

---

32 Grey, *Twenty-Five Years*, Vol II, p 51.
33 Grey, *Twenty-Five Years*, Vol II, p 51.

to London to see Grey and said he had not agreed to Austrian annexation with the Austrian Foreign Minister Aehrenthal, but Grey was rightly sceptical and refused the Russians' request for their warships to have clear passage through the Straits of Gibraltar. Already strains were developing in Russian relations, but the main consequence of the annexation of Bosnia was in 1909 a marked deterioration in Anglo-Austrian relations. Not that Grey was opposed personally to annexation, but he was disturbed by the adverse reaction from Russia, Serbia, Montenegro, Italy and Turkey. Another legacy of annexation was the problem of Serbian competition. Hardinge admitted that Britain was having a very strenuous time with Balkan affairs since there was no chance of Vienna making concessions.[34] Grey told Isvolsky that Britain would not give military support if war broke out between Serbia and Austria with Russia aiding Serbia. Berlin then put pressure on the Russians to accept Bosnia's annexation. So the issues that triggered the 1914 war were present from the summer of 1909 and simmered until 1912 when late in September Sazonov, who was by then the Russian Foreign Secretary, came to see Grey in Scotland. Both Grey and Nicolson underestimated the infinite capacity of the Balkan states for creating difficulties.[35] On 10 August 1913 the Second Balkan War ended with a defeat for Bulgaria. A difference of opinion developed between Grey and Nicolson, the latter being upset when Grey failed to give Russia firm support when they stood by Serbia and Montenegro.

Slowly Grey was starting to distance Britain from Russia, but without challenging the Triple Entente, which would have upset France. The mistake was not to sense that the special relationship was that between Germany and Austria, and that only Berlin could influence Vienna. Retrospection is all too easy in Foreign Affairs because the intricacies are not as apparent as in domestic matters.

---

34 Robbins, *Sir Edward Grey*, pp 192–4.
35 Robbins, *Sir Edward Grey*, pp 264–7.

The *War Memoirs* of Lloyd George[36] are a classic example of the perils of memoir writing. In them Lloyd George admonishes Grey for not telling the German leaders that Britain would go to war if they invaded Belgium much earlier than August 1914. Lloyd George knew better than anyone that the Liberal Cabinet would not have allowed Grey to have threatened Germany earlier. Even after the Sarajevo assassination of Archduke Franz Ferdinand, the British Cabinet, as will be clear later in this chapter, were divided over neutrality and had been painfully divided for some years. After Sarajevo, for over a week the Cabinet was in no mental, let alone political, condition to authorise Grey to take any major action, indeed Grey made it clear he wanted no such authority. Asquith told the King on the night of 24 July that happily Britain should be a 'spectator' to what would unfold. A material fact, too, was that Belgium did not ask for assistance from the guaranteeing Powers, but initially wanted to be left alone to deal with Germany as it thought fit.

So could Grey have done more to avoid Britain's continental military commitments in the First World War? The answer is 'yes'. The prime task of a Foreign Secretary is not to prevent war in all circumstances, but to do everything to avoid conflict wherever possible. Sadly, conflict sometimes becomes a necessity. The mistakes Grey made from 1906 were not that he did not try to avoid war. They were mistakes that flowed from a mindset, a mixture of rigid principles and a deeply held hidden perspective in relation to France. He talked to ambassadors in London, he did not see the importance of political engagement in person in Berlin, Paris, St Petersburg and Vienna. He was strangely divorced from military strategy, military options, creative negotiations and innovatory thinking. Douglas Hurd, Foreign Secretary from 1989–95, wrote a chapter on Grey as Foreign Secretary in his book written

---

36 David Lloyd George, *War Memoirs of David Lloyd George* (Odhams Press, London: 1938).

with Edward Young. 'Grey was walking a tightrope in a high wind. The political rationale behind his ambiguity was evident... "There would be a row with Parliament if I had used words which implied the possibility of a secret engagement unknown to Parliament all those years committing us to a European War ... I purposely worded the Parliamentary answer so as not to convey that the engagement of 1904 might not in certain circumstances be construed to have larger consequences than its strict letter." Grey was not by nature a devious man; but the double negative became a tool of his policy. It was for professional diplomats to wrestle with the complications.'[37]

As regards Naval policy, on 29 April 1912, Admiral Fisher wrote, despite having retired some two years earlier, to Lord Esher, chairman of the Committee of Imperial Defence, about Churchill as First Lord of the Admiralty, 'SO I'VE DONE WITH HIM'. This was despite their apparent meeting of minds in October 1911.

Fisher had pressed Churchill to build more submarines because he continued to see in them the key to domination of the North Sea. At the oil commission on 11 December 1912 and subsequently, Fisher heard evidence about German companies producing diesel engines for the German and other navies. Moreover, in 1913 the first four diesel-driven German U-Boats – essentially overseas submarines – came into service.[38]

Fisher believed 'my beloved submarines would magnify the naval power of England seven times more than at present'.[39] A typical Fisher memo (in capital letters) was: 'CONSIDERING THE SAFETY OF ENGLAND IT WOULD THEREFORE APPEAR THAT THE DEVELOPMENT OF THE SUBMARINE (PROVIDED WE KEEP AN EQUAL

37 Douglas Hurd and Edward Young, *Choose Your Weapons. The British Foreign Secretary. 200 Years of Argument, Success and Failure* (Weidenfeld & Nicolson, London: 2010) pp 226–7.
38 R F Mackay, *Fisher of Kilverstone* (Clarendon Press, Oxford: 1973), pp 441–2.
39 Nicholas A Lambert, *Sir John Fisher's Naval Revolution* (University of South Carolina Press, Columbia, SC: 1999), pp 12, 83.

OR LARGER NUMBER THAN PROSPECTIVE ENEMIES) WILL RESULT IN INCREASED SAFETY.[40] When Admiral Jellicoe received this, he wrote to Churchill reinforcing Fisher's arguments.

For far too long in Great Britain it was the Dreadnought debate that found the headlines and stirred passions: 'We want eight and we won't wait' was the public slogan in 1908. It was Asquith who brokered a compromise in Cabinet against the wishes of Lloyd George, then Chancellor, who was supported by Churchill in the Home Office. Both men wanted to slow the rate at which Dreadnoughts were being built in February 1909, but to save money for the domestic economy, not to use the money saved on submarines. What the Cabinet agreed was to start building four ships immediately and then another four the following spring. By the time war broke out Britain had 20 Dreadnoughts to Germany's 13. Yet by 1914 Britain had not built the submarine force that it needed as part of a distant blockade force, as distinct from a close blockade which was steadily going out of favour in naval operations. Nor did Britain have the mix of ships required for an intervention force to turn back or sink merchant ships supplying to or exporting from Germany. Fisher's boast in 1906 that on the day war broke out Britain would mop up German merchant steamers was never realised. On Fisher's return to the Admiralty once the war had started Churchill urgently charged him with the provision of more submarines.[41]

At Jutland, at the end of May 1916, the issues surrounding that naval debate were put to the test. In material terms the British lost more ships, yet in psychological terms were the victors. The German High Seas Fleet ventured forth only once more, on 16 August, but on hearing the British Grand Fleet had put to sea, the

---

40 Fisher, 16 May 1913, National Archives, Kew, London, Lord Hankey Papers, typescript 4pp., covered by F. to H.
41 Mackay, *Fisher of Kilverstone*, p 452.

Germans headed back to their home ports never to re-emerge.[42] Such a stand-off was a significant feat but it was as nothing to what might have been achieved had a massive economic maritime blockade been imposed on Germany in August 1914. Germany was vulnerable: over 66 per cent of its iron ore for steel production came from abroad, 25 per cent of its zinc, 50 per cent of its lead, 70 per cent of its copper and 66 per cent of its oil.[43] Britain initially made no attempt to block the flow of goods to the neutral countries under the wording 'contraband'. In the first nine months of the war, British exports and re-exports to northern neutrals increased from 10 to 24 per cent, and most of this went to Germany. By contrast, German submarines were able to reduce British foodstuffs by 1917 to 75 per cent of 1913 pre-war levels. They did not feel bound by international ties.

> The time for decision by Britain came five weeks after the Order in Council of 20 August [1914], when the American President [Wilson] suddenly initiated conversations about it by expressing informally his government's 'great concern' and 'conviction of the extreme gravity of the situation'. There were other factors also to be considered. France, already incensed at Britain's failure to consult her before important economic decisions were taken and sure that the Americans could be won round, thought it 'supreme folly and quite unnecessary weakness' not to cut off German supplies of foodstuffs and cotton. On top of this the Russians proposed a limited food blockade. Grey preferred friction with France to friction with America and his view carried the day against allies and colleagues.[44]

---

42 Arthur Herman, *To Rule the Waves: How the British Navy Shaped the Modern World* (HarperCollins, London: 2004) pp 503–9.

43 Paul Kennedy, *Strategy and Diplomacy, 1870–1945* (Fontana, London: 1984) p 137.

44 F H Hinsley (ed), *British Foreign Policy Under Sir Edward Grey* (Cambridge University Press, Cambridge: 1977) p 493.

Grey's decision was supported by Asquith to conciliate American views. It is interesting that Churchill at the Admiralty and Runciman at Trade were all for brinkmanship with America. It is in this context also worth recalling that Churchill had not opposed the Haldane Mission, though his speech in Britain on the day of Haldane's arrival in Berlin referring to the German navy as a 'luxury', a term even more offensive in German than in English, did not help. By August 1912, he appeared, however, resigned to war and wrote a memorandum to Grey:

> consider how tremendous would be the weapon which France would possess to compel our intervention, if she could say, 'On the advice of and by arrangement with your Naval authorities we have left our northern coasts defenceless' … everyone must feel who knows the facts that we have the obligations of an alliance without its advantages, and above all without precise definitions.[45]

This coming after the rather tortured Cabinet settlement dealing with the Military Conversations and the failure of the Haldane Mission was not inappropriate. He had spotted that there was by then a strong realpolitik case in the summer of 1912 for engaging the French in a joint naval strategy for concentrating the British Navy in the North, the French in the South. On 16 May the Cabinet, with some concern about totally leaving the Mediterranean, discussed such naval cooperation and it was argued over in a series of meetings that summer as well as at a special CID meeting on 4 July. A compromise was reached with a fleet of Royal Navy battleships still being based on a Mediterranean port. Esher wrote with some relief that 'it is cheaper than a conscript army and any entangling alliance.'[46] Britain was soon to have both.

---

45 Winston Churchill, *The World Crisis 1911–1918* (Odhams, London: 1938) Vol 1, p 113.
46 Robbins, *Sir Edward Grey*, pp 261–2

Yet in September Grey exaggerated his hidden perspective over France without the slightest evidence to support his claim, by telling C P Scott, the editor of the *Manchester Guardian*, 'if France is not supported against Germany she would join with her and the rest of Europe in an attack on us'. Described, quite correctly, by the historian Niall Ferguson as a 'simply fantastic' statement,[47] what it reveals, however, is how simplistically Grey still saw the strategic options.

On 22 November 1913, in a letter to the French Ambassador Cambon amended by the Cabinet, Grey gave the last significant definition before the war in 1914 of the government's position on the Military Conversations. He said that 'if either Government had grave reason to expect an unprovoked attack by a third Power, or something that threatened the general peace, it should immediately discuss with the other whether both Governments should act together to prevent aggression and to preserve peace, and, if so, what measures they would be prepared to take in common.'[48] Grey must have known at the time that it was a dishonest definition, in the deepest sense of the word dishonest, to pretend that there was no commitment to 'whether' or to 'what' measures would be taken in common.

In 1913 King George V wrote to Grey of his support and 'absolute reliance in your management of foreign policy'. It was not a view shared by the King's mother Queen Alexandra: 'E. Grey has certainly proved the worst Foreign Secretary England has ever had.'[49]

* * *

By 1914 the Whitehall view, broader than that of the Foreign Office, was that an expeditionary force was virtually certain to be sent if

---

47 Niall Ferguson, *The Pity of War* (Allen Lane, London: 1998) p 73.
48 *British Docs*, Vol X, Part II, Doc 416, pp 614–15.
49 Robbins, *Sir Edward Grey*, p 268.

France was attacked, but Grey knew that the Cabinet would still not face up to this. The prevailing view within the CID, the War Office and the Foreign Office was summed up by Lord Esher, with his long association with the CID: that the Military Conversations certainly committed Britain to fight whether the Cabinet liked it or not. That was the guiding principle governing Grey's actions but, in fairness, he was still ready to at least appear to contemplate other initiatives at the start of 1914.

Painstaking research from T G Otte, a considerable expert in the workings of the Foreign Office and author of *The Foreign Office Mind*, was published in a paper in the *Historical Journal*[50] as recently as February 2013. It reveals that a clandestine mission to Germany by Grey's private secretary in the Foreign Office, Sir William Tyrrell, was continuing to be planned in July 1914 just before war broke out.

Based on hitherto unused archival material, it is clear that though the mission never took place there was a growing sense of détente in Anglo-German relations on the eve of the First World War. Also that the plan involved the key official in Grey's private office in London. In Berlin it involved directly the then Foreign Minister. Anglo-German antagonism was no longer the central concern of British policy-makers. As Otte argues, relations with Germany had become a function of Anglo-Russian relations and the feared revival of Russian power from 1912 had provided a context for attempts by British and German officials to move relations between their countries on to what Otte calls 'a friendlier footing'. The article provides a powerful antidote to assumptions that the First World War was by the start of 1914 somehow inevitable.

William Tyrrell was described by the diplomat Sir Horace Rumbold, as Grey's 'very Papal Private Secretary [who kept] everything in the dark'.[51] In the two years before August 1914 Tyrrell's

---

50 T G Otte, 'Détente 1914: Sir William Tyrrell's Secret Mission to Germany', *The Historical Journal*, Vol 56, Issue 1, March 2013, pp 175–204.
51 Rumbold to Father, 15 Feb and 0 Oct 1908, Bodl. Rumbold dep. 13 and dep. 14.

influence over the Foreign Secretary grew as that of the PUS, Sir Arthur Nicolson, declined. Grey even sent Tyrrell to the United States in 1913 for talks with Colonel House, the right-hand man of Woodrow Wilson, the new US President; a clear sign of confidence. In December, Colonel House in the United States opened up to Tyrrell on his view that an understanding was possible between France, Germany, Great Britain and the United States. When Tyrrell was granted a knighthood in 1913, Charles MacDonald, a diplomat, quipped that he 'will be more autocratic than ever now', and the foreign affairs editor of *The Times*, Sir Valentine Chirol, noted to Hardinge that Tyrrell's influence was 'growing greater and greater – perhaps too great'. [52] Tyrrell acted with the authority of Grey but also responded to the desire for improved relations he and his German friends in London had detected in Gottlieb von Jagow, the Kaiser's last and least-known peacetime State Secretary for Foreign Affairs. It is also worth noting that Lloyd George, in an interview for the *Daily News* on 1 January 1914, singled out for praise the 'infinitely more friendly' relations between No. 10 Downing Street and Wilhelmstrasse in Germany and gave the credit for this to the 'wise and patient diplomacy' of Grey, a pretty clear sign that he wanted improved relations with Germany and was encouraging Grey to move in this direction with slightly tongue-in-cheek praise for his virtues. German journalists and historians were also picking up signs of détente and rapprochement.

Tyrrell used the fact that he had been educated at a *Gymnasium* in Bonn and at Göttingen University and spoke fluent German, and English with a slight accent, to make contact, in particular, with Blücher von Wahlstatt, a German businessman living in London. On 8 April 1914 von Wahlstatt wrote to Jagow, to suggest he meet Tyrrell. Jagow, who had known Tyrrell in Rome where he had been ambassador, welcomed the idea. As Tyrrell was reluctant to go to Berlin, initially a chateau at Dyck in the Lower Rhine

---

52 Otte, 'Détente 1914', p 188.

region, near the Dutch frontier, was chosen for the meeting, but that date and place slipped. Jagow was involved in budget debates in the Reichstag in May and was getting married in mid-June, when he was also due to return to Berlin. Tyrrell planned to leave on 8 July for Prussia's Polish province, Posen, where he and his family frequently spent their holidays, and which might have provided a place to meet, but he fell sick and did not return to work until 20 July.

Jagow did not approve of Admiral von Tirpitz and was worried about the bellicosity of Vienna and the Austrian interest in a military solution. He was also well aware of Harcourt's negotiations over Africa – yet one more sign that the Haldane Mission had had the potential to create agreement two years earlier. Jagow's acceptance of a meeting with Tyrrell was explicit: 'I believe that a confidential verbal discussion is more useful than the continued exchanges by means of notes and intermediaries.'[53] It also has to be noted that the British Ambassador in Berlin, Goschen, who retired at the end of 1913, had had very little close contact with key Germans in Berlin and not much influence in London either.

If only Tyrrell and Jagow had met in April, but delay followed delay. When Jagow returned from his honeymoon in early July, he still hoped to see Tyrrell, but decided not to press for a meeting because he did not want to give the impression that he was running after the English. Tyrrell invoked the Home Rule crisis over Ireland to defer an earlier, definite date, preferring 'some private house' possibly in Germany later in July. He stressed Grey 'approved very much of the idea'.[54]

Tyrrell's attitude to Grey and Germany changed over the years. Initially he shared the views of one of his closest colleagues in the Foreign Office, Sir Eyre Crowe, but this too was changing. Even

---

53 Otte, 'Détente 1914', p 184.
54 Tyrrell to Blücher (private), 18 April 1914, (TS copy), Nachlass Jagow, TNA (PRO) GFM, f 25/16.

Crowe was starting to recognise that the atmosphere was now different. On 17 February 1913, he wrote:

> one of the reasons why Anglo-German relations are now more cordial ... is that we have entirely ceased to discuss the question of limitations of [naval] armaments ... and that recent events in the Balkans with the growing risk of a weakened Austria and a strengthened Russia, are more likely to bring and keep us and Germany in touch than any amount of twaddle, Tirpitzian or otherwise about naval standards.[55]

Yet it was Crowe amongst other diplomats who had been involved in frustrating Haldane and Harcourt in 1912, raising difficult negotiating issues and helping Grey to block the Haldane Mission.

By 1914 Tyrrell, unlike Crowe, was ready to risk some French ire. Yet it has to be noted that throughout Tyrrell's initiative towards Berlin, Grey still believed he could continue entente with France, and his readiness to incur displeasure in Paris, hitherto an absolute, was never tested. Grey had as Otte admits 'little to lose by Tyrrell's proposed confidential exchanges with Jagow. His private secretary had demonstrated his discretion and his flair for unravelling complex foreign policy problems, most recently in America. He could rely on Tyrrell to conduct talks orally without anything compromising being recorded on paper.'[56]

On 23 April 1914 the exceptional first overseas visit by Grey as Foreign Secretary occurred to Paris, with Grey seeing his French opposite number, Gaston Doumergue, and the French President, Raymond Poincaré. The timing was accidental in that it was long planned he would accompany the King, but it was almost as if Grey was covering his base against any leakage from Germany of

---

55 Sir Eyre Crowe, 17 February 1913, National Archives, Kew, London, (PRO), FO 371/1649.
56 Otte, 'Détente 1914', p 203.

diplomatic conversations. His purpose was to kick the idea of military staff talks with Russia into the long grass. Grey was not keen on the joint initiative of the French government and the Russian Foreign Minister, Sergei Dmitrievich Sazonov, to forge closer Anglo-Russian ties, and was against active naval cooperation with Russia.

This is reflected in the despatch of 1 May 1914 from Grey to the British Ambassador to France after he had returned from Paris. It appears he had not been accompanied by Bertie in his Paris meetings but only by Tyrrell, a sign that he was conducting serious business and making a shift on policy in distancing the British Government from the more aggressive stance of Russia, but in a way calculated not to risk any misunderstanding with France. Hence his words reflected a reluctance to be sucked in: 'it would not be considered safe in time of war for the British fleet to enter the Baltic lest the fleet should be caught in a trap and find its communications cut off.' The draft, obviously written by Tyrrell on 26 April, was amended very slightly by Grey on 1 May 1914 and interestingly, the last sentence about everyone being 'immensely impressed by the growing strength of Russia' was in his own hand.

EASTERN EUROPE   May 1
SECRET SERIES
[19288]

No. 1

Sir Edward Grey to Sir F. Bertie

(No. 249) Secret.

Foreign Office, May 1, 1914.

Sir,
On the 23rd ultimo I had a long conversation with M. Doumergue

*at the Quai d'Orsay. Sir William Tyrrell was with me and M. Cambon
and M. Margerie were present also.*

*M. Doumergue spoke at length and with great emphasis on the
necessity for doing something to make relations with Russia more
secure. He evidently assumed that Germany would make great
efforts to detach Russia from the French Alliance, and might possibly be successful. In that case France and England would be left
alone; for Italy, who had at one time been the least certain and effective member of the Triple Alliance, was now taking Austria's place
in it. Italy had ambitions in the Mediterranean, and Germany was
showing a disposition to consolidate Italy's position in the Triple Alliance by keeping a German squadron in the Mediterranean. Russia
was anxious for some better understanding with us, and it was essential that we should do something. The French knew that an alliance
between Britain and Russia was out of the question, but could not we
at least promise to discuss matters with Russia, if necessary?*

*I said that I thought it not impossible, if the French agreed, that
we should communicate to the Russian Government exactly what the
state of things was between France and ourselves. We might let them
know of the Note that I had given to M. Cambon and of the conversations that had taken place between the military and naval staffs.
Russia would then be able to see exactly how things stood and what
scope they left for any conversations with her. She would understand
that both the French and British Governments were left entirely free
to decide whether, in case of war, they would support one another
or not. Russia would realise also that, if the British Government did
decide to engage in a continental war, any use that they could make
of their military forces would be on the French frontier; and, therefore, there could be no use in military conversations on the part of
Russia and England. In making the communication we could ask
Russia what she wanted.*

*M. Doumergue agreed with this, and said that Russia did not
want any military arrangement as far as we were concerned.*

I said that the matter would then be reduced to a conversation between the Russian and British naval staffs. It could not amount to very much, but it would be something, and I would consult the Prime Minister about it on my return to London and see whether we could agree to such a conversation.

I may inform your Excellency, though I did not enter upon this detail with M. Doumergue, that, unless it were to give the coup de grâce *at the very end of a war, when we had been practically victorious, it would not be considered safe in time of war for the British fleet to enter the Baltic lest the fleet should be caught in a trap and finds its communications cut off. If, therefore, there were naval conversations with Russia they would, so far as I can see, amount simply to letting Russia know that our naval forces would be used outside the Baltic, and that Russia could put her own naval forces to the best use inside the Baltic.*

Later in the evening, after dinner, M. Poincaré spoke to me and expressed himself satisfied with what he had heard that I had said to M. Doumergue.

I pointed out, in the course of conversation with M. Poincaré and M. Doumergue, that it was more difficult for us in the case of Russia than in the case of France – I would not say to enter into engagements, for we had no engagements with France – but to hold out to Russia any hopes of assistance from us. Whether we engaged in a continental war or kept aloof would depend upon public opinion in Great Britain when the time came. If there were a really aggressive and menacing attack made by Germany upon France, it was possible that public feeling in Great Britain would justify the Government in helping France. But it was not likely that Germany would make an aggressive and menacing attack upon Russia; and even if she did, people in Great Britain would be inclined to say that, though Germany might have successes at first, Russia's resources were so great that, in the long run, Germany would be exhausted without our helping Russia. Besides this, the French Government were a free Government, while the Russian Government were not; and this affected the sympathy of public opinion in Great Britain.

When I made this latter remark to M. Poincaré, he said that there was the same difficulty in the French feeling for Russia.

On this I observed that I knew this to be so, but in France the utility of an alliance with Russia was felt, while in England the matter required much more explanation.

M. Poincaré observed that it was not an alliance that was suggested, for there could be no question of anything more between England and Russia than existed between England and France.

I found that everyone conversant with politics, both those in Office and such men as M. Clémenceau and M. Delcassé, were immensely impressed by the growing strength of Russia, and her tremendous resources and potential power and wealth.[57]

Meanwhile Tyrrell's planned Mission was happening at an all too slow and measured pace. Grey was seriously under-estimating the amount of dry political tinder out in Europe, particularly relating to Vienna and the Balkans; as proof of that historians are still arguing as to whether it was Serb nationalism or Yugoslavism, Serbian secret societies or sheer local initiative that caused the assassination to happen. The Archduke's convoy of cars passed six potential assassins; five did not act, and one threw a bomb 'which bounced off the Archduke's car'. Then his car actually 'reversed back slowly past the exact spot from which Gavrilo Princip fired thrice with fatal results'.[58] The Balkans was ready to ignite and Grey should have sensed this and instructed Tyrrell – whom he saw every day in his private office – in April to go to Berlin straightaway, and ignore the Home Rule crisis which involved him as a politician but which was not strictly a matter requiring Tyrrell's attention. Grey could, and should, have been ready for Tyrrell to also say that he, Grey, would go and see Jagow himself and the

---

57 National Archives, Kew, London, No. 249, May 1914.
58 Noel Malcolm, *Bosnia: A Short History* (Macmillan, London: 1994) pp 155–6.

Chancellor in Berlin if the opening meeting went well. But it was not to be.

Why did Grey not recall this Tyrrell initiative when he came to muse in his memoirs about opportunities lost? The Cabinet in May had agreed with what Grey had said in Paris, that there could be no question of active naval cooperation with Russia, so that slight shift in British policy had democratic support. What was needed was to convince Germany that Britain shared their concerns about Russia. The work had started internally under Sir Edward Crowe, now head of the Eastern Department, through a draft memorandum, but it took a month. Nevertheless a highly critical memorandum was sent on 10 June, much of it the work of Grey, to Buchanan, the British Ambassador in St Petersburg.[59] The way for letting the German government know its contents was open and it clearly indicated that a renegotiation with Russia was underway. The Russians replied one month later, in the view of the British Ambassador in a 'weak' and 'childish' way. Three days later the Austrians sent their ultimatum to Serbia.[60] What was needed in the third week in June or preferably well before was for Grey to follow his visit to Paris and go to Berlin to state his concerns over Russia directly to the German Chancellor. There can only be one truthful answer as to why he never undertook such action. Grey did not, as over Haldane's Mission, sense the political opportunity in Berlin; he was not in the habit of seeing foreign politicians, he preferred to converse with diplomats. Tyrrell, by contrast, had concluded from Russia's dealings with Persia in 1911 onwards that there was a need to reorientate British foreign policy. A private secretary works so intimately with the Foreign Secretary that Tyrrell must have discussed all these issues with Grey. While the timing of Tyr-

---

59 *British Docs*, Vol X, Part II, p 547, and note 4, p 798.
60 D W Sweet and R T B Langhorne, Chapter 12, 'Great Britain and Russia, 1907–1914', in Hinsley (ed.), *British Foreign Policy under Sir Edward Grey*, p 254.

rell's proposed meeting with Jagow continued to be discussed, the actual meeting never materialised.

But how receptive really was the atmosphere in Germany and how influential was Jagow? That is the key question in weighing the importance of the abortive Tyrrell Mission to see Jagow.

It is a salutary fact that when Emperor Franz Joseph of Austria-Hungary's special emissary, Alexander, Count of Hoyos, met the Kaiser and Chancellor Bethmann-Hollweg on 5 July, and the latter made it clear that Vienna had a 'blank cheque', Jagow was neither present nor appears to have been fully aware of what was planned, a not unsurprising indication that he was not as crucial as the Chancellor in influencing the Kaiser. Bethmann-Hollweg was, however, still very powerful, a reason why Haldane's Mission, which engaged with him, was politically of greater importance to British foreign policy than Tyrrell's. Bethmann-Hollweg spent most of the rest of the month of July on his estate on the Oder, though he made discreet visits to Berlin to talk with the military. The Kaiser sailed off on 6 July for his annual three-week summer yachting trip in the North Sea. Some believe that this apparent nonchalance is evidence of orchestrated deception. But Max Hastings highlights the views of a German, Admiral Hopman, who 'persisted in his opinion, widely shared in Berlin, that Germany could gain important diplomatic capital from the Balkan crisis, at small cost' and wrote on 16 July 'personally I do not believe in war entanglement' and on 21 July 'Europe will not brawl because of Serbia'.[61]

On 6 July the German Ambassador saw Grey in the Foreign Office and, speaking privately, warned him about the 'anxiety and pessimism he had found in Berlin.' He later described how he had seen Bethmann-Hollweg, who did not share his optimism for Anglo-German relations and of how the talk in Berlin was of the Russians being about to raise 900,000 additional troops. 'The interview

---

61 Max Hastings, *Catastrophe: Europe Goes to War 1914* (William Collins, London: 2013) p 44.

left Grey full of foreboding.[62] But the Cabinet did not want to be caught up in Balkan affairs at a moment when the Ulster Crisis was coming to a head.[63] Grey did not intend to act decisively.'[64] Only a decisive break with Russia by Britain, coordinated with Germany changing its position of supporting Austria, could have made a big difference. To do this Grey would have had to go to Cabinet. In the event Grey brought these issues to Cabinet nearly three weeks later on 24 July, having been told the night before of the substance of the Austrian ultimatum. By then it was too late. The shift in British policy which had been occurring was needed in April, May and June 1914, the period when there was a new receptiveness at the very least from Jagow to a change in Anglo-German relations. Had he acted then Grey might well have influenced Bethmann-Hollweg to make another effort to improve relations with Britain.

It is hard to avoid the conclusion that once again in history a medical condition was a factor. Grey had arranged to go later that summer to Germany to consult the famous Wiesbaden eye specialist Dr Hermann Pagenstecher. He was getting into increasing difficulty with his eyesight, distressing for anyone and perhaps why he did not appear to envisage any political discussions while in Germany. There is no evidence that Grey ever intended to meet Jagow, nor that he put any pressure on Tyrrell to meet Jagow earlier. He had, however, written a favourable view of Jagow as early as 13 January 1913. 'If we could only have ten years of a man like Jagow to deal with really controlling the policy of Germany, we should be on intimate terms with her at the end of the time, and on increasingly good terms all through.'[65]

While it is reasonable for Otte to argue in his article 'Détente 1914' that the Tyrrell Mission meant Grey had not resigned himself

62 Michael Eckstein, 'Some notes on Sir Edward Grey's Policy in July 1914', *Historical Journal* (1972) pp 321–4.
63 Prince Lichnowsky, *Heading for the Abyss* (Payson & Clarke, New York: 1928).
64 Michael Eckstein and Zara Steiner, Chapter 23, 'The Sarajevo Crisis', in F H Hinsley (ed.) *British Foreign Policy under Sir Edward Grey*, p 398.
65 Robbins, *Sir Edward Grey*, p 269.

to the inevitability of war, there is no evidence to indicate that Grey had changed his basic foreign policy orientation from what he saw as the logic of the Military Conversations, namely for a British Expeditionary Force to be sent if France was attacked. This was also the prevailing 'Foreign Office view' from 1905 and 1914. Yet Grey underestimated throughout the extent to which giving the go-ahead to plan for an expeditionary force for France in 1906 took hold of departments like the War Office and created an atmosphere where obligations were undertaken, not just appeared to have been created, and where not to follow that course was a path of dishonour.

Was a British Expeditionary Force vital to avoid letting Germany beat France? Military historians differ. The German General Staff accepted that their Schlieffen proposal might lead to war with Britain, yet made the calculation that a small British Expeditionary Force would not alter the military battle in any fundamental way.[66] The suggestions by Algernon Cecil of what his relative Lord Salisbury might have done have more than a whiff of an age that had passed by 1914. He writes:

> A private letter to Berlin might have indicated at what point Austrian polemics must encounter British opposition; a private letter to St Petersburg have conveyed how long mobilisation must be restrained before the claims of Russian prestige could count upon British support; and a circular terminating in a Congress, with the British Foreign Secretary this time as broker, have sufficed to reconcile the claims of peace and honour for another quarter of a century.[67]

Yet this demanded a different, more engaged Prime Minister than Asquith. Heads of government communicating earlier would have

---

66 A J P Taylor, *The Struggle for Mastery in Europe, 1848–1918* (Oxford University Press, Oxford: 1954), p 525.
67 Algernon Cecil, cited in Andrew Roberts, *Salisbury: Victorian Titan* (Weidenfeld & Nicolson, London: 1999), p 845.

been a lot better than Asquith only acting on 30 July through the King to the Tsar.

* * *

From 1912 the British Cabinet was involved in matters of peace and war; there was a democratic debate. Grey as Foreign Secretary was made more accountable and two formidable, up-and-coming politicians, Lloyd George and Churchill, were engaged much more in foreign and defence policy. Yet on 24 July 1914, after many years of talk of war, it still came as a deep surprise to most members of the British Cabinet to hear that war was imminent. They had been discussing Ulster when Grey intervened to read a document that had just been brought into the Cabinet room. It was the brutal terms of the Austrian ultimatum to Serbia delivered the previous day. As ill-judged a document as it is possible to conceive, it unleashed a series of reactions and interactions that led by 4 August to Britain declaring war against Germany.

In *Diplomacy* Kissinger sums up the dire situation facing Europe: 'Prior to World War One, each member of the two main coalitions was in a position not only to start a war but to blackmail its allies into supporting it.'[68] Grey was urged in the Cabinet discussion to explore the possibility of a mediating group of states – England, Germany France and Italy – coming between Russia and Austria-Hungary.[69] The problem for Grey was that the Russian Foreign Minister Sazonov had sent him a message demanding solidarity as part of the Triple Entente; the French were supporting Russia and Poincaré the French President had just been in St Petersburg. On 26 July Grey authorised an ambassadorial conference in London. Lloyd George told Scott, the editor of the *Guardian*, that he knew of no Minister who would be in favour of our taking part in any war in the first instance.

---

68 Henry Kissinger, *Diplomacy* (Simon & Schuster, London: 1994) p 198.
69 Robbins, *Sir Edward Grey*, pp 289–1.

Asquith's initial view was contradictory that night, calling the situation 'the gravest event for many years past', but was more than somewhat detached from reality in also writing, 'happily there seems no reason why we should be anything other than a spectator'. Two countries who were locked into an arrangement where they could be blackmailed were Germany and Great Britain, who were all too late starting to look at loosening their respective ties. That Asquith could still believe that spectator status was feasible demonstrates the air of unreality that had hung around Downing Street for two years or more. But when writing to Venetia Stanley after the Cabinet he was more perceptive. 'This means almost inevitably that Russia will come on the scene in defence of Servia [Serbia] in defiance of Austria; if so, it is difficult both for Germany and France to refrain from lending a hand to one side or the other. So that we are in measurable, or imaginable, distance of a real Armageddon.'[70] Grey had only been 'authorised to inform the French and German Ambassadors that, at this stage, we were unable to pledge ourselves in advance either under all conditions to stand aside or in any conditions to join'.[71] There was no proposal from Grey to send a tough message to the Kaiser, who told a friend on 27 July, 'We are not at war yet and if I can I shall prevent it.'[72]

Grey, Haldane and Churchill were for supporting France militarily. John Morley, Lord President of the Council, Sir John Simon, Attorney General, John Burns, President of the Board of Trade, and some others, called for neutrality. The United States of America was committed to neutrality. No one, neither Lloyd George nor anyone else, and least of all Grey, put forward a brokering for peace strategy. There was a growing acceptance that the polarised choice was between sending a British Expeditionary Force or neutrality.

---

70 Michael and Eleanor Brock (eds.) *H H Asquith: Letters to Venetia Stanley* (Oxford University Press, Oxford: 1982) pp 122–3.
71 Roy Jenkins, *Asquith* (Collins, London: 1986), p 324.
72 Martin Gilbert, *First World War* (Weidenfeld & Nicolson, London: 1994) p 24.

Cabinet, most of whom were instinctively against war, were also desperately wanting to forge unity. Now much depended on the judgement and ambition of one man, David Lloyd George. Asquith could and did seek out a consensus but only Lloyd George had the power in that Cabinet, both because of his position as Chancellor of the Exchequer and because of the fertility of his mind and the intensity of his language, to polarise or to unite. He took a few days to make his position clear and the Cabinet needed all of that time to cohere behind a wish for unity in the face of, by then, inevitable war.

Lloyd George's motivation was analysed by his biographer, Roy Hattersley, as,

> a combination of idealism and self-interest – not an unknown partnership in politics – and his strategic judgement was changed by briefings he received in the Committee of Imperial Defence… Lloyd George was attempting to reconcile instinct with judgement, ambition with conviction and two conflicting principles. Liberals do not go lightly to war. But they also defend the integrity of small nations.[73]

His earlier biographer, John Grigg, wrote:

> Lloyd George was always a Concert of Europe man: he wanted the nations of the continent to live in a state of peace and harmony. But he was also a realist who could see that the maintenance of peace might depend on an approximate balance between potentially warring powers and who recognised vital national interests had to be defended.[74]

---

73 Roy Hattersley, *David Lloyd George: The Great Outsider* (Little, Brown, London: 2010), pp 354, 356.
74 John Grigg, *Lloyd George: War Leader 1916–1918* (Allen Lane, London: 2002) p 128.

Lloyd George had also grown a little closer to Grey, whatever the tough criticisms he made of him after the war was over, such as claiming he had dealt faithfully in his book with the charlatans and skunks, and 'Grey certainly belongs in my opinion in the first category.'[75] In June 1913 Grey had spoken for the government in a House of Commons debate directed against Lloyd George and the Attorney General Rufus Isaacs on the 'injudicious' share purchases in the American Marconi Company. After the success of Grey's defence, Lloyd George wrote to thank him for his support: 'The personal relations of all of us have not only stood the long strain but have gained an attachment to an extent that must be very rare if not unprecedented in the history of Cabinets.'[76]

The Cabinet meetings during this period have little formal record but a most fascinating informal account comes from Frank Owen, a journalist and biographer of Lloyd George, who put together a sequence of events from jottings and scribbled spontaneous notes passed between Cabinet Ministers.[77]

In democratic politics rapidly moving events usually dictate policies, reactions are more relevant than actions, and Cabinet solidarity can become a force for cohesion even when there are substantive differences. The records show how the Cabinet mood changed. A sense of realism slowly emerged. The differences of opinion about neutrality, naval strategy and a continental army were still present, but they were no longer seen as having as much relevance. The crisis was dominating every decision. How to respond was the issue as the facts changed hour by hour. Asquith allowed the debate to run and for views to emerge; it was as important a democratic debate as that which took place under Churchill in May 1940. On both occasions the Cabinet system was vindicated.

---

75 Robbins, *Sir Edward Grey*, p 370.
76 Robbins, *Sir Edward Grey*, pp 278–9.
77 Frank Owen, *Tempestuous Journey: Lloyd George, his Life and Times* (Hutchinson, London: 1954) pp 262–71.

The Cabinet was in effect sitting in almost continuous session over these days, sometimes in the Cabinet room, sometimes in smaller meetings in or near 10 Downing Street, from 28 July to 4 August. Most around the table knew that it was too late to go back to a policy of neutrality. The die had been largely cast for better or for worse on that issue in November 1911 when this Cabinet did not stop the Military Conversations. The overriding concern was now Cabinet cohesion and leadership, to give Britain's fighting forces the support they deserved and were going to need in great measure. Initially there was little popular jingoism outside on the streets of London. Everywhere the mood was sombre.

On Tuesday 28 July 1914 Austria-Hungary declared war on Serbia. It was its last independent political act. Four years later the Habsburg Empire had collapsed having existed for nearly seven centuries. The same day the Kaiser wrote in the margin of the Serbian reply to the ultimatum an hour before their noon declaration of war, 'A great moral victory for Vienna but with it every reason for war is removed and Giesl ought to remain quietly in Belgrade. On the strength of this I should never have ordered mobilisation.' [78] Baron Wladimir Giesl was the Austrian envoy to Belgrade. Asquith met Churchill and agreed the First Fleet in the English Channel should sail to its war station at Scapa Flow. Asquith went to see Grey and Haldane at Haldane's house and agreed with Grey there should be uncertainty about Britain's intentions.

On Wednesday 29 July the Kaiser promised Britain that he would not annex any French territory (in Europe) provided Britain remained neutral. He believed his brother, Prince Henry, who reported that when he had called on King George V after attending Cowes Regatta a few days earlier, the King had told him, 'We shall try all we can to keep out of this and shall remain neutral.'[79]

On Thursday 30 July that 'infamous offer' by the Kaiser was

---

78 Gilbert, *First World War*, p 24.
79 Gilbert, *First World War*, p 25.

unambiguously rejected by Edward Grey with Asquith's approval. The Tsar tried to countermand the partial mobilisation he had just ordered in the Russian Empire after a telegram from the Kaiser, who also contacted Britain for help with the Tsar, and Asquith with Tyrrell in attendance drafted a letter for the King to send to the Tsar.[80] It was all too late, for 'the wheels were already in motion all over the Empire'.[81]

On Friday 31 July Germany demanded from France, as a pledge of its neutrality, the keys for the fortress at Verdun and other forts. The French Prime Minister indicated that France would take care of its own business. On that Friday only two Ministers, Grey and Churchill, favoured Britain entering the war, with Asquith appearing to give support.

In Berlin on the question of Belgian neutrality, the British Ambassador was given to understand that the Germans rather doubted whether they could answer at all, as any reply they might give could not fail, in the event of war, to have the undesirable effect of disclosing to a certain extent part of their plan of campaign. Belgium, in their view, had already committed certain acts which could only qualify as hostile; for example, the Belgian government, they claimed, had already embargoed a consignment of grain destined for Germany.

On Saturday 1 August at 11 am Asquith received a wire from the official opposition leaders, Bonar Law and Lansdowne, offering unconditional support for any measures to resist German aggression. At noon the German ultimatum to Russia ran out. Germany declared war on Russia. The Governor of the Bank of England told Lloyd George the City of London was against intervening in the war. The Bank Rate went up to 8 per cent. The Stock Market was closed beyond the August Bank Holiday. The capitalists, as Lloyd

---

80 George H Cassar, *Asquith as War Leader* (Hambledon Press, London: 1994) p 19.
81 Cassar, *Asquith as War Leader*, p 27.

George subsequently often reiterated, were not in favour of the war. The financial strains and stresses were great but Lloyd George was inventive and optimistic, and he never used the grave financial pressure building up to challenge or manipulate the Prime Minister. Very different from Harold Macmillan as Chancellor, who under Anthony Eden as Prime Minister in 1956, when faced by direct financial pressure from President Eisenhower on sterling, advised withdrawing British troops only just after they had been sent in to take the Canal. Lloyd George focused on steadying the ship of state, on the economy. To describe him as vacillating is wrong; he was adjusting as any sensible Cabinet Minister was doing during this time to the horrendous military situation unfolding hour by hour, day by day.

> In Cabinet on the 1 August:
> Churchill to Lloyd George, 'I am most profoundly anxious that our long co-operation may not be severed. Remember your part at Agadir.'
> Lloyd George to Churchill: 'If patience prevails and you do not press it too hard tonight, we might come together.'

Churchill, by reminding Lloyd George of his Mansion House speech on Agadir in 1911, was also steadying the ship, but in the direction of war, not unreasonably given his responsibility as First Lord of the Admiralty.

> Lloyd George to Charles Masterman, 'What is your general view of what we ought to do?'
> Masterman to Lloyd George, 'If I had to decide now I would guarantee Belgium and the Fleet policy. If Germany accepts that, no war. But I am with McKenna and Runciman in fighting for *time*, sooner than break up the Cabinet. Twelve hours might find us united. Our collapse would be unthinkable – what is to happen to the Empire if we break to pieces! Do fight for unity.'

Edward Grey met the French Ambassador, Cambon, who was left white and speechless, feeling that he was not ready to honour the 1912 agreement where French ships were to stay in the Mediterranean. Harold Nicolson found Grey biting his lower lip and, when asked if he had refused to support France, made no answer beyond a gesture of despair.

* * *

Newspapers were divided as families were divided. The *Westminster Gazette*, a Liberal newspaper, deprecated 'the attempt to kindle a War fever'. The *Daily News*, the most widely read Liberal newspaper, which had campaigned to stop the Boer War, urged 'announce here and now neutrality'. The *Manchester Guardian* pleaded for neutrality. Other more Conservative supporting newspapers began to beat the drums for war.

Orders were given for the immediate mobilisation of the expeditionary force and the Territorial Army.

On Saturday night the Cabinet instructed Grey to tell the French Ambassador Britain would not stand by and see the German Fleet attack the French Channel ports.

Asquith's account was recorded in his book *Memories and Reflections* from his diary, since the normal messages to the King dropped away during the crisis. It reads:

> Lloyd George, all for peace, is more sensible and statesmanlike for keeping the position open. Grey declares that if an out and out and uncompromising policy of non-intervention at all costs is adopted he will go. Winston very bellicose and demanding immediate mobilisation … Of course, if Grey went, I should go, and the whole thing would break up.

On Sunday 2 August Lloyd George was telling Walter Runciman, who as President of the Board of Education had made an excellent contribution to the government and was now President of the

Board of Trade, right up to tea-time that he was doubtful what to do. He would not oppose Britain going to war but might then go to his home at Criccieth. Asquith drafted a reply between Cabinet meetings to the Opposition leaders, which was vague and somewhat confusing. At 6.30 pm, when the second Cabinet started, it was known that German troops had crossed into Luxembourg. A substantial violation of Belgian territory was now judged by a majority of the Cabinet as unacceptable, whatever the reaction of the Belgian government. After years of prevarication as to what would constitute a *casus belli* the Cabinet decided this was it. There was too great an obligation, it was judged, to protect the Channel coast of France from naval attack by Germany.

On Monday 3 August it was learnt that Belgium was refusing to allow the passage of German troops into France. Asquith saw Bonar Law and Lansdowne at 10.30 am in Downing Street. They wanted immediate action – he demurred. Asquith announced to Cabinet that he had received the resignation of Burns, Morley and Simon, whereupon Beauchamp at the Cabinet table said his name should be included too. The Prime Minister said, 'that is four out of our number and others have found it difficult to remain.' Lloyd George appealed for those who had resigned to delay their departure.

In Cabinet 3 August:

Lloyd George to Churchill, 'What is your policy?'

Churchill to Lloyd George, 'At the present moment I would act in such a way as to impress Germany with our intention to preserve the neutrality of Belgium. So much is still unknown as to the definite purpose of Germany that I would not go beyond this. Moreover, public opinion might veer round at any moment if Belgium is invaded and we must be ready to meet this opinion.'

Lloyd George to Churchill, 'Would you commit yourself in public *now* to war if Belgium is invaded whether Belgium asks for our protection or not?'

Churchill to Lloyd George, 'No.'

Belgium rejected the German ultimatum. Germany declared war on France.

Grey spoke in the House of Commons and an extremely emotional moment came when he read out the telegram from the King of Belgium making a 'supreme appeal to the diplomatic intervention of Your Majesty's Government to safeguard the integrity of Belgium'. Then Grey revealed the real feelings that had driven his hidden perspective since January 1906 with the Military Conversations and the Triple Entente. Speaking quietly, he said, 'How far that friendship entails obligations, it has been a friendship between the nations and ratified by the nations, how far that entails an obligation let every man look into his own heart and his own feelings, and construe the extent of the obligation for himself.'

Whereas Asquith, in a note to himself of six points, had as the first: 'We have no obligation of any kind either to France or Russia to give them military or naval help', Grey was correct to ask the House whether there was an obligation. There is a difference between a commitment and an obligation, as Grey was implying in his speech; there is a moral element in obligation that is not necessarily there in commitment. After the military conversations there was an obligation to France. Grey was right, Asquith was wrong.

The speech was considered by most to be a triumph, but there were others whose feeling was more apposite and who regarded it as the culminating point of a personal tragedy for the Foreign Secretary. Sir Maurice Hankey, looking back years later and having watched Grey from the vantage point of the Committee for Imperial Defence as he became Foreign Secretary, and who later became in 1916 the first Secretary to the War Cabinet, wrote in 1933: 'Much as I like the man, I have never had a high opinion of him as a statesman.'[82]

* * *

---

82 Hankey to Lloyd George, 4.4.33. G/212.

The Cabinet meeting at 6 pm was unlike any other since 24 July. There were no dissenting arguments exchanged, the legal basis for defending Belgium was clear and it was decided the ultimatum to Germany would be delivered the next day.

Late on 3 August the Prime Minister sent a handwritten note to the King:

> Mr Asquith with his humble duty to Your Majesty has the honour to report that the Cabinet met today.
>
> The time was exclusively occupied with a consideration of the diplomatic situation and of the statement to be made in the afternoon in the House of Commons by Sir E. Grey. That statement presents, exactly and exhaustively, the case put forward by the Government as the result of the full and anxious Cabinet consultations of the last three days.
>
> At a later meeting of the Cabinet Sir E. Grey communicated to his colleagues the telegram from Brussels to the Belgian Minister here which summarises the German ultimatum.
>
> Mr Asquith regrets to say that four of his colleagues – Lord Morley, Sir S. Simon, Lord Beauchamp & Mr Burns – have tendered their resignation. He hopes that some of them may be inclined to reconsider their position.
>
> 3 August 1914

On Tuesday 4 August the Germans started marching into Belgium. The German Foreign Minister, Jagow, sent a telegram via the German Ambassador in London that Germany had no intention of annexing Belgian territory. 'The sincerity of this declaration is borne out by the fact that we solemnly pledged our word to Holland strictly to respect their territory.' If serious, it showed a strange lack of understanding about neutrality, that just passing through with military forces was not a major violation. Had Tyrrell met him maybe such misconceptions could have been fully clarified. But way back, the Prussian government had, by insisting in 1839 that the Treaty guarantee in relation to Belgium should be a unilateral obligation as distinct from collective for Luxembourg, given an indication of their wish to keep their options open to attack France through Belgium. Asquith announced to the Cabinet that the British ultimatum had been dispatched and would expire at 11 pm in Berlin. Crowds had been filling Whitehall, and even before they knew about the German invasion there were banners up for 'poor little Belgium'. The public mood in the streets around Parliament seemed now for war. The German Chancellor Bethmann-Hollweg, speaking in the Reichstag, said rather unwisely: 'Our invasion of Belgium is contrary to international law.' Nevertheless, he was supported by Opposition Social Democrats as well as by fellow Conservatives. Bethmann-Hollweg also said, 'My blood boiled at this hypocritical harping on Belgium which was not the thing that drove England into war', and went on to say 'all for just a word – neutrality – just for a scrap of paper.'[83] But 'Bethmann did not will the war that broke out in August 1914.'[84]

Around 9 pm Asquith and a few colleagues were in the Cabinet room and Lloyd George joined them. It was clear to everyone that when Big Ben struck the appointed hour of 11 pm London time, Germany would have ignored Britain's demand that Belgium's neutrality should be respected. The authority for the declaration of war was Asquith's, interpreting the wishes of the Cabinet. Both Simon and Beauchamp had withdrawn their resignations. Asquith treated both Morley and Burns who went with respect, seeing them socially and considering their resignations a matter of conscience.

On 5 August the Committee of Imperial Defence, convened as a War Council, met at four o'clock. Seated around the table was the new Secretary of State for War, appointed by Asquith only hours before the meeting, Field Marshall Lord Kitchener. He was no more

---

83 Max Hastings, *Catastrophe*, p 95.
84 TG Otte, *July Crisis: The World's Descent into War, Summer 1914* (Cambridge University Press, Cambridge: 2014), p 517.

happy to be there than his colleagues were to have him. In the frank words of Barbara Tuchman, an American historian,

> The Government was nervous at having in their midst the first active soldier to enter the Cabinet since General Monck served under Charles II. The Generals were worried that he would use his position or be used by the government to interfere with the sending of an Expeditionary Force to France. No one's apprehensions were disappointed. Kitchener promptly expressed his profound contempt for the strategy, policy and role assigned to the British Army by the Anglo-French plan.[85]

At the War Council were Asquith, Grey, Churchill and Haldane along with eleven general officers including Sir John French, Commander-in-Chief designate of the Expeditionary Force, and 'representing no one quite knew what, was Lord Kitchener who regarded the purpose of the Expeditionary Force with deep misgivings and its Commander-in-Chief without admiration.' He told them that they had to be prepared to put armies of millions in the field and maintain them for several years, and that to fight and win Britain must have an army of seventy divisions which would take three years to reach full strength. The key to such a development was the officers, and particularly the non-commissioned officers, precious and indispensable as the nucleus for training the larger force. 'To throw this away in immediate battle under what he expected to be unfavourable circumstances, and where, from the long view, its presence could not be decisive, he regarded as criminal folly.' General Sir Douglas Haig at this same meeting advocated waiting for two or three months to see how things went and enable the 'immense sources of the Empire' to be developed. [86]

---

85 Barbara W Tuchman, *The Guns of August* (Robinson, London: 2000), pp 192–5.
86 Michael Howard, *The Continental Commitment: The Dilemma of British Defence Policy in the Era of the Two World Wars* (Temple Smith, London: 1972), p 54.

The British Expeditionary Force nevertheless was sent by the CID to cross the English Channel, a decision made by politicians. Grey assumed Kitchener reached his conclusion 'by some flash of instinct rather than by reasoning.' Churchill ruled out asking the Navy to transfer troops anywhere other than the shortest route across the Channel. Haldane supported him. All six divisions should embark as soon as possible. Within 24 hours the Council changed its opinion and sent only four divisions because of an ill-founded invasion scare. On 9 August embarkation began, while Kitchener was still arguing for going not to Maubeuge but further back to Amiens, and took the issue with Sir John French to Asquith, who found for the combined General Staffs against Kitchener.

Four years of carnage resulted. Britain was in no position militarily or politically alone to bring about a ceasefire or a negotiated settlement, for that was one of the consequences of taking up a continental military commitment. Peace was never seriously considered for over four years. In its own rather hesitant way the British Cabinet had shown the virtues of following the democratic process, listening to each other, feeling their way. It was not a dramatic or militaristic decision. There was a certain honour in its final determination. But it represented eight years of failed diplomacy.

How was it that those in power in Europe thought the war would be over by Christmas? How was it that the destructive power of war in the 19th and early 20th centuries had been so little understood? Even over a century later how is it that the full lessons of the run up from 1906 to the First World War have not been absorbed fully into the body politic in the United Kingdom? In particular the need for Cabinet government to be fully involved in matters of peace and war.

The hidden perspective of Edward Grey throughout had been that Great Britain would have to fight alongside France on the continent of Europe against Germany. It had proved to be the outcome. But how much had that been a self-fulfilling prophecy? Grey had agreed to plan to do so from 1906 while claiming to keep open to the Cabinet and Parliament any eventual decision, and later he always believed that that was what he had done.

The Military Conversations, however, had a momentum of their own. They were premature in 1906 and arguably should never have been undertaken, or certainly not until after the Haldane Mission had failed in the spring of 1912.

The fact that the German Chancellor Bethmann-Hollweg remarked as he did about the Haldane Mission to the Reichstag shows how deeply he resented his failure to forge an agreement with England in 1912. As he saw it then, and now on the eve of war, he had always been willing to limit the proposed neutrality agreement to cases in which Germany 'cannot be said to be the aggressor.' Furthermore, he had conceded that any agreement reached would have had no application insofar as it might not be reconcilable with existing agreements,[87] which the high contracting parties had already made. This meant that had such an agreement been entered into in 1912 it would not have stopped the British Cabinet deciding to act as they did. Britain lost out by not having built from 1912 a working relationship with Germany. Within such a relationship Asquith and Grey could have had far more influence. Both countries would have been better placed to discourage Austria from taking up arms against Serbia. Both countries might together have persuaded Russia not to side so completely with Serbia. That the Haldane Mission in 1912 was potentially a very serious negotiation is borne out by the documentary record and also by the African territorial negotiations agenda. These should have been fully supported by Grey and the Foreign Office, not undermined. Had they been supported the 1914 war might well never have taken place. This is not so much a 'what if' of history, as a documented fact of history; a negotiation blocked by a hidden perspective held by the Foreign Secretary and the prevailing Foreign Office view.

Some may feel I have been too harsh on Edward Grey and quote,

---

87 Clark, *The Sleepwalkers*, p 319.

in his favour, what supposedly happened on the 1–2 August 1914 in London with the German Ambassador as a great peace initiative. Indeed, this was the impression left by a three part television documentary, shown just prior to the 100th anniversary, of the weeks running up to the war, depicting Grey on the telephone to the German Ambassador; something disputed by historians.

The aborted Tyrrell Mission to meet with the German Foreign Minister, Jagrow, in the months before war was described in pages 187–198. Tyrrell was once again below the surface and involved with Grey .The most authoritative analysis comes from TG Otte in *July Crisis*.[88]

We know from German records that at 11.14 am on Saturday 1 August, a telegram was sent which reached Berlin at 4.23 pm from the German Ambassador. Lichnowsky wrote that Tyrrell had asked him to call on the Foreign Secretary that afternoon and that Grey would make a proposal that might 'avert catastrophe.' Tyrrell urged that no German troops should cross into French territory. Lichnowsky claimed Grey rang him just before 11 am to ask whether if France did not interfere in a Russo-German war, would Germany not fight in the west. There are significant problems with the recorded timing for this phone call as, at this time, Grey and Haldane were at a meeting with Asquith in No 10. Otte, usually favourable to Grey, and after studying the detail, argues that Lichnowsky, anxious for peace and so out of favour in Berlin, felt it necessary to carry conviction in these desperate circumstances and so claimed that Grey was involved, not just Tyrrell.

That afternoon, the Kaiser accepted no movement of troops into France until 7 pm on 3 August; his ambassador was told of this potentially important decision, although Germany was planning to attack first through Belgium. The Kaiser also wrote to the British King.

---

88 TG Otte, *July Crisis: The World's Descent into War, Summer 1914* (Cambridge University Press, Cambridge: 2014), pp 417–486.

A second telegram was sent at 7 pm in Berlin, arriving soon after the Kaiser's decision. Lichnowsky now wrote that Tyrrell had, at his most recent meeting, indicated that British neutrality might be possible. The word neutrality was key for the Germans; the Kaiser ordered champagne. Moltke, who had argued all day against any change to his plan, left 'broken and shed tears.' The exultant mood in Berlin was shattered however, when, just after 10 pm, a third telegram arrived from Lichnowsky detailing a 3pm meeting with Grey saying only that Germany's earlier equivocal statement on Belgian neutrality was 'a matter of very great regret.' He declined to give a pledge to remain neutral if Germany gave a pledge to respect Belgian neutrality. To cap that unsatisfactory statement, the King replied to the Kaiser later that night: 'there must be some misunderstanding,' and again at the end: 'Sir Edward will arrange to see Prince Lichnowsky early tomorrow morning to ascertain whether there has been a misunderstanding.'

Otte concludes, and I agree with him, that it was out of character for Grey to have authorised Tyrrell to refer to British neutrality, let alone to have referred to it himself. He had objected to Haldane using the term in 1912 and, though ambiguity was Tyrrell's stock in trade, it was not part of Grey's 'sober and straightforward pragmatism.' Just over three weeks later, Grey suggested it all stemmed from the two ambassadors and, since Tyrrell was still a serving diplomat, that was almost certainly a true description.

My perspective is that Grey lacked the imagination and the creativity to find peace. A concession on using the word neutrality in 1912 was required, but by 1 August 1914 it was too late and would only have sown confusion; the whole episode had to be dismissed as a misunderstanding. Just as every Foreign Minister had to visit Grey, so he could not put himself in their shoes and visualise the situation from their country's viewpoint. A rigid mind frame is a liability in a Foreign Secretary.

Democratic politics is a demanding master and on taking one's country to war there is no issue more corrosive to reputation than for politicians to be found to have shortcircuited democratic accountability. There is because of the necessary secrecy attached to waging war an alarming tendency to bypass the overriding responsibility for key politicians to tell the facts to Cabinet colleagues about military issues; also to make excuses for not keeping Parliament properly informed. But there is a price for doing this, and Britain paid that price from 1914–18 and in its aftermath – the Treaty of Versailles ushered in a far more aggressive and nationalistic Germany under Hitler which then started the Second World War. The Military Conversations from 1906–14 for war were never matched by comparable political conversations for peace. When Pope Benedict XV made his appeal on 7 December 1914 that 'the guns may fall silent at least upon the night the angels sang' not one government, nor a single statesman responded. The only government that had the political and military strength to force Germany and France to negotiate, Britain, was stuck in the mud of the continent. Britain should have been on the high seas, ready to block the shipping of any government who would not respond to its call for a Christmas ceasefire. It was left to the soldiers in the front line from Britain and Germany to come out from their trenches into no-man's-land, to play football, even to sing carols. Sadly there were no statesmen in England to hear and to be able to respond to this spontaneous longing for peace.

> When Statesmen gravely say 'We must be realistic',
> The chances are they're weak and, therefore, pacifistic,
> But when they speak of Principles, look out: perhaps
> Their generals are already poring over maps.[89]

In the embers of one war lie the flames of another. Remember that in 1906 Churchill was invited to attend German army manoeuvres

---

89 W H Auden, 'When Statesmen Gravely Say', in *The Double Man and Collected Shorter Poems* (Random House, London 1941).

at Wurzburg by the Kaiser and wrote to his wife with memories of the Boer War fresh in his mind: 'Much as war attracts me and fascinates my mind with its tremendous situations, I feel more deeply every year – & can measure the feeling here in the midst of arms – what vile & wicked folly & barbarism it all is.'

Remember the links between the First and Second World Wars and the mere 21 years that lay between them, and if that needs reinforcing, visit the woodlands near Rethondes in France and see the replica of the rail carriage in which the Germans signed the Armistice in November 1918 and where Hitler was determined to have the French surrender signed in June 1940.

Remember what Rudyard Kipling wrote of his son's death at the Battle of Loos in September 1915:

That flesh we had nursed from the first in all cleanness was given...
To be blanched or gay-painted by fumes – to be cindered by fires –
To be senselessly tossed and retossed in stale mutilation
From crater to crater. For that we shall take expiation.
But who shall return us our children?[90]

Remember that only five months earlier General Haig had told the British War Council: 'The machine gun is a much over-rated weapon and two per battalion is more than sufficient.' As Martin Gilbert wrote, 'he was once again proved terribly wrong.'[91]

Remember that for nearly six years – January 1906–November 1911 – the British Cabinet was not told about the Military Conversations, and from 1906 until April 1911 Asquith did not know, for three years of which he was Prime Minister.

Remember that for the next two and a half years, until August 1914, a sense of obligation built up that the joint planning with the

90 Rudyard Kipling, 'The Children', in *The Collected Poems of Rudyard Kipling* (Wordsworth Editions, Ware: 1994) p 544.
91 Gilbert, *First World War*, pp xviii, 199, 200.

French navy as well as the French army would lead to the deployment of a British Expeditionary Force to France, with little debate in Parliament or in public about its implications.

Remember that 100 years later when the Iraq Inquiry is published, many of these same issues about how to go to war in a democracy in relation to Cabinet and Parliament will need to be resolved anew, and senior politicians held to account.

Appendix

Memorandum by Mr. Eyre Crowe

*Memorandum on the Present State of British
Relations with France and Germany*

F.O. 371/257

(8882*) Secret. Foreign Office, January 1, 1907.

*The Anglo-French Agreement of the 8th April, 1904, was the
outcome of the honest and ardent desire, freely expressed among
all classes and parties of the two countries, that an earnest effort
should be made to compose, as far as possible, the many difference
[sic] which had been a source of perpetual friction between them. In
England the wish for improved relations with France was primarily
but a fresh manifestation of the general tendency of British Governments to take advantage of every opportunity to approach more
closely to the ideal condition of living in honourable peace with all
other States.*

*There were two difficulties: It was necessary, in the first instance,
that the French Government should realise the benefit which France
would derive from a policy of give and take, involving perhaps, from
her point of view some immediate sacrifice but resulting in the ban-
ishment of all occasions for quarrels with a powerful neighbour. It
was secondly indispensable, if French statesmen were to carry with
them the public opinion of their own country, without which they
would be powerless to act[,] that the suspiciousness of English designs
and intentions, with which years of hostile feelings and active political*

rivalry had poisoned the French mind, should give place to confidence in the straightforwardness and loyalty of British Governments not only in meeting present engagements, but also in dealing with any future points of difference, in a conciliatory and neighbourly spirit. It was natural to believe that the growth of such confidence could not be quickly forced, but that it might slowly emerge by a process of gradual evolution. That it declared itself with unexpected rapidity and unmistakable emphasis was without doubt due, in the first place, to the initiative and tactful perseverance of the King, warmly recognised and applauded on both sides of the Channel. The French nation having come to look upon the King as personally attached to their country, saw in His Majesty's words and actions a guarantee that the adjustment of political differences might well prepare the way for bringing about a genuine and lasting friendship, to be built up on community of interests and aspirations.

The conviction that the removal of causes of friction, apart from having an independent value of its own, as making directly for peace, would also confer on the Governments of both countries greater freedom in regulating their general foreign relations, can hardly be supposed to have been absent from the mind of the British and French negotiators. Whenever the Government of a country is confronted with external difficulties by the opposition of another State on a question of national rights or claims, the probable attitude of third Powers in regard to the point in dispute must always be a matter of anxious concern. The likelihood of other Powers actively taking sides in a quarrel which does not touch them directly may reasonably be expected, and, indeed, is shown by experience, very much to depend, quite apart from the merits of the dispute, on the general trend of relations existing between the several parties. It is impossible to over-estimate the importance in such a connection of the existence of a firmly established and broadly based system of friendly intercourse with those Powers whose position would enable them to throw a heavy weight into the balance of strength on the other side. If a country could be imagined whose foreign relations were so favourably disposed that, in the defence of its legitimate interests, it could always count upon the sympathy of its most powerful neighbours, such a country would never – or at least not so long as the national armaments were maintained at the proper standard of efficiency – need to entertain those fears and misgivings which, under the actual conditions of dominant international jealousies and rivalries, only too often compel the abandonment of a just cause as the only alternative to the more serious evil and risk of giving suspicious and unfriendly neighbours a welcome opportunity for aggression or hostile and humiliating interference. If both France and England were acutely conscious that, in the contingency of either of them being involved in a quarrel with this or that Power, an Anglo-French understanding would at least remove one serious danger inherent in such a situation, patriotic self-interest would, on this ground alone, justify and encourage any attempt to settle outstanding differences, if and so far as they were found capable of settlement without jeopardising vital interests.

It was creditable to M. Delcasse's sagacity and public spirit that he decided to grasp the hand which the British Government held out to him. The attempt has been made to represent this decision as mainly if not solely influenced by the desire to strengthen the hands of France in a struggle with Germany, since, as a result of the impending collapse of the Russian power in the Japanese war, she was incurring the danger of finding herself alone face to face with her great enemy. This criticism, even if it does not go so far as wrongly to ascribe to the Entente *an originally offensive character directed against Germany, will be seen, on a comparison of dates, to be founded in error. The war with Japan, which Russia herself did not believe to be imminent before it had actually begun, broke out in February 1904. It is true that the Anglo-French Agreements were signed two months later. But no one, certainly not the French Government, then anticipated the complete overthrow of Russia in the Far East, nor the disastrous reaction of defeat on the internal situation in the Czar's European dominions. In fact, the two chief criticisms directed against M. Delcasse's general policy in his own country were, first, that he would not believe those who foreshadowed a coming war between Russian and Japan, and, secondly, that when the war had broken out he remained almost to the last confident of Russia's ultimate success. Moreover, the negotiations which ultimately issued in the Agreements of the 8th April, 1904, were opened as far back as the early summer of 1903, when few would have ventured to prophesy that Russia was shortly to be brought to her knees by Japan. If one might go so far as to believe that the bare possibility of such a defeat may have begun to occupy the mind of M. Delcassé in the early spring of 1904, and that this reflection may have contributed to convincing him of the wisdom of persevering with the English negotiation, it would yet remain impossible to assert with truth that his primary object in entering upon that negotiation was to seek in a fresh quarter the general political support of which the temporary eclipse of Russia was threatening to deprive his country. But even if the weakening of the Franco-Russian alliance had been the principal and avowed reason why France sought an understanding with England, this would not justify the charge that the conclusion of such understanding constituted a provocation and deliberate menace to Germany. No one has ever seriously ascribed to the Franco-Russian alliance the character of a combination conceived in a spirit of bellicose aggression. That the association of so peace-loving a nation as England with France and Russia, or still less that the substitution of England for Russia in the association with France, would have the effect of turning an admittedly defensive organisation into an offensive alliance aimed directly at Germany cannot have been the honest belief of any competent student of contemporary history. Yet this accusation was actually made against M. Delcassé and, incidentally, against Lord Lansdowne in 1905. That, however, was at the time when the position of France appeared sufficiently weakened to expect that she could be insulted with impunity, when the battle of Mukden had made manifest the final defeat of France's ally, when internal disorders began to undermine Russia's whole position as a Power that must be reckoned with, and when the*

Anglo-French Entente was not credited with having as yet taken deep root in the popular imaginations of the two peoples so long politically estranged. No sound of alarm was heard, no such vindictive criticism of M. Delcasse's policy was even whispered, in 1904, at the moment when the Agreement was published, immediately after its signature. Then, although the world was somewhat taken by surprise, the Agreement was received by all foreign Governments without apparent misgiving, and even with signs of relief and satisfaction. At Berlin the Imperial Chancellor, in the course of an important debate in the Reichstag, formally declared that Germany could have no objection to the policy embodied in the Entente, and that, in regard more particularly to the stipulations respecting Morocco, she had no reason to fear that the interests would be ignored.

The history of the events that ensued, culminating in the Algeciras Conference, revealed to all the world how little Prince Bülow's declaration corresponded to the real feelings animating the German Government. Those events do not require to be more than briefly recalled. They are fresh in the public memory.

The maintenance of a state of tension and antagonism between third Powers had avowedly been one of the principal elements in Bismarck's political combinations by which he first secured and then endeavoured to preserve the predominant position of Germany on the continent. It is now no longer denied that he urged England to occupy Egypt and to continue in occupation, because he rightly foresaw that this would perpetuate the antagonism between England and France. Similarly, he consistently impressed upon Russia that it would be to her interest to divert her expansionist ambitions from the Balkan countries to Central Asia, where he hoped both Russia and England would, owing to the inevitable conflict of interests, keep one another fully occupied. The Penjdeh incident, which nearly brought about a war, was the outcome of his direct suggestion that the moment was favourable for Russia to act. Prince Bismarck had also succeeded by all sorts of devices – including the famous reinsurance Treaty with Russia – in keeping France and Russia apart so long as he remained in office. The conclusion of the Franco-Russian alliance sometime after Bismarck's fall filled Germany with concern and anxiety, and she never ceased in her efforts at least to neutralise it by establishing the closest possible relations with Russia for herself. From this point of view the weakening of Russia's general position presented simultaneously two advantages. It promised to free Germany for some time to come from any danger of aggression on her eastern frontier, and it deprived France of the powerful support which alone had hitherto enabled her to stand up to Germany in the political arena on terms of equality. It is only natural that the feeling of satisfaction derived from the relative accession of strength due to these two causes should have been somewhat rudely checked by the unexpected intelligence that France had come to an understanding with England.

It was, in fact, soon made apparent that, far from welcoming, as Prince Bülow pretended, an Anglo-French rapprochement, the Emperor's Government had been thoroughly alarmed at the mere disappearance of all causes of friction between the two Western Powers and was determined to resort to any measures likely to bring about the dissolution of a fresh political combination, which it was felt might ultimately prove another stumbling-block in the way of German supremacy, as the Franco-Russian alliance had previously been regarded. Nor is it possible to be blind to the fact that Germany is bound to be as strongly opposed to a possible Anglo-Russian understanding; and, indeed, there is already conclusive evidence of German activity to prevent any such contingency from happening in the near future.

The German view on this subject cannot be better stated than was done by Herr von Tschirschky, now Foreign Secretary at Berlin, then Prussian Minister at Hamburg, in speaking on New Year's Day 1906 to His Majesty's Consul-General at that place. He said:–

Germany's policy always had been, and would be, to try to frustrate any coalition between two States which might result in damaging Germany's interests and prestige; and Germany would, if she thought that such a coalition was being formed, even if its actual results had not yet been earned into practical effect, not hesitate to take such steps as she thought proper to break up the coalition.

In pursuance of this policy, which, whatever its merits or demerits, is certainly quite intelligible, Germany waited for the opportune moment for taking action, with the view of breaking up, if possible, the Anglo-French entente. When Russia was staggering under the crushing blows inflicted by Japan, and threatened by internal revolution, the German campaign was opened. The object of nipping in the bud the young friendship between France and England was to be attained by using as a stalking-horse those very interests in Morocco which the Imperial Chancellor had, barely a year before, publicly declared to be in no way imperilled.

The ground was not unskilfully chosen. By a direct threat of war, for which France was known to be unprepared, she was to be compelled to capitulate unconditionally. England had, on being questioned officially, admitted that beyond the terms of the Agreement which bound her to give France her diplomatic support in Morocco she was not pledged to further co-operation. Her reluctance for extreme measures, even under severe provocation, had only recently been tested on the occasion of the Dogger Bank incident. It was considered practically certain that she would shrink from lending armed assistance to France, but if she did, care had been taken to inflame French opinion by representing through the channels of a venal press that England was in her own selfish interest trying to push France into a war with Germany, so revealing the secret intentions which had inspired her in seeking the entente.

We now know that this was the policy which Herr von Holstein with the support of Prince Bülow succeeded in imposing on the German Emperor. It promised at the outset to succeed. M. Delcassé fell; France, thoroughly frightened, showed herself anxious to make concessions to Germany, and ready to believe that England's friendship, instead of being helpful, was proving disastrous. It is difficult to say what would have happened if at this critical moment Germany, under the skilful guidance of a Bismarck, had shown herself content with her decided triumph, and willing in every way to smooth the path for France by offering a friendly settlement of the Moroccan question in a sense that would have avoided wounding her national honour. Germany would, perhaps, have foregone some of the nominal advantages which she afterwards wrung from a reluctant and hostile France at the Algeciras Conference. This would not have hurt Germany, whose real interests, as Bismarck had long ago asserted, would be well served by France getting militarily and financially entangled in Morocco, just as England had got entangled in Egypt. On the other hand, a policy of graceful concessions on Germany's part, and the restriction of her demands to nothing more than the recognition of her existing rights in Morocco and the treatment of a friend, would have deepened the conviction which at this stage was forcing itself on the mind of the French Government, that the full enjoyment of benefits which the agreement concluded with England had been incapable of securing effectually, could be reaped from an amicable understanding with Germany.

At this point Herr von Holstein's policy overreached itself. The minatory attitude of the German Government continued. French overtures were left unanswered. A European Conference to be convoked under conditions peculiarly humiliating to France was insisted upon. Some manoeuvres of petty crookedness were executed at Fez by Count Tattenbach, in matters of concessions and loans, which were thought to have been already settled in a contrary sense by special agreements reluctantly assented to in Paris. It became clear to the successors of M. Delcassé that he had been sacrificed in vain. His original policy reasserted itself as the only one compatible with national dignity and ultimate independence. With it revived the confidence that safety lay in drawing closer to England. A bold demand was frankly made for her armed alliance in case of a German attack. This was perhaps the most critical moment for the entente.

Would France listen to and appreciate the arguments which the British Government were bound to advance against the conclusion of a definite alliance at this moment? If she saw reason, would the perhaps unavoidable sense of immediate disappointment tend, nevertheless, to react unfavourably on the only just rekindled trust in the loyalty of England? If so, Germany's object would have come near realisation. France would, however sorrowfully, have become convinced of the necessity of accepting unconditionally the terms for which Germany then held out, and which involved practically the recognition that French foreign policy must be shaped in accordance with orders from Berlin. The bitterness of such political abdication would naturally have engendered unmeasured hatred of the pretended friend who refused the helping hand in the hour of need.

The attitude adopted under these difficult conditions by His Majesty's Government has been justified by results. The difficulties in the way of there and then converting the entente into an alliance were frankly and firmly explained. At the same time Germany was explicitly warned, and the principal other Powers informed, that public opinion in England could not be expected to remain indifferent, and would almost certainly demand the active intervention of any British Government, should a quarrel be fastened upon France on account of her pursuing a policy in which England was under an honourable obligation to support her.

There can be no doubt that an element of bluff had entered into the original calculations of both Germany and France. M. Delcassé, who must be credited with sufficient foresight to have realised early in 1905, if not before, that his policy exposed his country to the resentment of its Teutonic neighbour, is proved, by his neglect to take military precautions, to have in his own mind discounted any German threats as unreal and empty of consequence. He had not counted on the capabilities for taking alarm and for working itself into a panic which reside in the nervous breast of an unprepared French public, nor on the want of loyalty characteristic of French statesmen in their attitude to each other. He paid for his mistake with his person.

Germany on her part had not really contemplated war, because she felt confident that France, knowing herself unprepared and unable to withstand an attack, would yield to threats. But she miscalculated the strength of British feeling and the character of His Majesty's Ministers. An Anglo-French coalition in arms against her was not in her forecast, and she could not face the possible danger of it. It is now known that Herr von Holstein, and, on his persuasion, Prince Bülow, practically staked their reputation on the prophecy that no British Government sufficiently bullied and frightened would stand by France, who had for centuries been England's ubiquitous opponent, and was still the ally of Russia, England's 'hereditary foe'. So lately as the time when the International Conference was sitting at Algeciras, the German delegates, on instructions emanating from Prince Bülow, confidentially pressed upon the British representative in all seriousness the folly and danger of supporting France, and painted in attractive colours a policy of co-operation with Germany for France's overthrow. Even at that hour it was believed that England could be won over. So grave a misapprehension as to what a British Government might be capable of, manifested at such a juncture, shows better than many a direct utterance the estimation in which England has been held in responsible quarters in Berlin. The error eventually proved fatal to the persistent inspirer of this policy, because its admitted failure on the present occasion apparently made it necessary to find a scapegoat. When, contrary to Herr von Holstein's advice, Germany finally made at Algeciras the concessions which alone rendered the conclusion of an international treaty possible, he was ignominiously dismissed by Prince Bülow, who had up to then consistently worked on the same lines, and must have had the principal share in recommending the unsuccessful policy to the Emperor.

When the signature of the Algeciras Act brought to a close the first chapter of the conflict respecting Morocco, the Anglo-French entente had acquired a different significance from that which it had at the moment of its inception. Then there had been but a friendly settlement of particular outstanding differences, giving hope for future harmonious relations between two neighbouring countries that had got into the habit of looking at one another askance; now there had emerged an element of common resistance to outside dictation and aggression, a unity of special interests tending to develop into active co-operation against a third Power. It is essential to bear in mind that this new feature of the entente *was the direct effect produced by Germany's effort to break it up, and that, failing the active or threatening hostility of Germany, such anti-German bias as the* entente *must be admitted to have at one time assumed, would certainly not exist at present, nor probably survive in the future. But whether the antagonism to Germany into which England had on this occasion been led without her wish or intention was but an ephemeral incident, or a symptomatic revelation of some deep-seated natural opposition between the policies and interests of the two countries, is a question which it clearly behoves British statesmen not to leave in any obscurity. To this point, then, inquiry must be directed.*

The general character of England's foreign policy is determined by the immutable conditions of her geographical situation on the ocean flank of Europe as an island State with vast oversea colonies and dependencies, whose existence and survival as an independent community are inseparably bound up with the possession of preponderant sea power. The tremendous influence of such preponderance has been described in the classical pages of Captain Mahan. No one now disputes it. Sea power is more potent than land power, because it is as pervading as the element in which it moves and has its being. Its formidable character makes itself felt the more directly that a maritime State is, in the literal sense of the word, the neighbour of every country accessible by sea. It would, therefore, be but natural that the power of a State supreme at sea should inspire universal jealousy and fear, and be ever exposed to the danger of being overthrown by a general combination of the world. Against such a combination no single nation could in the long run stand, least of all a small island kingdom not possessed of the military strength of a people trained to arms, and dependent for its food supply on overseas commerce. The danger can in practice only be averted – and history shows that it has been so averted – on condition that the national policy of the insular and naval State is so directed as to harmonise with the general desires and ideals common to all mankind, and more particularly that it is closely identified with the primary and vital interests of a majority, or as many as possible, of the other nations. Now, the first interest of all countries is the preservation of national independence. It follows that England, more than any other non-insular Power[,] has a direct and positive interest in the maintenance of the independence of nations, and therefore must be the natural enemy of any country threatening the independence of others, and the natural protector of the weaker communities.

Second only to the ideal of independence, nations have always cherished the right of free intercourse and trade in the world's markets, and in proportion as England champions the principle of the largest measure of general freedom of commerce, she undoubtedly strengthens her hold on the interested friendship of other nations, at least to the extent of making them feel less apprehensive of naval supremacy in the hands of a free trade England than they would in the face of a predominant protectionist Power. This is an aspect of the free trade question which is apt to be overlooked. It has been well said that every country, if it had the option, would, of course, prefer itself to hold the power of supremacy at sea, but that, this choice being excluded, it would rather see England hold that power than any other State.

History shows that the danger threatening the independence of this or that nation has generally arisen, at least in part, out of the momentary predominance of a neighbouring State at once militarily powerful, economically efficient, and ambitious to extend its frontiers or spread its influence, the danger being directly proportionate to the degree of its power and efficiency, and to the spontaneity or 'inevitableness' of its ambitions. The only check on the abuse of political predominance derived from such a position has always consisted in the opposition of an equally formidable rival, or of a combination of several countries forming leagues of defence. The equilibrium established by such a grouping of forces is technically known as the balance of power, and it has become almost an historical truism to identify England's secular policy with the maintenance of this balance by throwing her weight now in this scale and now in that, but ever on the side opposed to the political dictatorship of the strongest single State or group at a given time.

If this view of British policy is correct, the opposition into which England must inevitably be driven to any country aspiring to such a dictatorship assumes almost the form of a law of nature, as has indeed been theoretically demonstrated and illustrated historically, by an eminent writer on English national policy.

By applying this general law to a particular case, the attempt might be made to ascertain whether, at a given time, some powerful and ambitious State is or is not in a position of natural and necessary enmity towards England; and the present position of Germany might, perhaps, be so tested. Any such investigation must take the shape of an inquiry as to whether Germany is, in fact, aiming at a political hegemony with the object of promoting purely German schemes of expansion, and establishing a German primacy in the world of international politics at the cost and to the detriment of other nations.

For purposes of foreign policy the modern German Empire may be regarded as the heir, or descendant of Prussia. Of the history of Prussia, perhaps the most remarkable feature, next to the succession of talented Sovereigns and to the energy and love of honest work characteristic of their subjects, is the process by which on the narrow foundation of the modest Margraviate of Brandenburg there was erected in the space of a comparatively short period, the solid fabric of a European Great Power. That process was one of systematic territorial aggrandisement achieved mainly at the point of the sword, the most important and decisive conquests being deliberately embarked upon by ambitious rulers or statesmen for the avowed object of securing for Prussia the size, the cohesion, the square miles and the population necessary to elevate her to the rank and influence of a first class State. All other countries have made their conquests, many of them much larger and more bloody. There is no question now, or in this place, of weighing or discussing their relative merits or justification. Present interest lies in fixing attention on the special circumstances which have given the growth of Prussia its peculiar stamp. It has not been a case of a King's love of conquest as such, nor of the absorption of lands regarded geographically or ethnically as an integral part of the true national domain, nor of the more or less unconscious tendency of a people to expand under the influence of an exuberant vitality, for the fuller development of national life and resources. Here was rather the case of the Sovereign of a small and weak vassal State saying: 'I want my country to be independent and powerful. This it cannot be within its present frontiers and with its present population. I must have a larger territory and more inhabitants, and to this end I must organise strong military forces.'

The greatest and classic exponent in modern history of the policy of setting out deliberately to turn a small State into a big one was Frederick the Great. By his sudden seizure of Silesia in times of profound peace, and by the first partition of Poland, he practically doubled his inherited dominions. By keeping up the most efficient and powerful army of his time, and by joining England in her great effort to preserve the balance of power in face of the encroachments of France, he successfully maintained the position of his country as one of the European Great Powers. Prussian policy remained inspired by the same principles under his successors. It is hardly necessary to do more than mention the second and the third partitions of Poland; the repeated attempts to annex Hanover in complicity with Napoleon; the dismemberment of Saxony, and the exchange of the Rhenish Provinces for the relinquishment of Polish lands in 1815; the annexation of Schleswig-Holstein in 1864; the definite incorporation of Hanover and Electoral Hesse and other appropriations of territory in 1866; and, finally, the reconquest of Alsace-Lorraine from France in 1871. It is not, of course, pretended that all these acquisitions stand on the same footing. They have this in common – that they were all planned for the purpose of creating a big Prussia or Germany.

With the events of 1871 the spirit of Prussia passed into the new Germany. In no other country is there a conviction so deeply rooted in the very body and soul of all classes of the population that the preservation of national rights and the realisation of national ideals rest absolutely on the readiness of every citizen in the last resort to stake himself and his State on their assertion and vindication. With 'blood and iron' Prussia had forged her position in the councils of the Great Powers of Europe. In due course it came to pass that, with the impetus given to every branch of national activity by the newly-won unity, and, more especially by the growing development of overseas trade flowing in ever-increasing volume through the now Imperial ports of the formerly 'independent' but politically insignificant Hanse Towns, the young empire found opened to its energy a whole world outside Europe, of which it had previously hardly had the opportunity to become more than dimly conscious. Sailing across the ocean in German ships, German merchants began for the first time to divine the true position of countries such as England, the United States, France, and even the Netherlands, whose political influence extends to distant seas and continents. The colonies and foreign possessions of England more especially were seen to give to that country a recognised and enviable status in a world where the name of Germany, if mentioned at all, excited no particular interest. The effect of this discovery upon the German mind was curious and instructive. Here was a vast province of human activity to which the mere title and rank of a European Great Power were not in themselves a sufficient passport. Here in a field of portentous magnitude, dwarfing altogether the proportions of European countries, others, who had been perhaps rather looked down upon as comparatively smaller folk, were at home and commanded, whilst Germany was at best received but as an honoured guest. Here was distinct inequality, with a heavy bias in favour of the maritime and colonising Powers.

Such a state of things was not welcome to German patriotic pride. Germany had won her place as one of the leading, if not, in fact, the foremost Power on the European continent. But over and beyond the

European Great Powers there seemed to stand the 'World Powers'. It was at once clear that Germany must become a 'World Power'. The evolution of this idea and its translation into practical politics followed with similar consistency the line of thought that had inspired the Prussian Kings in their efforts to make Prussia great. 'If Prussia,' said Frederick the Great, 'is to count for something in the councils of Europe, she must be made a Great Power.' And the echo: 'If Germany wants to have a voice in the affairs of the larger oceanic world she must be made a "world power."' 'I want more territory,' said Prussia. 'Germany must have Colonies,' says the new world-policy. And Colonies were accordingly established, in such spots as were found to be still appropriate, or out of which others could be pushed by the vigorous assertion of a German demand for 'a place in the sun': Damaraland [now part of Namibia], Cameroons, Togoland, German East Africa, New Guinea, and groups of other islands in the Pacific. The German example, as was only natural, found ready followers, and the map of unclaimed territories was filled up with surprising rapidity. When the final reckoning was made up[,] the actual German gain seemed, even in German eyes, somewhat meagre. A few fresh possessions were added by purchase or by international agreement – the Carolines, Samoa, Heligoland. A transaction in the old Prussian style secured Kiao-chau. On the whole, however, the 'Colonies' have proved assets of somewhat doubtful value.

Meanwhile the dream of a Colonial Empire had taken deep hold on the German imagination. Emperor, statesmen, journalists, geographers, economists, commercial and shipping houses, and the whole mass of educated and uneducated public opinion continue with one voice to declare: We must have real Colonies where German emigrants can settle and spread the national ideals of the Fatherland, and we must have a fleet and coaling stations to keep together the Colonies which we are bound to acquire. To the question, 'Why must?' the ready answer is: 'A healthy and powerful State like Germany, with its 60,000,000 inhabitants, must expand, it cannot stand still, it must have territories to which its overflowing population can emigrate without giving up its nationality.' When it is objected that the world is now actually parcelled out among independent States, and that territory for colonisation cannot be had except by taking it from the rightful possessor, the reply again is: 'We cannot enter into such considerations. Necessity has no law. The world belongs to the strong. A vigorous nation cannot allow its growth to be hampered by blind adherence to the status quo. We have no designs on other people's possessions, but where States are too feeble to put their territory to the best possible use, it is the manifest destiny of those who can and will do so to take their places.'

No one who has a knowledge of German political thought, and who enjoys the confidence of German friends speaking their minds openly and freely, can deny that these are the ideas which are proclaimed on the housetops, and that inability to sympathise with them is regarded in Germany as the mark of the prejudiced foreigner who cannot enter into the real feelings of Germans. Nor is it amiss to refer in this connection to the series of Imperial apothegms, which have from time to time served to crystallise the prevailing German sentiments, and some of which deserve quotation: 'Our future lies in the water.' 'The trident must be in our hand.' 'Germany must re-enter into her heritage of maritime dominion once unchallenged in the hands of the old Hansa.' 'No question of world politics must be settled without the consent of the German Emperor.' 'The Emperor of the Atlantic greets the Emperor of the Pacific,' &c.

The significance of these individual utterances may easily be exaggerated. Taken together, their cumulative effect is to confirm the impression that Germany distinctly aims at playing on the world's political stage a much larger and much more dominant part than she finds allotted to herself under the present distribution of material power. It would be taking a narrow view of the function of political criticism to judge this theory of national self-assertion as if it were a problem of morals to be solved by the casuistical application of the principles governing private conduct in modern societies. History is apt to justify the action of States by its general results, with often but faint regard to the ethical character of the means employed. The ruthless conquests of the Roman Republic and Empire are recognised to have brought about an organisation of the world's best energies, which, by the characteristic and lasting impulse it gave to the civilisation of the ancients, fully compensated for the obliqueness of the conquerors' political morals. Peter the Great and Katharine II [sic] are rightly heroes in the eyes of Russia, who largely owes to their unscrupulous and crafty policies her existence as a powerful and united nation. The high-handed seizure of Silesia by Frederick the Great, the low intrigues by which the first partition of Poland was brought about, the tortuous manoeuvres by which Bismarck secured Schleswig-Holstein for Prussia are forgotten or condoned in the contemplation of a powerful Germany that has brought to these and all her other territories a more enlightened government, a wider conception of national life, and a greater share in a glorious national tradition than could have been their lot in other conditions. Germans would after all be only logical if they did not hesitate to apply to their current politics the lesson conveyed in such historical judgements, and were ready to leave to posterity the burden of vindicating the employment of force for the purpose of spreading the benefits of German rule over now unwilling peoples. No modern German would plead guilty to a mere lust of conquest for the sake of conquest. But the vague and undefined schemes of Teutonic expansion ('die Ausbreitung des deutschen Volkstums') are but the expression of the deeply rooted feeling that Germany has by the strength and purity of her national purpose, the fervour of her patriotism, the depth of her religious feeling, the high standard of competency, and the perspicuous honesty of her administration, the successful pursuit of every branch of public and scientific activity, and the elevated character of her philosophy, art, and ethics, established for herself the right to assert the primacy of German national ideals. And as it is an axiom of her political faith that right, in order that it may prevail, must be backed by force, the transition is easy to the belief that the 'good German sword', which plays so large a part in patriotic speech, is there to solve any difficulties that may be in the way of establishing the reign of those ideals in a Germanised world.

The above very fragmentary sketch has given prominence to certain general features of Germany's foreign policy, which may, with some claim to impartiality, accuracy, and clearness, be deduced from her history, from the utterances and known designs of her rulers and statesmen, and from the unmistakable manifestations of public opinion. It remains to consider whether, and to what extent, the principles so elucidated may be said, on the one hand, to govern actual present policy, and, on the other, to conflict with the vital interests of England and of other independent and vigorous States, with the free exercise of their national rights, and the fulfillment of what they, on their part, may regard as their own mission in this world.

It cannot for a moment be questioned that the mere existence and healthy activity of a powerful Germany is an undoubted blessing to the world. Germany represents in a pre-eminent degree those highest qualities and virtues of good citizenship, in the largest sense of the word, which constitute the glory and triumph of modern civilization. The world would be immeasurably the poorer if everything that is specifically associated with German character, German ideas, and German methods were to cease having power and influence. For England particularly, intellectual and moral kinship creates a sympathy and appreciation of what is best in the German mind, which has made her naturally predisposed to welcome, in the interest of the general progress of mankind, everything tending to strengthen that power and influence – on one condition: there must be respect for the individualities of other nations, equally valuable coadjutors, in their way, in the work of human progress, equally entitled to full elbow-room in which to contribute, in freedom, to the evolution of a higher civilisation. England has, by a sound instinct, always stood for the unhampered play and interaction of national forces as most in accord with Nature's own process of development. No other State has ever gone so far and so steadily as the British Empire in the direction of giving free scope to the play of national forces in the internal organisation of the divers peoples gathered under the King's sceptre. It is perhaps England's good fortune, as much as her merit, that taking this view of the manner in which the solution of the higher problems of national life must be sought, she has had but to apply the same principle to the field of external policy in order to arrive at the theory and practice governing her action as one of the international community of States.

So long, then, as Germany competes for an intellectual and moral leadership of the world in reliance on her own national advantages and energies[,] England can but admire, applaud, and join in the race. If, on the other hand, Germany believes that greater relative preponderance of material power, wider extent of territory, inviola-ble frontiers, and supremacy at sea are the necessary and preliminary possessions without which any aspirations to such leadership must end in failure, then England must expect that Germany will surely seek to diminish the power of any rivals, to enhance her own by extending her dominion, to hinder the co-operation of other States, and ultimately to break up and supplant the British Empire.

Now, it is quite possible that Germany does not, nor ever will, con-sciously cherish any schemes of so subversive a nature. Her statesmen have openly repudiated them with indignation. Their denial may be perfectly honest, and their indignation justified. If so, they will be most unlikely to come into any kind of armed conflict with England, because, as she knows of no causes of present dispute between the two countries, so she would have difficulty in imagining where, on the hypothesis stated, any such should arise in the future. England seeks no quarrels, and will never give Germany cause for legitimate offence.

But this is not a matter in which England can safely run any risks. The assurances of German statesmen may after all be no more genuine than they were found to be on the subject of the Anglo-French entente and German interests in Morocco, or they may be honestly given but incapable of fulfilment. It would not be unjust to say that ambitious designs against one's neighbours are not as a rule openly proclaimed, and that therefore the absence of such proclamation, and even the profession of unlimited and universal political benevolence are not in themselves conclusive evidence for or against the existence of unpublished intentions. The aspect of German policy in the past, to which attention has already been called, would warrant a belief that a further development on the same general lines would not constitute a break with former traditions, and must be considered as at least possible. In the presence of such a possibility it may well be asked whether it would be right, or even prudent, for England to incur any sacrifices or see other, friendly, nations sacrificed merely in order to assist Germany in building up step by step the fabric of a universal preponderance, in the blind confidence that in the exercise of such preponderance Germany will confer unmixed benefits on the world at large, and promote the welfare and happiness of all other peoples without doing injury to anyone. There are, as a matter of fact, weighty reasons which make it particularly difficult for England to entertain that confidence. These will have to be set out in their place.

Meanwhile it is important to make it quite clear that a recognition of the dangers of the situation need not and does not imply any hostility to Germany. England herself would be the last to expect any other nation to associate itself with her in the active support of purely British interests, except in cases where it was found practicable as a matter of business to give service for counter-service. Nevertheless, no Englishman would be so foolish as to regard such want of foreign co-operation for the realisation of British aims as a symptom of an anti-British animus. All that England on her part asks – and that is more than she has been in the habit of getting – is that, in the pursuit of political schemes which in no way affect injuriously the interests of third parties, such, for instance, as the introduction of reforms in Egypt for the sole benefit of the native population, England shall not be wantonly hampered by factious opposition. The same measure, and even a fuller measure, England will always be ready to mete out to other countries, including Germany. Of such readiness in the past instances are as numerous as they are instructive; and this is perhaps the place where to say a few words respecting the peculiar complexion of the series of transactions which have been characteristic of Anglo-German relations in recent years.

It has been so often declared as to have become almost a diplomatic platitude, that between England and Germany, as there has never been any real clashing of material interests, so there are no unsettled controversies over outstanding questions. Yet for the last twenty years, as the archives of our Foreign Office show, German Governments have never ceased reproaching British Cabinets with want of friendliness and with persistent opposition to German political plans. A review of British relations during the same period with France, with Russia, and with the United States reveals ancient and real sources of conflict, springing from imperfectly patched-up differences of past centuries, the inelastic stipulations of antiquated treaties, or the troubles incidental to unsettled colonial frontiers. Although with these countries England has fortunately managed to continue to live in peace, there always remained sufficient elements of divergence to make the preservation of good, not to say cordial, relations an anxious problem requiring constant alertness, care, moderation, good temper, and conciliatory disposition. When particular causes of friction became too acute, special arrangements entered into succeeded as a rule in avoiding an open rupture without, however, solving the difficulties, but rather leaving the seed of further irritation behind. This was eminently the case with France until and right up to the conclusion of the Agreement of the 8th April, 1904.

A very different picture is presented by the succession of incidents which punctuate the record of contemporary Anglo-German relations. From 1884 onward, when Bismarck first launched his country into colonial and maritime enterprise, numerous quarrels arose between the two countries. They all have in common this feature – that they were opened by acts of direct and unmistakable hostility to England on the part of the German Government, and that this hostility was displayed with a disregard of the elementary rules of straightforward and honourable dealing, which was deeply resented by successive British Secretaries of State for Foreign Affairs. But perhaps even more remarkable is this other feature, also common to all these quarrels, that the British Ministers, in spite of the genuine indignation felt at the treatment to which they were subjected, in each case readily agreed to make concessions or accept compromises which not only appeared to satisfy all German demands, but were by the avowal of both parties calculated and designed to re-establish, if possible, on a firmer basis the fabric of Anglo-German friendship. To all outward appearance absolute harmony was restored on each occasion after these separate settlements, and in the intervals of fresh outbreaks it seemed true, and was persistently reiterated, that there could be no further occasion for disagreement.

The peculiar diplomatic methods employed by Bismarck in connection with the first German annexation in South-West Africa, the persistent way in which he deceived Lord Ampthill up to the last moment as to Germany's colonial ambitions, and then turned round to complain of the want of sympathy shown for Germany's 'well-known' policy; the sudden seizure of the Cameroons by a German doctor armed with officially obtained British letters of recommendation to the local people, at a time when the intention of England to grant the natives' petition for a British Protectorate had been proclaimed; the deliberate deception practised on the Reichstag and the German public by the publication of pretended communications to Lord Granville which were never made, a mystification of which Germans to this day are probably ignorant; the arousing of a profound outburst of anti-English feeling throughout Germany by Bismarck's warlike and threatening speeches in Parliament; the abortive German raid on St. Lucia Bay, only just frustrated by the vigilance of Mr. Rhodes; the dubious proceedings by which German claims were established over a large portion of the Sultan of Zanzibar's dominions; the hoisting of the German flag over vast parts of New Guinea, immediately after inducing England to postpone her already-announced intention to occupy some of those very parts by representing that a friendly settlement might first determine the dividing line of rival territorial claims; the German pretensions to oust British settlers from Fiji and Samoa: these incidents constitute the first experience by a British Cabinet of German hostility disguised as injured friendship and innocence. It was only England's precarious position resulting from the recent occupation of Egypt (carefully encouraged by Bismarck), the danger of the troubles with Russia in Central Asia (directly fomented by a German special mission to St. Petersburg), and the comparative weakness of the British Navy at the time, which prevented Mr. Gladstone's Government from contemplating a determined resistance to these German proceedings. It was, however, felt rightly that, apart from the offensiveness of the methods employed, the desires entertained by Germany, and so bluntly translated into practice, were not seriously antagonistic to British policy. Most of the territory ultimately acquired by Bismarck had at some previous time been refused by England, and in the cases where British occupation had lately been contemplated, the object had been not so much to acquire fresh provinces, as to prevent their falling into the hands of protectionist France, who would inevitably have killed all British trade. It seems almost certain that had Germany from the outset sought to gain by friendly overtures to England what she eventually secured after a display of unprovoked aggressiveness, there would have been no difficulty in the way of an amicable arrangement satisfactory to both parties.

As it was, the British Cabinet was determined to avoid a continuance of the quarrel, and having loyally accepted the situation created by Germany's violent action, it promptly assured her of England's honest desire to live with her on terms of absolute neighbourliness, and to maintain the former cordial relations. The whole chapter of these incidents was typical of many of the fresh complications of a similar nature which rose in the following years. With the advent of Lord Salisbury's administration in 1885, Bismarck thought the moment come for inviting England to take sides with the Triple Alliance. Repeated and pressing proposals appear to have been made thenceforward for some considerable time with this end.[1] Whilst the British Government was too prudent to abandon altogether the traditional policy of holding the balance between the continental Powers, it decided eventually, in view of the then threateningly hostile attitude of France and Russia, to go so far in the direction of co-operation with the Triple Alliance as to conclude the two secret Mediterranean Agreements of 1887. At the same time Lord Salisbury intimated his readiness to acquiesce in the German annexation of Samoa, the consummation of which was only shipwrecked owing to the refusal of the United States on their part to abandon their treaty rights in that group of islands in Germany's favour. These fresh manifestations of close relations with Germany were, however, shortly followed by the serious disagreements caused by the proceedings of the notorious Dr. Carl Peters and other German agents in East Africa. Dr. Peters' design, in defiance of existing treaties, to establish German power in Uganda, athwart the line of communication running from Egypt to the head-waters of the Nile, failed, but England, having previously abandoned the Sultan of Zanzibar to Germany's territorial ambitions, now recognised the German annexation of extensive portions of his mainland dominions, saving the rest by the belated declaration of a British protectorate. The cession of Heligoland sealed the reassertion of Anglo-German brotherhood, and was accompanied by the customary assurance of general German support to British policy, notably in Egypt.

On this and on other occasions England's spirit of accommodation went so far as to sacrifice the career of subordinate British officials, who had done no more than carry out the policy of their Government in as dignified a manner as circumstances allowed, and to

---

1 For the whole of Lord Salisbury's two Administrations our official records are sadly incomplete, all the most important business having been transacted under the cover of 'private' correspondence. It is not known even to what extent that correspondence may have been integrally preserved. A methodical study of our relations with Germany during that interesting period is likely to remain for ever impossible. [E. A. C.]

whose conduct that Government attached no blame, to the relentless vindictiveness of Germany, by agreeing to their withdrawal as one of the conditions of a settlement. In several instances the German Government admitted that no fault attached to the British official, whilst the German officer alone was acknowledged to be at fault, but asked that the latter's inevitable removal should be facilitated, and the outside world misled, by the simultaneous withdrawal of his British colleagues. In one such case indeed, a German Consul, after being transferred with promotion to another post, was only a few years afterwards reinstated on the scene of his original blunders with the higher rank of Consul-General without any British protest being made.

The number of British officials innocently branded in this manner in the course of some years is not inconsiderable, and it is instructive to observe how readily and con amore the German Government, imitating in this one of the great Bismarck's worst and least respectable foibles, habitually descend to attacking the personal character and position of any agents of a foreign State, often regardless of their humble rank, whose knowledge, honesty, and efficient performance of their duties are thought to be in the way of the realisation of some particular, probably not very straightforward, piece of business. Such machinations were conspicuous in connection with the fall of M. Delcassé, but tales could be told of similar efforts directed against men in the service of the Spanish, Italian, and Austrian, as well as of the British Government.

It seems unnecessary to go at length into the disputes about the frontiers of the German Colonies in West Africa and the hinterland spheres of influence in 1903–1904, except to record the ready sacrifice of undoubted British treaty rights to the desire to conciliate Germany, notwithstanding the provocative and insulting proceedings of her agents and officials; nor into the agreement entered into between Germany and France for giving the latter access to the Niger, a transaction which, as the German Government blandly informed the British Embassy at Berlin, was intended to show how unpleasant it could make itself to England if she did not manifest greater alacrity in meeting German wishes.

It was perhaps partly the same feeling that inspired Germany in offering determined resistance to the scheme negotiated by Lord Rosebery's Government with the Congo Free State for connecting the British Protectorate of Uganda by a railway with Lake Tanganyika. No cession of territory was involved, the whole object being to allow of an all-British through communication by rail and lake steamers from the Cape to Cairo. It was to this that Germany objected, although it was not explained in what way her interests would be injuriously affected. She adopted on this occasion a most minatory tone towards England, and also joined France, who objected to other portions of the Anglo-Congolese Agreement, in putting pressure on King Leopold. In the end the British Government consented to the cancellation of the clauses respecting the lease of the strip of land required for the construction of the railway, and Germany declared herself satisfied.

More extraordinary still was the behaviour of the German Government in respect to the Transvaal. The special treaty arrangements, which placed the foreign of that country under the control of England, were, of course, well known and understood. Nevertheless, it is certain that Germany believed she might by some fortuitous circumstances hope someday to establish her political dominion over the Boers, and realise her dream of occupying a belt of territory running from east to west right across Africa. She may have thought that England could be brought amicably to cede her rights in those regions as she had done before in other quarters, but, meanwhile, a good deal of intriguing went on which cannot be called otherwise than actively hostile. Opposition to British interests was deliberately encouraged in the most demonstrative fashion at Pretoria, which went so far in 1895 that the British Ambassador at Berlin had to make a protest. German financial assistance was promised to the Transvaal for the purpose of buying the Delagoa Bay Railway, a British concern which had been illegally confiscated by the Portuguese Government, and was then *the subject of an international arbitration. When this offer failed, Germany approached the Lisbon Cabinet direct with the demand that, immediately on the arbitration being concluded, Germany and Portugal should deal with the railway by common agreement. It was also significant that at the time of the British annexation of Amatongaland (1895), just south of the Portuguese frontier on the East Coast, Germany thought it necessary to warn England that this annexation was not recognised by the Transvaal, and that she encouraged the feverish activity of German traders to buy up all available land round Delagoa Bay. In the same year, following up an intimation that England's 'opposition to German interests at Delagoa Bay' – interests of which no British Government had ever previously been informed – was considered by Germany as one of the legitimate causes of her ill-will towards England, the German Government went out of its way to declare the maintenance of the independence of the Transvaal to be a German national interest. Then followed the chapter of the Jameson Raid and the Emperor's famous telegram to President Kruger. The hostile character of that demonstration was thoroughly understood by the Emperor's Government, because we know that preparations were made for safe-guarding the German fleet in the contingency of a British attack. But in a way the most important aspect of the incident was that for the first time the fact of the hostile character of Germany's official policy was realised by the British public, who up to then, owing to the anxious care of their Government to minimise the results of the perpetual friction with Germany, and to prevent any aggravation of that friction by conceal-ing as far as possible the unpleasant details of Germany's aggressive behaviour, had been practically unaware of the persistently contemp-tuous treatment of their country by their Teutonic cousins. The very decided view taken by British public opinion of the nature of any possible German intervention in South Africa led the German Gov-ernment, though not the German public, to abandon the design of supplanting England at Pretoria. But for this 'sacrifice' Germany, in accordance with her wont, demanded a price – namely, British acquiescence in the reversion to her of certain Portuguese Colonies in the event of their eventual division and appropriation by other Powers. The price was paid. But the manner in which Germany first bullied the Portuguese Government and then practically drove an indignant British Cabinet into agreeing in anticipation to this partic- ular scheme of spoliation of England's most ancient ally, was deeply resented by Lord Salisbury, all the more, no doubt, as by this time he was fully aware that this new 'friendly' settlement of misunderstand- ings with Germany would be no more lasting than its many predeces- sors. When, barely twelve months later, the Emperor unabashed by his recent formal 'abandonment of the Boers', threatened that unless the question of the final ownership of Samoa, then under negotiation, was promptly settled in Germany's favour, he would have to recon- sider his attitude in the British conflict with the Transvaal which was then on the point of being submitted to the arbitrament of war, it cannot be wondered at that the British Government began to despair of ever reaching a state of satisfactory relations with Germany by continuing in the path of friendly concessions and compromises. Yet no attempt was even then made to seek a new way. The agreement by which Samoa definitely became German was duly signed, despite the serious protests of our Australian Colonies, whose feelings had been incensed by the cynical disregard with which the German agents in the group, with the open support of their Government, had for a long time violated the distinct stipulations of the Samoan Act agreed to at Berlin by the three interested Powers in 1889. And when shortly after the outbreak of the South African war, Germany threatened the most determined hostility unless England waived the exercise of one of the most ancient and most firmly-established belligerent rights of naval warfare, namely, the search and citation before a Prize Court of neutral mercantile vessel[s] suspected of carrying contra- band, England once more preferred an amicable arrangement under which her undoubted rights were practically waived, to embarking on a fresh quarrel with Germany. The spirit in which this more than conciliatory attitude was appreciated at Berlin became clear when immediately afterwards the German Chancellor openly boasted in the Reichstag that he had compelled England by the display of German firmness to abandon her absolutely unjust claim to interference with the unquestioned rights of neutrals, and when the Emperor subsequently appealed to his nation to hasten on the building of an overwhelming German fleet, since the want of superior naval strength alone had on this occasion prevented Germany from a still more drastic vindication of Germany's interests.*

A bare allusion must here suffice to the way in which the German Government at the time of the South African war abetted the campaign of odious calumny carried on throughout the length and breadth of Germany against the character of the British army, without any Government official once opening his mouth in contradiction; and this in the face of the faithful reports known to have been addressed to their Government by the German military officers attached to the British forces in the field. When the Reichstag proceeded in an unprecedented fashion to impugn the conduct of a British Cabinet Minister, it was open to Prince Bülow to enlighten his hearers as to the real facts, which had been grossly mis-represented. We know that he was aware of the truth. We have the report of his long interview with a distinguished and representative English gentleman, a fortnight after Mr. Chamberlain's famous speech, which was alleged to be the cause of offence, but of which a correct version revealing the groundlessness of the accusation had been reported in a widely-read German paper. The Prince then stated that his Government had at that moment no cause to complain of anything in the attitude of British Ministers, yet he descended a few days afterwards to expressing in the Reichstag his sympathy with the whole German outcry against Mr. Chamberlain's supposed statement and the alleged atrocities of the British army, which he knew to be based on falsehoods. Mr. Chamberlain's dignified reply led to extraordinarily persistent efforts on the Chancellor's part to obtain from the British Government an apology for the offence of resenting his dishonouring insinuations and, after all these efforts had failed, he nevertheless intimated to the Reichstag that the British Government had given an explanation repudiating any intention on its part to imply any insult to Germany by what had been said.[2]

As if none of these things had happened, fresh German demands in another field, accompanied by all the same manifestations of hostility, were again met, though with perhaps increasing reluctance, by the old willingness to oblige. The action of Germany in China has long been distinctly unfriendly to England. In 1895 she tried to obtain from the Chinese Government a coaling station in the Chusan Islands, at the mouth of the Yang-tsze, without any previous communication with the British Government, whose preferential rights over the group, as established by Treaty, were of course well known. The manner in which Kiao-chau was obtained, however unjustified it may be considered by any recognised standard of political conduct, did not concern England more than the other Powers who professed in their Treaties to respect China's integrity and independence. But Germany was not content with the seizure of the harbour; she also planned the absorption of the whole of the large and fertile province of Shantung. The concession of the privileged rights which she wrung from the Chinese Government was obtained owing in no small degree to her official assurance that her claims had the support of England who, needless to say, had never been informed or consulted, and who was, of course, known to be absolutely opposed to stipulations by which, contrary to solemn British treaty rights, it was intended to close a valuable province to British trade and enterprise.

About this time Germany secretly approached Russia with a view to the conclusion of an Agreement, by which Germany would have also obtained the much desired foothold on the Yang-tsze, then considered to be practically a British preserve. These overtures being rejected, Germany wished at least to prevent England from obtaining what she herself had failed to secure. She proposed to the British

---

[2] This and the preceding paragraph are printed in Gooch and Temperley, *British Documents*, Vol I, pp 276–7.

Cabinet a self-denying Agreement stipulating that neither Power should endeavour to obtain any territorial advantages in Chinese dominions, and that if any third Power attempted to do so both should take common action.

The British Government did not conceal their great reluctance to this arrangement, rightly foreseeing that Germany would tacitly exempt from its operation her own designs on Shantung, and also any Russian aggression in Manchuria, whilst England would solemnly give up any chances she might have of establishing on a firm basis her well-won position on the Yang-tsze. That is, of course, exactly what subsequently did happen. There was no obvious reason why England should lend herself to this gratuitous tying of her own hands. No counter-advantage was offered or even suggested, and the British taste for these one-sided transactions had not been stimulated by past experience. Nevertheless, the policy of conciliating Germany by meeting her expressed wishes once more triumphed, and the Agreement was signed – with the foreseen consequences: Russian aggression in Manchuria was declared to be altogether outside the scope of the stipulations of what the German Chancellor took care to style the 'Yang-tsze' Agreement, as if its terms had referred specially to that restricted area of China, and the German designs on Shantung continue to this day to be tenaciously pursued.

But Germany was not content with the British renunciation of any territorial claims. The underhand and disloyal manoeuvres by which, on the strength of purely fictitious stories of British plans for the seizure of various Chinese places of strategical importance (stories also sedulously communicated to the French Government), Germany wrung out of the Peking Court further separate and secret guarantees against alleged British designs, on the occasion of the termination of the joint Anglo-France-German occupation of Shanghai, betrayed such an obliquity of mind in dealing with her ostensible friends that Lord Lansdowne characterised it in the most severe terms, which did not prevent him from presenting the incident to Parliament in the form of papers from which almost every trace of the offensive attitude *of Germany had been carefully removed, so as not to embitter our German relations. And this was after the reports from our officers had shown that the proceeding of the German troops in Northern China, and the extraordinary treatment meted out by the German General Staff to the British and Indian contingents serving, with a loyalty not approached by any of the other international forces, under the supreme command of Count Waldersee, had created the deepest possible resentment among all ranks, from the British General Commanding to the lowest Indian follower.[3]*

Nor was any difficulty made by the British Government in shortly afterwards cordially co-operating with Germany in the dispute with Venezuela, and it was only the pressure of public opinion, which had gradually come to look upon such cooperation for any political purpose whatsoever as not in accord with either British interests or British dignity, that brought this joint venture to a very sudden and somewhat lame end.

It is as true to-day as it has been at any time since 1884, in the intervals of successive incidents and their settlements, that, practically every known German demand having been met, there is not just now any cause troubling the serenity of Anglo-German relations. So much so, that the German Ambassador in London, in reply to repeated inquiries as to what specific points his Government had in mind in constantly referring to its earnest wish to see those relations improved, invariably seeks refuge in the vaguest of generalities, such as the burning desire which consumes the German Chancellor to be on the most intimate terms of friendship with France, and to obtain the fulfillment of this desire through the good offices of the British Government.

Nothing has been said in the present paper of the campaign carried on against this country in the German press, and in some measure responded to in English papers. It is exceedingly doubtful

---

3 This and the preceding three paragraphs are printed in Gooch and Temperley, *British Documents*, Vol II, pp 152–3.

whether this campaign has had any share whatever in determining the attitude of the two Governments, and those people who see in the newspaper controversy the main cause of friction between Germany and England, and who consequently believe that the friction can be removed by fraternisations of journalists and the mutual visits of more or less distinguished and more or less disinterested bodies of tourists, have not sufficiently studied – in most cases could not possibly be in a position to study – the records of the actual occurrences which have taken place, and which clearly show that it is the direct action of the German Government which has been the all-sufficient cause of whatever obstacle there may be to the maintenance of normally friendly relations between the two countries. If any importance is in this connection to be attributed to the German press, it is only in so far as it is manipulated and influenced by the official Press Bureau, a branch of the Chancellor's Office at Berlin of which the occult influence is not limited to the confines of the German Empire. That influence is perceived at work in New York, at St. Petersburg, at Vienna, at Madrid, Lisbon, Rome, and Cairo, and even in London, where the German Embassy entertains confidential and largely unsuspected relations with a number of respectable and widely read papers. This somewhat unsavoury business was until recently in the clumsy hands of the late Chancellor of the Embassy, whose energies are now transferred to Cairo. But, by whomsoever carried on, it is known that the tradition of giving expression to the views of the German Government for the benefit of the British public, and even of the British Cabinet, by using other and less direct methods than the prescribed channel of open communication with the Secretary of State for Foreign Affairs, survives at Carlton House Terrace.

There is no pretence to completeness in the foregoing survey of Anglo-German relations, which, in fact, gives no more than a brief reference to certain salient and typical incidents that have characterised those relations during the last twenty years. The more difficult task remains of drawing the logical conclusions. The immediate object of the present inquiry was to ascertain whether there is any real and natural ground for opposition between England and Germany. It has been shown that such opposition has, in fact, existed in an ample measure for a long period, but that it has been caused by an entirely one-sided aggressiveness and that on the part of England the moot conciliatory disposition has been coupled with never-failing readiness to purchase the resumption of friendly relations by concession after concession.

It might be deduced that the antagonism is too deeply rooted in the relative position of the two countries to allow of its being bridged over by the kind of temporary expedients to which England has so long and so patiently resorted. On this view of the case it would have to be assumed that Germany is deliberately following a policy which is essentially opposed to vital British interests, and that an armed conflict cannot in the long run be averted, except by England either sacrificing those interests, with the result that she would lose her position as an independent Great Power, or making herself too strong to give Germany the chance of succeeding in a war. This is the opinion of those who see in the whole trend of Germany's policy conclusive evidence that she is consciously aiming at the establishment of a German hegemony, at first in Europe, and eventually in the world.

After all that has been said in the preceding paragraphs, it would be idle to deny that this may be the correct interpretation of the facts. There is this further seemingly corroborative evidence that such a conception of world-policy offers perhaps the only quite consistent explanation of the tenacity with which Germany pursues the construction of a powerful navy with the avowed object of creating slowly, but surely, a weapon fit to overawe any possible enemy, however formidable[,] at sea.

There is, however, one obvious flaw in the argument. If the German design were so far-reaching and deeply thought out as this view implies, then it ought to be clear to the meanest German understanding that its success must depend very materially on England's remaining blind to it, and being kept in good humour until the moment arrived for striking the blow fatal to her power. It would be not merely worth Germany's while, it would be her imperative duty, pending the development of her forces, to win and retain England's friendship by every means in her power. No candid critic could say that this elementary strategical rule had been even remotely followed hitherto by the German Government.

It is not unprofitable in this connection to refer to a remarkable article in one of the recent numbers of the 'Preussische Jahrbücher,' written by Dr. Hans Delbrück, the distinguished editor of that ably conducted and influential magazine. This article discusses very candidly and dispassionately the question whether Germany could, even if she would, carry out successfully an ambitious policy of expansion which would make her follow in the footsteps of Louis XIV and of Napoleon I. The conclusion arrived at is that, unless Germany wishes to expose herself to the same overwhelming combinations which ruined the French dreams of a universal ascendency, she must make up her mind definitely and openly to renounce all thoughts of further extending her frontiers and substitute for the plan of territorial annexations the nobler ambition of spreading German culture by propagating German ideals in the many quarters of the globe where the German language is spoken, or at least taught and understood.

It would not do to attribute too much importance to the appearance of such an article in a country where the influence of public opinion on the conduct of the affairs of State is notoriously feeble. But this much may probably be rightly gathered from it[:] that the design attributed by other nations to Germany has been, and perhaps is still being, cherished in some intermediate way by influential classes, including, perhaps the Government itself, but that responsible statesmen must be well aware of the practical impossibility of carrying it out.

There is then, perhaps, another way of looking at the problem: It might be suggested that the great German design is in reality no more than the expression of a vague, confused and unpractical statesmanship, not fully realising its own drift. A charitable critic might add in a way of explanation, that the well-known qualities of mind and temperament distinguishing for good or for evil the present Ruler of Germany may not improbably be largely responsible for the erratic, domineering, and often frankly aggressive spirit which is recognisable at present in every branch of German public life, not merely in the region of foreign policy; and that this spirit has called forth those manifestations of discontent and alarm both at home and abroad with which the world is becoming familiar; that, in fact, Germany does not really know what she is driving at, and that all her excursions and alarums[,] all her underhand intrigues[,] do not contribute to the steady working out of a well-conceived and relentlessly followed system of policy, because they do not really form part of any such system. This is an hypothesis not flattering to the German Government and it must be admitted that much might be urged against its validity. But it remains true that on this hypothesis also most of the facts of the present situation could be explained.

It is, of course, necessary to except the period of Bismarck's Chancellorship. To assume that so great a statesman was not quite clear as to the objects of his policy would be the reductio ad absurdum *of any hypothesis. If, then, the hypothesis is to be held sound, there must be forthcoming a reasonable explanation for Bismarck's conduct towards England after 1884, and a different explanation for the continuance of German hostility after his fall in 1890. This view can be shown to be less absurd than it may at first sight appear.*

Bismarck suffered from what Count Schuvaloff called le cauchemar des coalitions *[the nightmare of coalitions]. It is beyond doubt that he particularly dreaded the hostile combination against his country of France and Russia, and that as one certain means of counteracting that danger, he desired to bring England into the Triple Alliance, or at least to force her into independent collision with France and Russia, which would inevitably have placed her by Germany's side. He knew England's aversion to the entanglement of alliances, and to any policy of determined assertion of national rights, such as would have made her a Power to be seriously reckoned with by France and Russia. But Bismarck had also a poor opinion of the*

*power of English Ministers to resist determined pressure. He appar-
ently believed he could compel them to choose between Germany
and a universal opposition to England. When the colonial agitation
in Germany gave him an opening, he most probably determined to
bring it home to England that meekness and want of determination
in foreign affairs do not constitute a policy; that it was wisest, and
certainly least disagreeable, for her to shape a decided course in a
direction which would secure her Germany's friendship; and that in
co-operation with Germany lay freedom from international troubles
as well as safety, whilst a refusal to co-operate brought inglorious
conflicts, and the prospect of finding Germany ranged with France
and Russia for the specific purpose of damaging British interests.*

*Such an explanation gains plausibility from the fact that, accord-
ing to Bismarck's own confession, a strictly analogous policy was followed by him before 1866 in his dealings with the minor German
States. Prussia deliberately bullied and made herself disagreeable to
them all, in the firm expectation that, for the sake of peace and quiet,
they would follow Prussia's lead rather than Austria's. When the war
of 1866 broke out Bismarck had to realise that, with the exception
of a few small principalities which were practically enclaves in the
Kingdom of Prussia, the whole of the minor German States sided
with Austria. Similarly he must have begun to see towards the end
of his career that his policy of browbeating England into friendship
had failed, in spite of some fugitive appearance of success. But by that
time the habit of bullying and offending England had almost become
a tradition in the Berlin Foreign Office, and Bismarck's successors,
who, there is other evidence to show, inherited very little of his political capacity and singleness of purpose, seem to have regarded the
habit as a policy in itself, instead of as a method of diplomacy calculated to gain an ulterior end. Whilst the great Chancellor made
England concede demands objectionable more in the manner of pres-
entation than in themselves, treating her somewhat in the style of
Richard III wooing the Lady Anne, Bismarck's successors have apparently come to regard it as their ultimate and self-contained purpose*

to extract valuable concessions from England by offensive bluster and persistent nagging, Bismarck's experience having shown her to be amenable to this form of persuasion without any risk of her lasting animosity being excited.

If, merely by way of analogy and illustration, a comparison not intended to be either literally exact or disrespectful be permitted, the action of Germany towards this country since 1890 might be likened not inappropriately to that of a professional blackmailer, whose extortion[s] are wrung from his victims by the threat of some vague and dreadful consequences in case of a refusal. To give way to the blackmailer's menaces enriches him, but it has long been proved by uniform experience that, although this may secure for the victim temporary peace, it is certain to lead to renewed molestation and higher demands after ever-shortening periods of amicable forbearance. The blackmailer's trade is generally ruined by the first resolute stand made against his exactions and determination rather to face all risks of a possibly disagreeable situation than to continue in the path of endless concessions. But, failing such determination, it is more than probable that the relations between the two parties will grow steadily worse.

If it be possible, in this perhaps not very flattering way, to account for the German Government's persistently aggressive demeanour towards England, and the resulting state of almost perpetual friction, notwithstanding the pretence of friendship, the generally restless, explosive, and disconcerting activity of Germany in relation to all other States would find its explanation partly in the same attitude towards them and partly in the suggested want of definite political aims and purposes. A wise German statesman would recognise the limits within which any world-policy that is not to provoke a hostile combination of all the nations in arms must confine itself. He would realise that the edifice of Pan-Germanism, with its outlying bastions in the Netherlands, in the Scandinavian countries, in Switzerland, in the German provinces of Austria, and on the Adriatic, could never be built up on any other foundation than the wreckage of the liberties of Europe. A German maritime supremacy must be acknowledged to be incompatible with the existence of the British Empire, and even if that Empire disappeared, the union of the greatest military with the greatest naval Power in one State would compel the world to combine for the riddance of such an incubus. The acquisition of colonies fit for German settlement in South America cannot be reconciled with the Monroe Doctrine, which is a fundamental principle of the political faith of the United States. The creation of a German India in Asia Minor must in the end stand or fall with either a German command of the sea or a German conquest of Constantinople and the countries intervening between Germany's present south-eastern frontiers and the Bosphorus. Whilst each of these grandiose schemes seems incapable of fulfilment under anything like the present conditions of the world it looks as if Germany were playing with them all together simultaneously, and thereby wilfully concentrating in her own path all the obstacles and oppositions of a world set at defiance. That she should do this helps to prove how little of logical and consistent design and of unrelenting purpose lies behind the impetuous mobility, the bewildering surprises, and the heedless disregard of the susceptibilities of other people that have been so characteristic of recent manifestations of German policy.

If it be considered necessary to formulate and accept a theory that will fit all the ascertained facts of German foreign policy, the choice must lie between the two hypotheses here presented:–

Either Germany is definitely aiming at a general political hegemony and maritime ascendancy, threatening the independence of her neighbours and ultimately the existence of England;

Or Germany, free from any such clear-cut ambition, and thinking for the present merely of using her legitimate position and influence as one of the leading Powers in the council of nations, is seeking to promote her foreign commerce, spread the benefits of German culture, extend the scope of her national energies, and create fresh German interests all over the world wherever and whenever a peaceful opportunity offers, leaving it to an uncertain future to decide whether the occurrence of great changes in the world may not someday assign to Germany a larger share of direct political action over regions not now a part of her dominions, without that violation of the established rights of other countries which would be involved in any such action under existing political conditions.

In either case Germany would clearly be wise to build as powerful a navy as she can afford.

The above alternatives seem to exhaust the possibilities of explaining the given facts. The choice offered is a narrow one, nor easy to make with any close approach to certainty. It will, however, be seen, on reflection, that there is no actual necessity for a British Government to determine definitely which of the two theories of German policy it will accept. For it is clear that the second scheme (of semi-independent evolution, not entirely unaided by statecraft) may at any stage merge into the first, or conscious-design scheme. Moreover, if ever the evolution scheme should come to be realised, the position thereby accruing to Germany would obviously constitute as formidable a menace to the rest of the world as would be presented by any deliberate conquest of a similar position by 'malice aforethought'.

It appears, then, that the element of danger present as a visible factor in one case, also enters, though under some disguise, into the second; and against such danger, whether actual or contingent, the same general line of conduct seems prescribed. It should not be difficult briefly to indicate that line in such a way as to command the assent of all persons competent to form a judgment in this matter.

So long as England remains faithful to the general principle of the preservation of the balance of power, her interests would not be served by Germany being reduced to the rank of a weak Power, as this might easily lead to a Franco-Russian predominance equally, if not more, formidable to the British Empire. There are no existing German rights, territorial or other, which this country could wish to see diminished. Therefore, so long as Germany's action does not overstep the line of legitimate protection of existing rights she can always count upon the sympathy and good-will, and even the moral support, of England.

Further, it would be neither just nor politic to ignore the claims to a healthy expansion which a vigorous and growing country like Germany has a natural right to assert in the field of legitimate endeavour. The frank recognition of this right has never been grudged or refused by England to any foreign country. It may be recalled that the German Empire owes such expansion as has already taken place in no small measure to England's co-operation or spirit of accommodation, and to the British principle of equal opportunity and no favour. It cannot be good policy for England to thwart such a process of development where it does not directly conflict either with British interests or with those of other nations to which England is bound by solemn treaty obligations. If Germany, within the limits imposed by these two conditions, finds the means peacefully and honourably to increase her trade and shipping, to gain coaling stations or other harbours, to acquire landing rights for cables, or to secure concessions for the employment of German capital or industries, she should never find England in her way.

Nor is it for British Governments to oppose Germany's building as large a fleet as she may consider necessary or desirable for the defence of her national interests. It is the mark of an independent State that it decides such matters for itself, free from any outside interference, and it would ill become England with her large fleets to dictate to another State what is good for it in matters of supreme national concern. Apart from the question of right and wrong, it may also be urged that nothing would be more likely than any attempt at such dictation, to impel Germany to persevere with her shipbuilding programmes. And also, it may be said in parenthesis, nothing is more likely to produce in Germany the impression of the practical hopelessness of a never-ending succession of costly naval programs than the conviction, based on ocular demonstration, that for every

German ship England will inevitably lay down two, so maintaining the present relative British preponderance.

It would be of real advantage if the determination not to bar Germany's legitimate and peaceful expansion, nor her schemes of naval development, were made as patent and pronounced as authoritatively as possible, provided care were taken at the same time to make it quite clear that this benevolent attitude will give way to determined opposition at the first sign of British or allied interests being adversely affected. This alone would probably do more to bring about lastingly satisfactory relations with Germany than any other course.

It is not unlikely that Germany will before long again ask, as she has so often done hitherto, for a 'close understanding' with England. To meet this contingency, the first thing to consider is what exactly is meant by the request. The Anglo-French entente had a very material basis and tangible object[ive] – namely, the adjustment of a number of actually-existing serious differences. The efforts now being made by England to arrive at an understanding with Russia are justified by a very similar situation. But for an Anglo-German understanding on the same lines there is no room, since none could be built up on the same foundation. It has been shown that there are no questions of any importance now at issue between the two countries. Any understanding must therefore be entirely different in object and scope. Germany's wish may be for an understanding to co-operate for specific purposes, whether offensive or defensive or generally political or economical, circumscribed by certain geographical limits, or for an agreement of a self-denying order, binding the parties not to do, or not to interfere with, certain things or acts. Or the coveted arrangement might contain a mixture of any or all of these various ingredients. Into offensive or defensive alliances with Germany there is, under the prevailing political conditions, no occasion for England to enter, and it would hardly be honest at present to treat such a possibility as an open question. British assent to any other form of co-operation or system of non-interference must depend absolutely on circumstances, on the particular features, and on the merits of *any proposals that may be made. All such proposals England will be as ready as she always has been to weigh and discuss from the point of view of how British interests will be affected. Germany must be content, in this respect to receive exactly the same treatment as every other Power.*

There is no suggestion more untrue or more unjust than that England has on any recent occasion shown, or is likely to show in the future, a parti pris *against Germany or German proposals as such, or displayed any unfairness in dealing strictly on their own merits with any question having a bearing on her relations with Germany. This accusation has been freely made. It is the stock-in-trade of all the inspired tirades against the British Government which emanate directly or indirectly from the Berlin Press Bureau. But no one has ever been able to bring forward a tittle of evidence in its support that will bear examination. The fact, of course, is that, as Mr. Balfour felt impelled to remark to the German Ambassador on a certain occasion, German communications to the British Government have not generally been of a very agreeable character, and, unless that character is a good deal modified, it is more than likely that such communications will in future receive unpalatable answers. For there is one road which, if past experience is any guide to the future, will most certainly not lead to any permanent improvement of relations with any Power, least of all Germany, and which must therefore be abandoned: that is the road paved with graceful British concessions – concessions made without any conviction either of their justice or of their being set off by equivalent counter-services. The vain hopes that in this manner Germany can be 'conciliated' and made more friendly must be definitely given up. It may be that such hopes are still honestly cherished by irresponsible people, ignorant, perhaps necessarily ignorant, of the history of Anglo-German relations during the last twenty years, which cannot be better described than as the history of a systematic policy of gratuitous concessions, a policy which has led to the highly disappointing result disclosed by the almost perpetual state of tension existing between the two countries. Men in responsible positions, whose business it is to inform themselves and to see things as they really are, cannot conscientiously retain any illusions on this subject.*

Here, again, however, it would be wrong to suppose that any discrimination is intended to Germany's disadvantage. On the contrary, the same rule will naturally impose itself in the case of all other Powers. It may, indeed, be useful to cast back a glance on British relations with France before and after 1898. A reference to the official records will show that ever since 1882 England had met a growing number of French demands and infringements of British rights in the same spirit of ready accommodation which inspired her dealings with Germany. The not unnatural result was that every successive French Government embarked on a policy of 'squeezing' England, until the crisis came in the year of Fashoda, when the stake at issue was the maintenance of the British position on the Upper Nile. The French Minister for Foreign Affairs of that day argued, like his predecessors, that England's apparent opposition was only half-hearted, and would collapse before the persistent threat of French displeasure. Nothing would persuade him that England could in a question of this kind assume an attitude of unbending resistance. It was this erroneous impression, justified in the eyes of the French Cabinet by their deductions from British political practice, that brought the two countries to the verge of war. When the Fashoda chapter had ended with the just discomfiture of France, she remained for a time very sullen, and the enemies of England rejoiced, because they believed that an impassable gulf had now been fixed between the two nations. As a matter of fact, the events at Fashoda proved to be the opening of a new chapter of Anglo-French relations. These, after remaining for some years rather formal, have not since been disturbed by any disagreeable incidents. France behaved more correctly and seemed less suspicious and inconsiderate than had been her wont, and no fresh obstacle arose in the way which ultimately led to the Agreement of 1904.

Although Germany has not been exposed to such a rebuff as

France encountered in 1898[,] the events connected with the Algeci-
ras Conference appear to have had on the German Government the
effect of an unexpected revelation, clearly showing indications of a
new spirit in which England proposes to regulate her own conduct
towards France on the one hand and to Germany on the other. That
the result was a very serious disappointment to Germany has been
made abundantly manifest by the turmoil which the signature of the
Algeciras Act has created in the country, the official, semi-official,
and unofficial classes vying with each other in giving expression to
their astonished discontent. The time which has since elapsed has,
no doubt, been short. But during that time it may be observed that
our relations with Germany, if not exactly cordial, have at least been
practically free from all symptoms of direct friction, and there is an
impression that Germany will think twice before she now gives rise
to any fresh disagreement. In this attitude she will be encouraged if
she meets on England's part with unvarying courtesy and considera-
tion in all matter of concern, but also with a prompt and firm refusal
to enter into any one-sided bargains or arrangements, and the most
unbending determination to uphold British rights and interests in
every part of the globe. There will be no surer or quicker way to win
the respect of the German Government and of the German nation.

E.A.C.

MINUTES

Mr. Crowe's Memorandum should go to the Prime Minister, Lord
Ripon, Mr. Asquith, Mr. Morley, Mr. Haldane, with my comment
upon it. – E. G.

This Memorandum by Mr. Crowe is most valuable. The review
of the present situation is both interesting and suggestive, and the
connected account of the diplomatic incidents of past years is most
helpful as a guide to policy. The whole Memorandum contains infor-
mation and reflections, which should be carefully studied. The part

of our foreign policy with which it is concerned involves the greatest issues, and requires constant attention. – E. GREY. January 28, 1907.

The observations at p. 11 [supra p 277] on the beneficial results of our free trade policy on our international position are very well put. The only other remark I make on this most able and interesting Memo[randum] is to suggest whether the restless and uncertain personal character of the Emperor William is sufficiently taken into account in the estimate of the present situation. There was at least method in Prince Bismarck's madness; but the Emperor is like a cat in a cupboard. He may jump out anywhere. The whole situation would be changed in a moment if this personal factor were changed, and another Minister like General Caprivi also came into office in consequence. – F.

Index